Tyninghame

Tyninghame

Landscapes and Lives

JUDY RILEY

ORIGIN

First published in 2022
by Origin, an imprint of
Birlinn Limited
West Newington House
10 Newington Road
Edinburgh
EH9 1QS

ISBN: 978 1 83983 011 2

British Library Cataloguing-in-Publication Data
A catalogue record for this book is available
from the British Library

Designed and typeset by Mark Blackadder

Printed and bound by Bell & Bain Ltd, Glasgow

Contents

For Vanessa,
plant lover and garden detective,
whose helping hand set me on the path

To North Berwick

Bruce's Circle

Binning Wood

Thomas's Circle

Helen's Circle

Garleton Walk

Limetree Walk

Lodge

Walled Garden

Old Hard Gait

Lawhead

Tyninghame
Village

Lodge

Old Saw Mill

Mill Lade

Foreword

Tyninghame House in its earlier phases was an unremarkable building. It was, however, transformed from 1828 by Thomas the 9th Earl of Haddington, in association with the architect William Burn, into a magnificent baronial mansion. Many of the architectural features were clearly taken from Jacques Androuet du Cerceau's *Les plus excellents batiments de France*, published in Paris in 1576. The original walled garden provided fruit and vegetables, whilst other garden areas were planted for the delight of the Haddington family and have been enjoyed by all who have lived at Tyninghame more recently.

My wife, Jane, daughter, Pandora and I lived for many happy years in the West Wing at Tyninghame. The great red sandstone pile had been sold by the delightful but eccentric John Baillie-Hamilton, 13th Earl of Haddington (known to all his friends as Binning) to Kit Martin, who brilliantly saw the possibilities of the house, dividing it up skilfully into flats while keeping the gardens together, with the exception of the magnificent walled garden which was sold separately and owned by Charnisay Gwyn and her husband, Charles, both knowledgeable and indefatigable gardeners.

The first to be tempted to buy a section of the house were Sir Alistair and Lady Grant. Alistair – sadly no longer with us – was the celebrated banker, grocer and entrepreneur born nearby at Haddington who acquired the Library Wing, which was entered via the original front door and included the grand staircase and a handsome library. Our section, next door, was blessed with a magnificent drawing room, over sixty feet long and equipped with matching marble chimney pieces by Lorenzo Bartolini. It had an extensive bay window overlooking the intricately designed rose parterre, which is dominated by a tile red sandstone sundial at its centre.

Jane reminded me that soon after we moved to Scotland, she had taken tea with Sarah, Lady Haddington (Binning's mother). Sitting in what later became our own drawing room, the view from the window was as if she were standing on the bridge of a liner watching white-capped waves crashing below. But instead of white-capped waves it was a sea of Iceberg roses.

Our flat was contained on the other side by the Tower Wing, which we had persuaded our old friends Asa and Susan Briggs to buy. Lord Briggs had just retired from being President of Worcester College, Oxford and had been desperate to find a suitable additional space to contain much of his extensive library. We discussed collaborating on a book on Tyninghame and undertook considerable research, but sadly it never came to anything.

Opposite: The Secret Garden

Over the years other families were to fill up the remaining sections of the house, and one of these neighbours was the delightful and learned author of this book. The detailed research that Judy Riley has undertaken is remarkable, and in relating the history of the Tyninghame estate, the gardens and the house from the earliest times, she has brilliantly told the history of Scotland in microcosm. It is almost certainly the most comprehensive study of a Scottish garden ever to have been written.

Timothy Clifford
Director, National Galleries of Scotland, 1984–2006

Other echoes
Inhabit the garden. Shall we follow?
T. S. ELIOT

Preface

This is a story of the designs on the landscape at Tyninghame. To me, the most intriguing part of the landscape story has been the part played by a woman, Lady Helen Hope. It is her story, or rather the lack of it, which inspired the detective work that is the origin of this book. She and her husband are commemorated by an obelisk, designed by William Burn and erected in 1856 at the end of a mile-long avenue of ancient beech and oak trees terminating by the sea at Hedderwick Bay. My interest was piqued by a simple question: who was Helen? I hope I have found some of the answers.

In setting her Tyninghame story into context, it became impossible to ignore the deeper historical layers as well as the more recent ones. The evidence uncovered is patchy, though much, of necessity, has been omitted: the farming history, for example. I have tried to bring the threads together to make a convincing story. Any mistakes are mine.

I am grateful for the generosity of many people; in particular that of Jane, Dowager Countess of Haddington and of Sir Timothy Clifford. My deepest thanks go to my husband, David, whose encouragement and support knew no bounds.

The book was completed before Storm Arwen devastated the southern shore of Hedderwick Bay on 26 November 2021. The damage to the Binning Wood and to the woodlands around Tyninghame was more sporadic and less extensive, although many veteran oaks, beeches and Scots pine came down that night. Their place will eventually be taken by other trees, and the cycle will continue.

Understanding the evolution of designs on the land can be the key that unlocks the door to the future. Those of us who love and respect the Tyninghame landscape with its farmland, woodlands, beaches and buildings, want it to maintain its integrity, to evolve and to endure.

Judy Riley
Tyninghame, March 2022

CHAPTER 1

Marks and Makers

A solitary stone finger points to the sky in the middle of a field by Kirklandhill, about a mile from Tyninghame. It is an imposing 3.36 metres high, roughly square in section with a slight lean to the south. There are two other standing stones in the area, one on Pencraig Hill, and another at Easter Broomhouse. This latter is hewn from old red sandstone and has three cup markings at the base of the western face. Three more stones are close by Traprain Law. All are at least 4,000, but possibly even 6,000, years old.

These standing stones tantalise us. What function did they have? Do they align with other features in the landscape at the equinoxes? Did they have a ceremonial purpose? Were they route markers? Their function or meaning remains elusive, but what we do know is that they were erected by East Lothian's early settlers in the Neolithic or New Stone Age period (*c.* 4,000–2,500 BC): farmers who raised crops, grazed animals, fished, made pots and buried their dead with ceremony. The standing stone at Kirklandhill[1] is one of over a thousand in Scotland, petrified voices, announcing: 'We did this. We were here. This is our mark.'

On Orkney and on Lewis, the stone circles of the Ring of Brogdar and Callanish are famous; stone-built houses at Skara Brae are the best preserved in Western Europe, perhaps blinding us to the fact that New Stone Age builders also used timber extensively. In East

Lothian this was certainly the case. Houses, halls and stockades were made of timber which could be impressive yet, unlike the standing stones, today what is left of these wooden structures lies buried, hidden underground, out of sight and out of mind, unless dry weather reveals telltale crop marks in the fields above.

In the vicinity of Tyninghame there are many such crop marks revealing dwellings, halls, enclosures and ritual funereal monuments, as well as others whose purpose remain a mystery. One of the earliest known dwellings in Scotland was excavated in advance of quarrying between 2002 and 2003 at East Barns, a few miles down the coast. Roughly circular in structure, it had post holes indicating internal 'room' divisions and a central fireplace, and may have accommodated six or seven people. The sheer number of flint tools and scraps from tool making – over 25,000 in total – indicated that this was no temporary shelter for nomadic hunter gatherers but a more permanent home.[2] Charcoal found there has been dated to 8,300 BC, revealing that not all Mesolithic, or Middle Stone Age, people were nomadic: in this part of East Lothian, some also lived in round houses.

Our understanding of these ancient structures is continually being refined, and occasionally previous

Opposite: Kirklandhill standing stone

1

Neolithic Hall at Doon Hill being burned to the ground (Courtesy of Historic Environment Scotland)

research is overturned. On Doon Hill, at the eastern end of the Lammermuirs, two timber halls were excavated between 1964 and 1966. The larger one, some twenty-three metres long and half as wide, was long thought to have been constructed *c.* AD 550 by a native lord, and the smaller one, which eventually replaced it, was thought to be the work of Anglo-Saxon invaders sometime after AD 600. Only recently has radiocarbon dating confirmed that both were made by Neolithic farmers, 6,000 years ago.[3] Some years after its construction it was set alight and deliberately destroyed, as were many of the other Neolithic halls across the country. The interpretation board shows an artist's impression of the event.

In a field by Paradise Wood, just north of Tyninghame, lies evidence of more 'timber halls with associated enclosures, together with a number of ring ditches and enclosures, of prehistoric and Early Historic date'.[4]

They represent both early and late prehistoric farming settlements, together with timber halls which are believed to be Anglo-Saxon.[5]

These early farmers, those who built the first hall at Doon Hill and those who erected the stone at Kirklandhill, would have found on the nearby beaches not only an abundance of shellfish and fish but also flint for harpoons, arrows and spears, and the woods inland would have provided good hunting. Over time, the settlements became more established and parts of the forest were cleared to make fields. Those who were living near present-day Tyninghame would have been attracted to the fertile soil and to the estuary of the Tyne, either for grazing or growing crops, and certainly for fishing, for access to the sea and for the stone in abundant supply on the shore.

The earliest settlers in Tyninghame itself remain elusive: nearby there is evidence of prehistoric enclosures and a settlement at Hedderwickhill[6] on the opposite bank of the river, an enclosure to the east of the present Tyninghame road bridge[7] as well as another in the field by the Kirklandhill standing stone, but the sites have not yet been fully excavated. Nor is there hard evidence for the areas around the site of the old village of Tyninghame, as no archaeological research has taken place there.

However, snapshots of these early times emerge from the preliminary archaeological assessment of the A1 corridor between Haddington and Dunbar, prior to the upgrading of the A1 to dual carriageway which took place between 2001 and 2004. Hundreds of trenches were dug along the proposed nine-mile route and radiocarbon dating determined the ages of the prehistoric samples. Eleven new archaeological sites were discovered which shed light on early farming settlements along the banks of the Tyne and give tantalising glimpses of their rituals.[8]

Most of the archaeology from these sites dated from the Neolithic period, 4,000 BC and later, but some was even earlier. The charcoal from Overhailes indicated people were living here around 7600–7525 BC, and charcoal from other sites dated from the sixth and fifth millennia BC. Flint tools, including arrow blades and scrapers (found at Pencraig and Phantassie), indicated that people were hunting and skinning animals just as at East Barns. This was at a time when oak, elm and hazel were increasing in the birch woodland that first established after the retreat of the last Ice Age. Much of East Lothian would have been covered by such woodland. Small communities were skilled at surviving in this environment, hunting and gathering fruit and nuts in the forests and fishing by the rivers and along the coast.

By the fourth millennium BC, a technological revolution was taking place throughout the Lothians and all over the British Isles. The Mesolithic people had lived off the land, now Neolithic people were beginning to dominate it. Communities began cutting down forests creating more agricultural land, and knowledge of pottery and stone axes spread. They created dwellings and also built other structures such as the communal timber hall at Doon Hill. Farming began to develop as animals were domesticated and plants were bred, though they still hunted and gathered from the wild. Evidence of domesticated cattle and sheep or goats was found (Eweford West) as well as pigs (Overhailes), although the latter could have been from wild boar hunted in the forests.[9] There was little evidence of early actual Neolithic settlements along this new A1 route (which had been designed to avoid known, scheduled, sites). Instead, excavations revealed two roughly contemporary sites where elaborate funerary rites took place: Pencraig Hill and Eweford West.

Over many generations, people returned to these places where they constructed mounds, funeral pyres and enclosures. They placed the cremated remains of

Overleaf: Paradise Wood crop marks showing two timber halls, enclosures and riggs (Courtesy of Historic Environment Scotland)

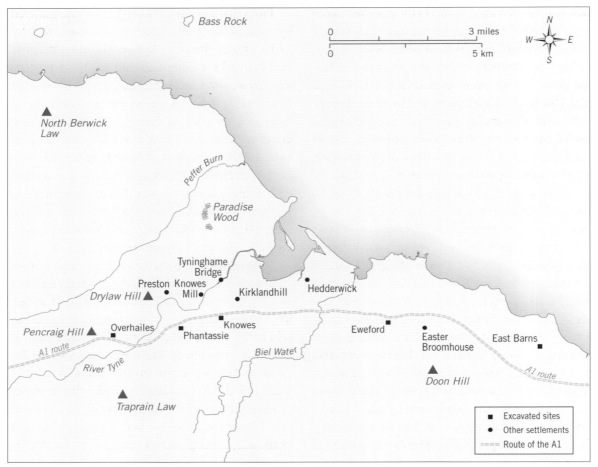

Map of some of the archaeological sites by Tyninghame

their dead, together with pieces of decorated pottery bowls, in structures that were then burned. At Pencraig Hill, a large trapeze-shaped enclosure was made of oak timbers which dated from 3950–3650 BC. Here the remains of at least two people were found, cremated on a funerary pyre, inside the enclosure. Other human remains were found in pits together with pot sherds.

At Eweford West, two funerary pyres were found, one of oak dating from 3800–3650 BC and the other of stone. Burnt human bones were found indicating that successive generations had returned to both sites for over 1,000 years.

Early Neolithic pottery found at these funerary sites, known as 'Carinated Bowl' pottery, is found all over Britain and Ireland and seems to have appeared around 3900 BC in north-eastern France and the European mainland. Given its widespread distribution, it was probably made by European farmer immigrants.[10] However, it might have been made by the descendants of the earlier hunter-gatherers. Other pottery from Overhailes was Fengate Ware, which was first identified in the Fens around the Wash in south-eastern England. Most of these had been used for cooking.

Deposits of charcoal in pits (Eweford West) also

indicated the increasing variety of the tree cover: alder (3960–3710 BC), hazel, blackthorn and willow (3660–3510 BC). Surprisingly, evidence of birch was absent, and yet it was one of the most widespread trees. Whatever else it may have been used for, it was not burned here. One pit contained barley and small amounts of emmer wheat, an ancient grain. The grains had all been burned and then placed in the pit, perhaps as part of a funereal rite.[11] It did not seem to be part of domestic activity in which grain was dried over gentle heat.

Closer to Tyninghame, on the site south of the Knowes, a curious line of twelve pits or pit alignments, twelve metres long was found. Many of these exist in East Lothian, often as crop marks seen in aerial photographs. Three had sherds of incised pottery layered at the bottom. These had then been packed with charcoal from alder, hazel and hazel-nut shell, blackthorn, rose, cherry, willow and oak. Eventually they were set alight and destroyed, and although their meaning remains a mystery, the charcoal is concrete evidence of the tree cover at the time: '. . . woven together, the A1 discoveries take us on a journey from a landscape of forests punctuated by open ground 7,000 years ago, through ones that were gradually cleared, to landscapes that were fields with pockets of scrub and managed woodland about 2,000 years ago'.[12]

Typical of development in south-east Scotland at this time were settlements which had been enclosed by ditches in the first millennium BC, then deliberately filled in and abandoned by the early first millennium AD. This happened at Howmuir and Eweford cottages. The most complete evidence of a settlement found was on land above the River Tyne, near Phantassie. Here a later Iron Age (800 BC–AD 400) farmstead was established which included 'a substantial house . . . approached by a gated passage, areas of hard standing for cattle and a stone wall around part of the settlement'.[13] Expanded by later generations, another house was eventually built over it, but by the second or third century AD, it too had been abandoned.

From all the evidence along the A1 route gathered by the team of archaeologists from Glasgow University Archaeological Research Division (GUARD), it is clear that the earliest fishermen and hunter-gatherers, together with the earliest farmers, were active around Tyninghame. Looking across the landscape today, there is barely a sign of their hidden existence; even imposing man-made landforms like the cursus at Drylawhill have disappeared. Here, huge parallel earthworks with ditches indicated earth-moving on a grand scale some 6,000 years ago.[14] There is another at Preston Mains nearby. It extended for over a kilometre; today it is only visible as crop marks and its purpose remains a mystery – though theories abound.

Crop marks have been the key to identifying most of the early prehistoric sites which lie buried; even later Iron Age sites in East Lothian have only been identified by the telltale pale lines on aerial photographs. In the field to the west of the Kirklandhill standing stone is an Iron Age enclosure which was excavated by the Traprain Law Environs Project team in 2003.[15] Surrounded by a rectilinear ditch, the dwelling consisted of a series of roughly circular 'rooms', with paved floors connected by cobbled passageways as at Phantassie, although only a small part of the interior was excavated here. One room had a clay oven. By the entrance to the enclosure, a stone cist had been constructed in the wall and used for cremation burials. Again, as at Phantassie, the site was eventually abandoned. The investigating team considered the assemblage of finds 'exceptional': besides cremated bone and animal bone, there were several quernstones (though most were broken), sections of four Roman glass bangles, Iron Age tradition pottery and some Roman pottery together with a selection of tools, proof that the site was occupied during the Roman and possibly pre-Roman Iron Age.

Now, as then, rising above the Tyninghame landscape are the distinctive volcanic intrusions of Traprain Law (221m) to the west, North Berwick Law (187m) to

Traprain Law, North Berwick Law and the Bass Rock

the north with the Bass Rock (107m) just out to sea; to the south the Lammermuir Hills form the horizon with Doon Hill at the easterly end.

They are visible for miles and from each other, and can be seen from different parts of Tyninghame. They all had deep significance in prehistoric times: Traprain and North Berwick Laws are both important archaeological sites with their own Iron Age forts which are still evident.[16] The routes between these prominent features and those that linked the vanished settlements and burial sites have long disappeared. Some of these ancient tracks undoubtedly lie beneath the roads we use today.

One physical link is the Tyne which flows close by Traprain Law and five of the western A1 sites – Pencraig Hill and Pencraig, Overhailes, Phantassie and the Knowes – and then to Tyninghame itself, on the northern bank of the estuary. It is the river and its name that holds the key to unlocking the later history.

CHAPTER 2

Monastery and St Baldred

The earliest record of the name Tyninghame is found in the *Annals of Lindisfarne*, written in the first quarter of the twelfth century, where Symeon of Durham writes for the year 756, '*Balthere obiit in Tininghami anachorita*',[1] in other words, 'Baldred, the anchorite died in Tiningham'. In the Annals, the place name is important only because Baldred, one of the saints of the early Northumbrian Church, died here. An anchorite was a religious recluse, a hermit like Baldred, who withdrew from the world from time to time. His life gave rise to several legends, but the place name itself, now spelt Tyninghame, has a story of its own to tell.

It has three parts to it: Tīn-, meaning river in a

The River Tyne at Tyninghame

Lindisfarne Castle from the Priory ruins

regional variant of Old Celtic, now the River Tyne; then Anglo-Saxon -īnga, meaning here the people of, or the settlers of; and finally -hām ('hame' in Scots, 'home' in English), meaning a settlement. Just as 'farm' is both a landholding and a set of buildings, so, in place names, '-hām may have referred to quite a substantial area, comparable to a later parish . . .'[2] So the name Tīn-īnga-hām, Tyninghame, signifies 'the place of the settlers of the Tyne'. How long the settlement had been in existence before Baldred arrived there is uncertain, but we know, from evidence described in the previous chapter, that settlements close to the banks of the river had waxed and waned over many thousands of years.

There are several place names in East Lothian ending in -ham(e), or -ingham(e): Morham, Auldhame, Oldhamstocks, Pefferham, Coldingham,

Whittingehame, Lyneryngam (the old name for East Linton). All appear to be evidence of the English-speaking colonisation north of Hadrian's Wall by the early eighth century. Much of East Lothian and the Borders was then in what was the kingdom of Bernicia, part of Northumbria, with Bamburgh as the probable centre of secular power, and religious power in the hands of the bishops of the Holy Island of Lindisfarne.

It is possible that rather than extensive colonisation by English speakers, land grants were given 'to religious communities able to provide civil and ideological leadership favourable to the house of Banborough'.[3] This may well have been the case with Tyninghame as the appellation -ham could be used up to the early ninth century in order to refer to a religious foundation.[4] Significantly, Morham, Auldhame, Coldingham and

Traprain Law. The Tyne is hidden by trees and the dip of the land in the foreground

Tyninghame all have early Christian connections.

The background to the arrival of the Angles in East Lothian and the eventual establishment of a monastery at Tyninghame is complex; it may or may not have been peaceful. The warrior leaders of the British Gododdin (whom the Romans called Votadini), originally had their capital at Traprain Law, and when they set off from Edinburgh around 600 to fight against the pagan Angles at Catterick, passing within a mile of Tyninghame, it is thought they had already converted to Christianity.[5]

Their defeat at the hands of the Angles however opened the way for the expansion north of the Anglo-Saxons. Not many years after the battle at Catterick, the kingdoms of Bernicia and Deira were united to form Northumbria, and Christianity became more

established. In 616, Edwin defeated his brother-in-law, Æthelfrith, and became the first Christian king of Northumbria. His motives for conversion may have been political rather than spiritual as it coincided with his strategic marriage to Æthelburh of Kent who brought the Roman missionary Paulinus to Northumbria. In one of his most poignant similes, Bede describes how, after Paulinus has explained the Christian doctrine, King Edwin asks his counsellors for their opinion. One answers:

Your majesty, when we compare the present life of man on earth with that time of which we have no knowledge, it seems to me like the swift flight of a single sparrow . . . This sparrow flies swiftly in through one door of the hall, and out

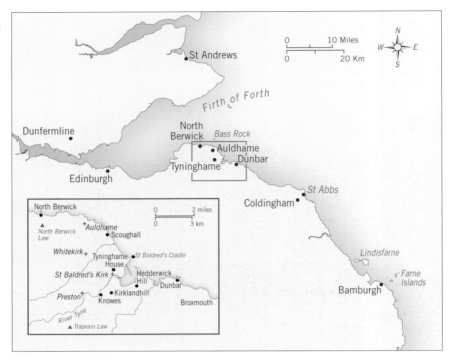

through another. While he is inside, he is safe
from the winter storms; but after a few
moments of comfort, he vanishes from sight
into the wintry world from which he came.
Even so, man appears on earth for a little while;
but of what went before this life or of what
follows, we know nothing. Therefore, if this new
teaching has brought any more certain knowledge, it seems only right that we should follow
it.[6]

Even with such an endorsement, the conversions at
his court may not have run very deep for when Edwin
was killed *c.*632, Paulinus returned to Kent with Queen
Æthelburh and her sons, and Christianity was
renounced by his immediate pagan successors. Nevertheless, the tide was turning in favour of the Church
through Æthelfrith's son, Oswald.

After the death of his father, Oswald, his mother,

brother and sister had all been exiled. They sought
refuge on Iona in the Scottish kingdom of Dál Riada
where all were converted to Christianity. In 634 Oswald
was finally successful in battle and became a powerful
ruler. In a determined effort to re-establish Christianity,
he looked to his friends from St Columba's monastery
on Iona for support and asked for a bishop 'by whose
teaching and ministry the English people over whom
he ruled might receive the blessings of the Christian
faith and the sacraments'.[7] Bishop Aidan was sent and
was given the island of Lindisfarne to be his see, but
he succeeded where Paulinus had failed.

In 638, Oswald extended his kingdom to the north,
successfully besieging Edinburgh and conquering the
Gododdin. Historians assume that by this time most
of the Lothians to the south and east of Edinburgh
would have been annexed by the Angles, and though
there is some evidence of possible Anglo-Saxon presence in East Lothian at this period, the crop marks at

Paradise Wood for example, it is scarce. The excavations which took place at Auldhame in 2005 and 2008 cast more light on this period: they revealed a monastic settlement, 'that flourished between mid seventh and mid ninth century'.[8] This raises questions about the possible origins of the monastery at Tyninghame.

In her book *Scotland's Lost Gardens*, Marilyn Brown writes: 'From the sixth and seventh centuries onwards monasteries and hermitages were founded across Scotland. The ideal was a remote place, cut off from the world, where monks and nuns would be undisturbed by secular affairs.'[9] Oswald's sister, Æbbe, chose such a site for the double separate monastery for monks and nuns she established on what is now known as Kirk Hill on St Abb's Head. The site at Auldhame, though far less well known, follows this pattern. The site itself is flat, on a steep rocky promontory overlooking the Bass Rock to the north-east. According to Symeon of Durham, St Baldred sometimes withdrew

to a small hermitage and chapel that he built on this tiny island, just as St Cuthbert had withdrawn from Lindisfarne to one of the Farne islands at different times during his life.

Monastic sites often use natural features, a river for example, to form part of the enclosure. At Auldhame, the cliffs of the promontory and the sea afford a natural boundary on three sides. A *vallum*, or surrounding bank with ditch, was found during the excavation which would have created a small enclosure. Within the boundary the archaeologists discovered the remains of two early Christian chapels, both timber constructions. Soon after the first was built, another appears to have replaced it sometime in the mid-eighth to mid-ninth century. It was a simple, rectangular room with an entrance at the west gable end and a rounded wall to the east.[10] The monastery was abandoned around AD 900 but the cemetery continued to be used.

Several different grave types were found ranging

The site of the early Christian monastery at Auldhame, with the Bass Rock in the distance

from simple earth-cut graves, to a single late eighth to tenth-century Viking grave. They were those of men, women and children; men and women were not buried in separate areas, which might suggest this was not a monastic site, however other evidence suggests that it was. Two adjoining shards of a glass inkwell were found, 'perhaps the most significant in the strands of the case for a monastic settlement'.[11] Only six other monastic inkwells are known in Britain. There were also large quantities of dog-whelk or sea-snail shells on the site. These could be crushed to extract a gland that produces a purple dye used in Anglo-Saxon illuminated manuscripts. The shells at Auldhame had not been cracked, suggesting that they had been stockpiled but then not used.

No archaeological excavations have taken place around the ruins of St Baldred's church at Tyninghame, so it is impossible to give a date for its origin or size and many of the comparisons between Auldhame and Tyninghame must remain hypothetical. The findings at Auldhame suggest that it may have been the older

of the two, dating from the mid seventh-century, a hundred years before the death of St Baldred in 756, so could not have been founded by him. The very name Auld -hām, the old religious establishment, suggests that it might pre-date Tyninghame but later functioned as 'a satellite, with a more significant monastic establishment'.[12] The landscape features that may have accounted for the establishment of a monastery in the first place – an exposed rocky promontory – were those that prevented its expansion; the south facing site on the banks of the Tyne estuary was larger, provided more shelter and safer access to the sea. By the middle of the tenth century, Tyninghame was the more important site; both settlements had co-existed for many years until Auldhame was abandoned in the late ninth century.

The one piece of physical evidence of Tyninghame's monastic past is a fragment of an elaborately carved Anglian sandstone cross, found around 1930 in the core of the old church tower. It has been dated as late ninth century.[13] It is the upper part of a free-standing

Seated figure with bushy hair and crossed arms
with two animals with intertwined tongues

Two birds with long beaks and a spray of leaves and berries

An animal with curling lips, lying on its back
eating berries dangling from a branch

Fragment showing double strand interlace pattern
on the back of ninth-century Anglo Saxon Cross

cross. On the front panel is a seated a figure with some damage to the hands. On the right side of the shaft are two birds with gannet like beaks and necks and on the opposite side is a curious animal, partly truncated but the rest of the upside-down body and legs fill the space beneath the branch. The construction of a cross like this required a patron of some means – a nobleman or woman, or someone of importance and wealth. It indicates that Tyninghame was a place of some standing in the ninth century.

Early documentary evidence is more plentiful and comes from different sources: histories, liturgy and poetry. The earliest, 'are notes made by the historian, Symeon of Durham, in the first quarter of the twelfth century. He recorded Baldred's death in AD 756 in the *Annals of Lindisfarne* and again in the *Historia Regum* that he edited. (Many of the earlier textual sources he used are preserved and so the authenticity of his information is not in question.)'[14] In his *Historia Dunelmensis ecclesiae*, Symeon repeats again the detail that Baldred led the life of an anchorite in Tyninghame. Anchorites, being part of the ecclesiastical tradition brought to Iona from Ireland, were venerated for their fortitude as well as for their piety, and their asceticism became a strong thread in the aspirations of the early Church in Northumbria and in Scotland.

Proof of this and of Baldred's connection with Lindisfarne are found in the *Liber Vitae* (Book of Life) of Durham, now in the British Library. It consists of lists of names of those members to be remembered by the community of St Cuthbert in their liturgy and prayers.[15] The book would have originally been kept on the altar at Lindisfarne (and until the Reformation it lay on the high altar in Durham Cathedral). It ensured that the monks following in St Cuthbert's footsteps honoured his example of endurance and solitude by remembering and praying for others who, like Baldred, had done the same. There are ten lists of names arranged in order of importance: kings and *duces*, queens and abbesses, and anchorites (after these

come abbots of different ranks, priests, deacons, clerics and monks). It is a striking indication of their prestige that the list of anchorites is third; Baldred's name is the thirteenth on the list.[16] Together the names in the *Liber Vitae* served to strengthen the self-belief of the community and kept alive the memory of its past.

In the oral traditions that developed alongside learned writing, the deeds and miracles of holy men and women needed to impress and strengthen belief. And they needed to match the stories from the Celtic and Scandinavian oral traditions where violence and heroism were on an epic scale, often with supernatural interventions. Baldred's name had first appeared in writing in a poem: *The Bishops, Kings and Saints of York* by Alcuin of York (735–805) where the poet described Baldred (Balthere) as 'a mighty warrior':

> There is a place completely encircled by the
>   ocean waves,
> hemmed by terrible crags and steep cliffs, where
> Balthere, the mighty warrior, during his life on
>   this earth
> vanquished time and again the hosts of the air
> that waged war on him in countless shapes.
> This saint fearlessly crushed his enemy's forces
>   and the arms
> of wicked demons, always opposing them with
>   the weapons of
> the Cross, the helmet and shield of Faith, in
>   successful combat.[17]

Alcuin goes on to describe Baldred's miracles including one in which he walked on water. Although Alcuin does not mention any place names, the Bass Rock has traditionally been associated with St Baldred and the ruins of the chapel there are said to mark his cell; the poem describes that terrain well. Exactly what kind of shelter St Baldred occupied is not known. *Clochans*, or beehive cells, belong to the tradition of the early Celtic Church and are found on rocky islands off the coast of

The Bass Rock. The remains of the chapel can just be seen to the right, above the lighthouse

south-west Ireland and also in Scotland, for example on Eileach an Naoimh, an uninhabited island between Mull and Argyll. Few survive, except in place names: a Gaelic word for church, *cill*, comes from the Latin, *cella*, and referred to small church buildings and settlements.

By 1507 when James IV requested the printing of a Scottish breviary containing brief biographies of Scottish saints together with a standardised church liturgy, their legends had accumulated. William Elphinstone, Bishop of Aberdeen, was charged with its composition with the help of the historian Hector Boece. Two Edinburgh booksellers acquired a printing press for this purpose and it appeared in 1510, the first book to be printed in Scotland. Every diocese in Scotland was approached for legends of their saints and they did not disappoint. The Aberdeen Breviary set out what the parishes wanted to be written about them – the fame and sanctity of their founders, their relics and shrines,

the extent of their properties – often to the detriment of historical accuracy.[18] Ownership of a relic, shrine or holy well had pecuniary as well as ecclesiastical advantages. Pilgrims and visitors to shrines were important to the local economy and miracle stories did the marketing.

St Baldred is now associated with three parishes: Auldhame, Tyninghame and Preston (Prestonkirk, East Linton). His feast day is 6 March, and he is described as a pupil of St Kentigern, who sought out remote places and islands in the sea where he meditated for long periods but did not forget his parishioners.

Two further miracles were added to those described by Alcuin: one concerns the origin of St Baldred's Boat, or St Baldred's Rock. In its original position, midway between the Bass Rock and the mainland it caused many shipwrecks. St Baldred placed himself on this rock, and 'like a ship driven by a fair wind, it came to

Reconstruction of a clochan at Kilmartin, Argyll

the hither shore'. Today it is situated on the rocks below Auldhame, marked with a beacon since it remains a hazard. Other places associated with the saint bear witness to a strong local cult: St Baldred's Cave on the beach near Auldhame, St Baldred's Cradle at Whitberry Point, Tyninghame, and a whirlpool in the Tyne, together with a well, below the church at Prestonkirk, East Linton.

The last miracle occurred after his death, which Boece records as occurring at Auldhame, not Tyninghame. The parishioners from the three churches each requested the body for their own kirk, but since they could not agree they left the body overnight and went away to pray for a sign from God. On returning the next morning, they found three identical bodies laid out for burial. Each parish gave thanks and carried the bodies with their shrines to their respective churches.

Although we know little about St Baldred's life and the monastery at Tyninghame, his cult grew and so did the settlement. By the middle of the tenth century Tyninghame was large enough and wealthy enough to attract a Viking attack. In the *Historia Regum*, for the year 941, Symeon of Durham writes: 'Anlaf laid waste

the church of St Baldred and burned Tyninghame.'[19] Anlaf, or Olaf (Guthfrithson), was the Norse King of York and Dublin; he died immediately after the attack. A late-eighth- to tenth-century Viking grave was found at the excavations at Auldhame. The skeleton had been buried with a belt with a copper alloy buckle and strap end, part of a cloth garment, iron spurs with buckles and an iron spearhead. While this was evidently a high-ranking individual, it is not possible to confirm that the skeleton is that of Olaf. Nevertheless, it is reasonable to associate this burial with the Viking attacks in the area. The site of Olaf's grave is unknown. Perhaps he was buried at Tyninghame.

Viking raids on Northumbria had begun with the destruction of the abbey on Lindisfarne in 793. In 795, Iona was attacked for the first time. The early Viking raids seem to have been hit-and-run affairs but by the end of the ninth century, large armies were arriving with the aim of settling permanently. At first pagan, they later converted to Christianity. In Scotland, and in the south-east in particular, the story of their impact is far from simple and the archaeological evidence is sparse, however, there is one further piece of evidence of Viking presence in Tyninghame.

In a field at Kirklandhill farm, a red sandstone drinking trough, now in the care of the National Museum of Scotland, was identified in the 1950s as a late tenth-century hogback stone.[20] Hogback monuments of this period are shaped like Viking longhouses, with curved roof ridges, some with stylised roof tiles and 'walls' decorated with animals or interlace patterns. They are found in areas of southern Scotland, usually close to maritime routes, in areas that had been settled by Scandinavians, and also in northern England.

On one side, there is a simple ring knot and two canine animals, with their forepaws on a disc, possibly the moon or the sun. On the other face, on the left-hand side there is a single animal in an identical position, a bold, chequered pattern in the centre and a simple pattern of small roof shingles with pointed ends on the right. The animals could represent the Norse mythological wolves, devouring the sun and the moon. Hogback stones rarely have Christian imagery and the images on the Kirklandhill stone are decidedly pagan, nevertheless, it very probably originated in the church-yard by the kirk across the river and would have been made for a wealthy Scandinavian Christian.

As the name implies, Kirklandhill was part of the land belonging to the kirk at Tyninghame, and in the past was easily reached across the ford. Before the parish at Tyninghame was united with Whitekirk in 1761, the cemetery was an impressive two acres in size, but after the merger, most was absorbed into the park-land. It is quite possible that a member of the Shirreff family, factors to the Earls of Haddington, who lived at Kirklandhill at the time 'saved' the hogback stone and found a new use for it in their fields.

Although there is no evidence of the re-establishment of a monastic settlement at Tyninghame after the Viking raid in 941, the site continued to have powerful significance through its association with St Baldred and the community from Lindisfarne. The

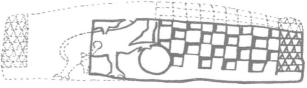

Reconstruction of the damaged hogback stone found at Kirklandhill (Courtesy of the Society of Antiquaries of Scotland)

Viking hogback gravestone indicated that although the village had been burned and the church 'laid waste', the cemetery was still in use and a church must have been rebuilt on the site by the end of the tenth century. Early in the eleventh century, Ælfred, a zealous priest of Durham, 'raised from the earth the bones . . . of those saints . . . and enshrined them above ground, so that they might be . . . venerated . . . (including) the bones . . . (of) Balthere and Bilfrith . . .'[21] Part of the relics were then taken to Durham where the community of Lindisfarne had eventually resettled in AD 995. No mention is made of the other identical bodies and shrines described in the Aberdeen Breviary. Perhaps the remaining parts were divided between the three churches of Auldhame, Preston and Tyninghame, thus giving rise to the legend.

In spite of the lack of evidence of a re-established monastery, the connection with the church family of Lindisfarne remained strong. The existence of a church with administrative responsibilities within the community of St Cuthbert is evidenced in the *Historia de Sancto Cuthberto*, produced in the middle of eleventh century. It contains a detailed record of the land-holdings – of which there were many. In fact, establishing property rights seems to have been the primary motive for the composition of the *Historia* 'as a record of the places and regions of (St Cuthbert's) ancient patrimony'.[22] These lands extended: 'beyond the Tweed . . . and all the land which lies between . . . (the) Blackadder and . . . Leader . . . and all the land that pertains to the monastery of St Balthere, which is called Tyningham (*quod locatur Tinningaham*), from the Lammermuir Hills as far as the mouth of the Esk'.

The extent of the land owned by Tyninghame seems exaggerated, but this might be explained if St Baldred's mission in Lothian had been as a 'daughter house', a manor, administered from Lindisfarne, having control over the land between the Lammermuir Hills and the mouth of the river Esk.[23] Historically, this might have been the case and undoubtedly in the eleventh century, the bishopric of Durham was keen to establish as large a sphere of influence (and pecuniary advantage) as possible.

The next documented reference to Tyninghame occurs in Scotland's earliest surviving charter, that of King Duncan II of Scotland, *c.*1094. It gives a different, more specific picture:

> I Dunecan, son of King Malcolumb, by hereditary right King of Scotland, have given in alms to Saint Cuthbert and to his servants, Tiningeham, Aldeham, Scuchale, Cnolle, Hatheruuich, and of Broccesmuthe all the service which Fodan the bishop thence had. And these I have given in such quittance with sac and soc, as ever Saint Cuthbert has had best from those from whom he holds his alms. And this I have given for myself, for the soul of my father, for my brothers, and for my wife, and for my children. And because I would that this gift should be firm to Saint Cuthbert, I have made my brothers join in the grant. But whosoever would destroy this or take from the servants of Saint Cuthbert anything of it, let him bear the curse of God and of Saint Cuthbert and mine. Amen.[24]

Tyninghame is mentioned first, suggesting it was the most important, followed, from north to south, by Scoughal, Knowes, Hedderwick and Broxmouth, just south of Dunbar. ('Sac and soc' is a medieval term referring to the right of local jurisdiction.) The charter refers to 'Fodan the bishop', as a previous 'superior'. He was in fact bishop of St Andrews from *c.*1070 and had married Duncan's father and stepmother, King Malcolm and Queen Margaret in 1071. He probably died around 1093–4, just before the charter was signed. This is the earliest reference to St Andrews in connection with Tyninghame but how or why Bishop Fodan gained this 'service' is not known.

This was a time when the Scottish monarchs, and the Church, were consolidating their control over Lothian. It appears that Tyninghame had become the centre of an administrative tug-of-war between the diocese of Durham to the south, and the cathedral priory of St Andrews to the north. It caught the early attention of Duncan II, whose motive in making this gift to the servants of St Cuthbert must have been to bolster support for his claim to the throne, and not just as a simple act of piety. As a child, Duncan had been sent as hostage to the court of William the Conqueror in 1072 and he grew up in the Anglo-Norman culture of the time. When his uncle Donald laid claim to the throne, Duncan moved north with an invading army and was successful. He was seen as a Norman 'outsider' and his brief reign ended after only seven months, when he was ambushed and killed in battle.

Had it worked, such an arrangement should have been mutually beneficial, but the charter, which reaffirmed the ancient patrimony, was never realised and the monks of St Cuthbert at Durham were not able to capitalise on Duncan's apparent generosity. In spirit, Auldhame and Tyninghame belonged to the tradition of Lindisfarne but the tide had turned and, in reality, their ecclesiastical centre had shifted to the north, to St Andrews.

CHAPTER 3

Lords Spiritual and Temporal

Reform and reorganisation were occurring throughout Scotland in the first half of the twelfth century. As far as the Church was concerned it involved new, Norman, forms of management and administration, at least on the surface. At St Andrews, for example, Celtic bishops, such as Fodan (or Fothad) mentioned in Duncan's Charter as having been associated with Tyninghame, made way for 'a series of "Norman" bishops: that is, bishops who were foreign-born or (foreign)-trained and who brought to their diocese a concern to bring it into conformity with the practices of the western church'.[1] Tyninghame provides a good example of how the old ways continued to influence these modernising trends.

When the cathedral priory of St Andrews was established in 1140, the church at Tyninghame featured in its foundation as a possession of the priest Robert, who became one of its first canons.[2] It not known how, or why, the priest Robert came into the possession of Tyninghame, but it reveals a continuing connection with the bishops of St Andrews, at this time the most important and the richest diocese in Scotland. 'It seems possible that these lands, which surrounded the site of the ancient monastery of St Baldred, came into the possession of the bishops as part of the extension of royal power into Lothian in the tenth and eleventh centuries. Along with the Bass Rock they formed the basis of the episcopal barony of Tyninghame, which remained a constant administrative unit throughout the middle ages.'[3] This link with St Andrews continued for over 600 years, well after the parish of Tyninghame was annexed to the parish of Whitekirk in 1761.

Another important record of the existence of a church at Tyninghame is the famous illuminated *Kelso Charter* of King Malcolm IV, of 1159. This was once in the possession of the Earls of Haddington and is now in the National Library of Scotland and is celebrated as it contains the earliest portraits of the kings of Scotland.

The portraits contrast the aged King David I and his young successor, King Malcolm IV. The charter granted to the abbot and monks of Kelso, for their church at Innerleithen, the same privilege of 'girth' (sanctuary) as at Tyninghame and Stow.[4] There is no reference to a monastery, but the evidence from these very different texts is proof there was a well-established church here by the mid twelfth century.

At Tyninghame, the surviving decorated arches and pillars testify that this was one of the finest examples of a Romanesque parish church. Its architectural details bear similarities to Dunfermline Abbey, 'the most quintessential of all Romanesque churches in mainland Scotland.'[5]

As the first stages of the parish network were estab-

King David I as a bearded old man with grey hair and his clean-shaven grandson, young King Malcolm IV, Kelso Charter, 1159
(By kind permission of the Duke of Roxburgh and the National Library of Scotland)

St Baldred's Kirk

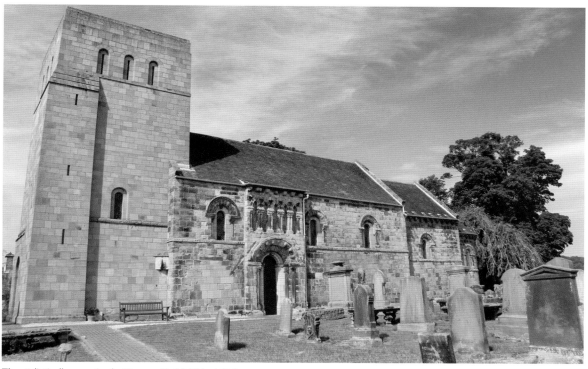

The stylistically pure Anglo-Norman Parish Kirk at Dalmeny

lished during the reign of David I, a demand was created for new churches. There was an unprecedented demand for experienced stonemasons and craftsmen, which could not be met without importing skilled tradesmen from England. Dunfermline Abbey is a case in point. Re-established in 1128 and dedicated in 1150, David invited monks from Canterbury as its first community, but the masons came from Durham. For the church of St Baldred, whose remains were possibly still interred at Tyninghame, this significant link with Durham would have been even more appropriate.

All that remains of the church today are an outline of the foundations, two decorated arches and twin pillars or wall shafts of the apse. (The fifteenth-century tomb to an unknown lady was introduced at a later date from elsewhere.) Yet there is enough to show that this was originally an important church dating from the mid twelfth century. It was thirty-five metres in length and had a semi-circular apse with stone vaulting, chancel, nave and a bell tower at the western end. Many less important churches were simple rectangular structures, possibly with a distinct nave and chancel, but without the apse or tower.[6] In addition, the twin arched recesses in the eastern end of the nave are an extra refinement, suggesting a sophisticated building.

The roof and the masonry of the walls were taken down sometime in the late eighteenth century in order to leave a picturesque ruin. The church at Dalmeny, the most complete Romanesque church in Scotland and contemporary with Tyninghame, gives an idea of what the original church may have looked like. The dominating architectural influences at this time were the monastic and cathedral foundations and many of the masons who worked on parish churches, including Tyninghame and Dalmeny, had served their apprenticeships at these greater churches.[7] At Dalmeny, for

Arches with chevron patterns and capitals with typical Romanesque decoration

example, the same mason's marks there also occur at Dunfermline, and some of these are also found at Durham. No such marks have been found at Tyninghame but there are enough similarities for architectural historians to note the 'debts to Dunfermline at Tyninghame'.[8]

The decoration on the pale pink sandstone arches is a case in point. The chevron, or zigzag, pattern which prevails here in different forms is characteristic of the period and widespread, from Kirkwall to Durham. The paired capitals (the top section of the pillar) all have different decorations, and are all found at Dunfermline.[9] Those at the nave are patterned with overlapping 'fish scales' and those between the chancel and the curved apse have scroll-like, volute curves with further palmette decoration above. The fluted scalloped decoration on the capitals of the surviving wall shafts of the apse, resembling organ pipes, would have supported a stone roof, as at Dalmeny.

When the parish was merged with nearby Whitekirk in 1761, stone from the redundant building was gradually removed and then re-used locally. Some of the carved stones were inserted as decorations into the walls of the stables. In concluding his entry for the church at Tyninghame in *The Buildings of Scotland*, Colin McWilliam wrote, 'Who can have paid for these splendours? We know the bishop of St Andrews owned both the church and the lordship, but is this in itself sufficient explanation? There is no reason to think that the church was anything more than parochial.'[10] While it is true that the church was a parish church, its connection with the bishops of St Andrews gives it a far more prominent status than just 'parochial'. It was the bishops' chapel and they owned the manor house. Richard Fawcett, in his book *The Architecture of the Scottish Medieval Church, 1100–1560*, agrees that the church could have been built by one of the bishops of St Andrews, who were the 'high bishops of Scotland' – *ardescop Alban* in Gaelic.[11]

In medieval Scotland, the Church was sandwiched between the archdiocese of Trondheim in Norway and the English archdioceses of York and Canterbury, both wanting ecclesiastical superiority over Scotland. Instead, Scotland looked to Rome and Pope Honorarius III (1216–27), as the head of the independent Scottish Church, issued a charter in 1218 offering 'Protection to the Bishop of St Andrews, and his successors, for their church and its possessions'. 'Tiningham, with its belongings'[12] is one of the churches listed, and the phrasing suggests that its landholdings (possessions) must have been significant enough to warrant a separate mention.

When choosing sites for their residences, bishops were drawn to holy places already imbued with sacred authority, what the sites had in common was their previous association with a saint or holy relic. The asso-

ciation with St Baldred and Lindisfarne, together with the physical remains of the free-standing cross and the cemetery, including the hogback tombstone, made Tyninghame a particularly attractive place for the bishops of St Andrews. Here they could capitalise on its spiritual heritage and strengthen the diocese.

Medieval scribes variously used the terms castle, palace or manor in charters describing a bishop's residence, and these terms suggest a worldly, rather than ecclesiastical, authority.[13] In the case of Tyninghame, the residence was modest, probably a simple tower house. Although there are no surviving records to cast light on the first building, there are indications of a small, three storey tower house at the heart of what is now Tyninghame House. There is no way of knowing whether this fortified manor house dates from the thirteenth century, or whether a timber structure preceded it, as at the Bishop's Castle at St Andrews, but either would be entirely consistent with the programme of building bishop's residences that accompanied the organisational reform of the dioceses in the late twelfth and early thirteenth centuries.

Pastoral responsibility was administered by the archdeacon and rural deans. The diocese of St Andrews had two archdeaconries in existence by the middle of the twelfth century, one to the north of the Firth of Forth and one to the south, which was known as Lothian, Tyninghame or Liston. The area of the eastern deanery north of the Lammermuirs, corresponded almost exactly with the original lands of the ancient monastery of Tyninghame.[14] Clearly, what had 'aye been' the territory associated with St Baldred, remained in place, though with new layers of administration.

As far as the administration of the bishop's territorial demesne was concerned, the three episcopal baronies in Lothian were based on ancient ecclesiastical sites: Tyninghame, Stow and Kirkliston. In each of these a bailie, the bishop's agent, was appointed and was responsible to the bishop's chamberlain. In 1316, Bishop Lamberton granted lands on the Bass Rock to

Robert Lauder in return for his services as heritable bailie of Tyninghame, though the charter is now lost.[15]

From 1316 successive generations of the powerful Lauder family were responsible, as bailies, for Tyninghame, and would have resided there from time to time. There are no records indicating a separate dwelling place for the rector. One important figure, Nicholas de Moffat, bishop-elect of Glasgow had been rector and his burial here in 1270 is recorded.[16] In the 1274–5 accounts of the papal tax collector in Scotland, it is shown that the rector paid nine merks.[17] Teinds or tithes would also have been paid to the diocese of St Andrews, the superior.

More records survive in the fifteenth century, mostly in papal letters, naming some of the rectors of Tyninghame: Patrick de Lochris, Alexander de Newton, George Carmichael, Andrew Martin, Hugh Douglas, Thomas Vaus, and George Brown, who was replaced by Nicholas Greenshaw when he became Bishop of Dunkeld.[18] When George Brown resigned in 1484, the independence of the parish church was threatened as there was an effort to annex it to St Salvator's, one of the colleges of St Andrew's University. In 1473 the diocese of St Andrews had become an archdiocese and no time was lost in attempting to bring Tyninghame more closely into the fold, along with other churches in the diocese, by annexing them to the *mensa* of the new archbishopric. The archbishop would then have enjoyed these revenues for his personal expenses. Both St Salvator's College and the archbishopric were keen to get the revenues from the parish, but neither fully achieved their goal and for another fifty years, from 1487 to 1537, Tyninghame remained an independent parish church. Archbishop Beaton, the last archbishop of St Andrews, succeeded where his predecessors had failed: the teinds were annexed to the New College of St Mary in the university.[19]

When the parish of Tyninghame was annexed to that of Whitekirk, the College raised no objection but stipulated that the sum of 200 merks from the teinds of Tyninghame should be reserved and paid to their factor.[20]

For most of the intervening 400 years, only two families were associated with Tyninghame: the Lauders of the Bass, who were bailies and tenants for most of this time, and the Earls of Haddington who were owners. There was a brief period in the 1530s when the Lauders were pushed aside when James V intervened to procure Tyninghame for his eldest natural son, James Stewart, confirmed in a charter issued by Cardinal Beaton in 1535. But having obtained the far more lucrative forfeited estates of Douglas, James Stewart assumed the title of Lord Douglas and promptly leased the barony back to Robert Lauder in 1537. He surrendered the lordship of Tyninghame to his younger sibling the Earl of Moray, brother of Mary, Queen of Scots, and regent of Scotland (1567–70).

The charter of 1535 is interesting because it details for the first time, the extent of the lands of Tyninghame: 'the lands of the mains of Tyninghame, twenty husbandlands and twenty cotlands, five brewlands, the mill of Tyninghame, lands called Warrilandis, Gilliescot and Smithyland, with fishing in the water of Tyne and lochs and cunningars (rabbit warrens) of the lands of Tyninghame and with the office of bailiary of the Lordship'.[21] A husbandland equates to roughly twenty-six acres, a cotland was the land attached to a cottage and a brewland was the land associated with the brewing on an estate. The impression is that the estate was not vast, something over 500 acres, but not insignificant; its value lay in the spiritual association with St Baldred and its connection to the early Church, as important to the Lauders as it was to the New College of St Andrews.

The Lauders finally became owners of Tyninghame in September 1568 when Sir Robert Lauder and his son purchased it from Sir William Maitland of Lethington for 11,000 merks. William had been Secretary to Mary, Queen of Scots, and had acquired the property from

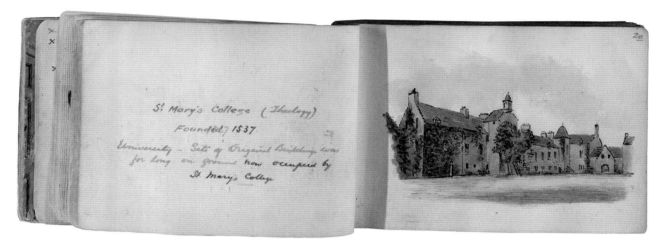

St Mary's College which today houses the School of Divinity, from J. N. Bonthron's sketchbook of St Andrews, 1907–9 (Courtesy of the University of St Andrews)

his friend, the Earl of Moray, in a private sale in 1562.[22] They also added the lands of the Knowes and Kirklandhill, adjacent to Tyninghame. Sadly for the Lauders, their ownership was to be relatively short lived.

They borrowed extensively to raise the money for the purchase but then had to mortgage the land to their creditors. This was to prove their downfall for even though they had friends at court and extensive landholdings, they had overstretched themselves. Robert died in 1576, his grandson, George, was still a minor when he inherited Tyninghame in 1611 and his mother, the Dowager Lady Bass, managed their properties. By all accounts she was inept and did not acknowledge the precariousness of their finances, even enlarging Tyninghame.

Evidence that she was employing builders from Edinburgh at the mansion house comes from the Tyninghame kirk session minutes for 12 October 1617. The 'maisonis qua wer bigging [building] the Ladyis hous to come befor ye session, because he [the minister] hard that ye last Sabbothe at efternoone ye saidis maisonis wer playing at ye golf . . .'[23] Lady Bass would not have employed builders from Edinburgh had she

not been undertaking a serious (and costly) building project as there were masons to be found locally. The minutes also record that the builders had been living in the village for a while, further proof that the work was extensive. Medieval towers were not large and her extension may have been the west wing, doubling the size and making the building L-shaped. However, there are no historical records and later additions have obscured what went before so this must remain conjectural. What is clear is that in post-Reformation Scotland, the days of the tower house as an occasional bishop's residence were past. By the early seventeenth century it was being further transformed into a country seat.

The Lauders had been bailies and tenants at Tyninghame for more than 250 years, but Sir Robert's purchase could not be sustained by his daughter-in-law and his grandson. The house was sold to John Murray (later Lord Annandale) for 200,000 merks and the contract of sale was signed on 2 June 1621.

It marked the end of an era and the beginning of a period of uncertainty and transition for all who lived and worked in Tyninghame. It also coincided with a famine which was to last three years. The entry in the session minutes for 14 October 1621 describes 'verie tempestious . . . verie vehement' weather. A note in the margin of that day adds, 'At this tyme the famin began; for the vehement rain began the 3 day of Octr., and lastit till the tenth day without intermission. Famin for thre yeirs continuit, viz., 1621, 1622, 1623.'[24]

The fact that John Murray never lived at Tyninghame made life even more difficult for the residents. On 10 March 1622 the minister, John Lauder, or 'Maister Jhone' as he was known, was concerned for the schoolmaster ('have ane cair for the schoolmaister') as there was no provision for the school. They asked for help from their landowner's factor, Sir James Baillie: 'Lady Bass did give befor four bolls of victual for the schoole' and they asked that 'my Lord of Annandale wald do the lyke'.[25] Lord Annandale's response is not noted. He is remembered for his gifts of a bell for the steeple and a bible in 1625, though both the bell and the bible were moved to Whitekirk in 1761 but, sadly, did not survive the fire there in 1914.

At the turn of the year, in January 1628, the Earl of Annandale again sold Tyninghame for 200,000 merks, the same sum that he had paid nearly seven years before, to his friend Thomas Hamilton, the new Earl of Haddington. It was to remain in the Hamilton family until 1987.

It may not have been a coincidence that the purchase followed his new honour so quickly. The illustrious public career of Thomas Hamilton, previously Earl of Melrose, was drawing to a close. The title of Haddington, with the rank of viscount, was granted to him in August 1627, suggesting that the purchase of Tyninghame was probably already under way. Hamilton had given faithful service to James VI throughout his career, but after the king's death in 1625 he found it more difficult to give the same allegiance to his successor, Charles I. Nevertheless, it was King Charles who bestowed this last honour.

Thomas Hamilton (1563–1635), the eldest son of Thomas Hamilton of Priestfield, attended the Royal High School in Edinburgh before going to Paris to study law, as his father had done before him. There he was under the supervision of his uncle, John Hamilton, a Catholic priest and something of a zealot, who 'organised the Paris clergy as shock-troops of the Holy League against Henry IV, said mass in his cuirass, (and) baptised children in full armour . . .'[26] For the rest of his life, Thomas was wary of religious extremists, though his opponents noted his scruples did not impede his rise to power.

On his return to Edinburgh in 1587 his ascent was swift: he became an advocate, married Margaret Borthwick the following year, four years later he became a Law Lord (Lord Drumcairn after his Perthshire estate) and, in 1593, a privy councillor. He was appointed to a committee to manage Queen Anne's estates and finances, and its success in increasing her revenues brought him to the king's notice.[27] In 1596 he became one of the eight commissioners appointed for life known as the Octavians, joint commissioners of the exchequer, with full powers to collect and disburse royal revenue. The responsibilities and the temptations came in equal measure and Thomas appears to have shouldered the one and succumbed to the other. The commissioners brought about the necessary reforms but rewarded themselves (and family members) with high offices of state; Thomas Hamilton was made Lord Advocate. Inevitably the Octavians attracted criticism and jealousy: they were mostly 'new men', upwardly mobile professionals from outside the old, landed aristocracy, educated abroad and keen to modernise the State. But it was the suspicion that they favoured Roman Catholicism that brought them into conflict with the Church and which was their downfall. They disbanded after only a year. Nevertheless, the eight commissioners had manoeuvred themselves into positions of power and they re-emerged in a subsequent,

Opposite: Portrait of Thomas, 1st Earl of Haddington, after Adam de Colone by an unknown artist, after 1630 (Courtesy of the National Galleries of Scotland)

larger commission of the exchequer as members for life.

The two strands that formed the basis of Thomas's rise to power and were the bedrock of his career were already in evidence. On the one hand he was a powerful and effective advocate and, on the other, he understood and participated in the management of the exchequer. There is no doubt he was also conscientious and hard working; there can have been little time for family life with Margaret and their two daughters. Margaret died in December 1596 and by August 1597 Thomas had married Margaret Foulis, daughter of James Foulis of Colinton, who was to bear him three sons and four more daughters. When James VI succeeded to the English throne in 1603, he left Scotland but not before passing an Act that gave even more power to the Lord Advocate. In the king's absence, few if any had more authority in Scotland than Thomas Hamilton, or 'Tam o' the Cowgate' as James VI affectionately called him.

In 1607 James made his famous boast to the English Parliament: 'This I may say for Scotland and may truly vaunt it; here I sit and govern it with my pen; I write, and it is done, and by a Clerk of the Council I govern Scotland now, which others could not do with the sword.' The truth was rather different. James had been King of Scotland, man and boy, for over thirty years and left behind statesmen who were perfectly capable of governing in his absence. Thomas Hamilton was part of this established elite and his power continued to increase during James' lifetime. But in his private life there was sadness as his second wife also died young in 1609, just a year after giving birth to their daughter Lady Anne, who was named after the queen. He did not remarry until 1613, this time to the widow of Patrick Hume of Polwarth, Juliana Ker, the same year he was created Lord Binning. They had one son. This was the marriage that was to last the longest and they died within weeks of each other in 1637.

Thomas became Scottish Secretary of State from 1612, Lord President of the Court of Session in 1616 and in 1618, Commissioner to the Assembly. He regarded the latter as something of a poisoned chalice, or at least a chalice for which he had no taste, as he quickly asked to be relieved of the office. There was considerable tension over the Five Articles of Perth which the king wished to impose in order to integrate the Church in Scotland with the Episcopalian Church of England. Although eventually, and reluctantly, the Articles were authorised by Parliament in 1621, the whole affair succeeded in galvanising Presbyterian opposition. In a letter quoted by Sir William Fraser, Lord Binning wrote to the king: 'If your continouall caire of the good of this cuntrie and church move your royall mynd to intend heirefter any church matters of such consequence, I beseech your Maiestie, for the good of your own service, to employ ane more fit commissioner in my place, who am als unskilfull in thir subiectis as I am ungracious to the opposites.'[28] However Lord Binning did what he was asked and promoted public worship according to the king's wishes. Shortly afterwards, he was raised another rung in the peerage and created Earl of Melrose. A contemporary historian, resolutely opposed to the introduction of bishops in Scotland, noted 'noe doubt for the good service he had done in advancing the state of bishops and course of conformitie'.[29] The earl's eldest son, also Thomas, then aged nineteen, took the courtesy title, Lord Binning.

When James VI died on 27 March 1625, the fortunes of Thomas Hamilton, Earl of Melrose, began to change. Charles I lost no time in bringing in new policies and superseding parliamentary procedures which angered the country. Within a year of James' death, the Earl of Melrose was replaced as president of the Court of Session. He was still nominally the Secretary and Keeper of the Signet, but after such long and faithful service he resented this treatment and protested but he was not reinstated.

Behind the scenes, during the turbulent years that

followed, it seems that the Earl of Melrose continued to try to persuade the new king of the need to involve Parliament if consent to his proposals were to be achieved. However, he helped to formulate the tithes and annual rents the king demanded. When the king requested help raising forces in Scotland for the ill-fated expedition to France in 1627, not only did the earl give his assistance but sent his second eldest son, James, in charge of a company.[30] Later that year he received royal letters patent changing his title from Melrose to Haddington, which coincided with his purchase of Tyninghame. Although still involved in affairs of state, he knew his days of real influence were over.

The 1st Earl was the ablest statesman of all the succeeding generations of his family; though many held public office, none held as many high positions of state nor accrued as much wealth. Wealth that attracted attention during his lifetime, with a contemporary historian, Robert Chambers, telling the story that during his visit to Scotland in 1617, James VI found Lord Binning to be very rich 'and was informed that the people believed him to be in possession of the philosopher's stone, there being no other feasible means of accounting for his immense wealth'.[31]

Although much of his wealth was invested in property, the imposing Edinburgh mansion, which was the family town house, was leased. It occupied the site between Merchant Street and the Cowgate until it was demolished around 1829 to make way for the George IV Bridge.

Thomas Hamilton's first properties were inherited from his father: Priestfield (now Prestonfield), together with Balnabein and Drumcairn in Perthshire. The first land that he bought was fifty-two acres of the 'common myre' or marsh adjoining Priestfield and bordering Duddingston Loch. Soon afterwards he bought land in what was then Linlithgowshire: Humbie, including the church lands of Binny, or Binning, named after the Binny or Binning family who once owned them and

also acquired mineral rights in the Bathgate area. The following year (1608) he bought land in East Lothian: the Byres, and later Balgone and Luffness. By the time he was made Lord Melrose in 1621 his landholdings had further increased. The long list given by Sir William Fraser included several more temple lands in Edinburgh and Leith, from Berwick to Inverness and from East Lothian to Kirkcudbright and Ayr.[32] In the Borders he bought land and baronies which had belonged to the abbey of Melrose and later Coldstream and Coldenknows. But it was Tyninghame that became his major country residence.

The sasine of 29 January 1628 describes the same lands as had been given to James Stewart in 1535.[33] Of the mansion itself, little is known, apart from the reference in the kirk session record to building work by Lady Bass. His residence in the Cowgate suggests that he lived in some grandeur, but the building at Tyninghame was more modest when Thomas acquired it. But whatever the extended tower house may have lacked in magnificence in 1628, it had a splendid location, a splendid church, a splendid history and was potentially a splendid country seat. It is highly likely that Lord Haddington extended it further. In an inventory dated 9 June 1635, completed by the earl's servant, Archibald Elliot,[34] mention is made of the 'easterwork', suggesting recent building. This could refer to a wing extending at the east of the house to balance the west wing that had previously been added by the Lauder family. Charles McKean suggests that it was the 1st Earl of Haddington who added both wings at the same time, concluding that 'the west wing must have been the family wing, and the east wing the public and guest wing'.[35] While it is possible that both wings were added simultaneously after 1628, it implies that the important Lauder family had lived for many years confined in the old tower four metres wide and seven metres in length whenever they came to Tyninghame. The massive walls of the tower and projecting jamb (wing) are now hidden at the heart of the house but are

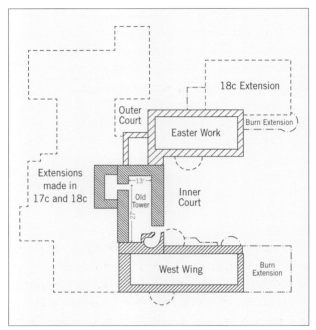

Plan of Tyninghame House showing possible phases of development

with the outer close or outer court, from where estate business was usually conducted and where the bakehouse, brewhouse, stable and yards were found. This section of the building may have been of a single storey whereas the next section described had three storeys and bounded the inner close. Charles McKean describes this inner close as typical of a Scottish country seat, 'Guests were received in the inner court, the inner close or the *cour d'honneur* . . . which was lined by offices, guest lodgings, woman house and occasionally a chapel. The well was the dominant feature . . . The inner court was a place of arrival and departure, reception and hospitality.'[38]

This 'easterwork', formed the eastern third side, or wing, of the now U-shaped mansion. It contained a 'grit hall' on the principal floor and two bedchambers on each of the floors above and below. Moving across to the older, west wing, Elliot describes the 'wasterhall' with its 'chalmber of dease'. This may have been the first extension to the tower, begun by one of the Lauder family or by Lady Bass whose 'biggin' was noted earlier. As Charles McKean notes: 'Additional accommodation could be provided by building a new module alongside; hence the Scots habit of architecture by accretion . . . the compressions and constrictions of the tower were incompatible with the changes of living patterns that occurred during the sixteenth century.'[39] In Scotland, the hall was always on the first floor, away from the damp ground floor, and from it opened the 'chalmber of dease', or chamber of dais, a formal, small private room often sumptuously furnished, and which could contain the principal bed. In 1635 it was being used as a bedroom, but it was not the most lavishly furnished. There were two further rooms above the wester hall: one was a lavish bathroom with a mirror and a marble table, chamber pot and pan, and the other, a bedroom with flowered taffeta curtains and valance, stitched and woven covers, and an oak table with an (expensive) woven tablecloth. The adjacent room above the chamber of dais was the finest. It had an oak four-

revealed in the plans of the house made by William Burn in 1829.[36]

If the Lauders extended the house prior to 1628, they were following an earlier trend for expansion that had begun in the sixteenth century, 'There was usually a sequence of three rooms on the principal floor in country houses, sometimes characterised as antechamber, chamber and bed chamber; or Hall, Chamber of Dais and Bedchamber. An identical apartment for the lady of the house might lie on the floor above.'[37] This is roughly the sequence in the west wing at Tyninghame as the inventory makes clear. By adding an east wing, if this hypothesis is correct, Thomas was in effect balancing that to the west and creating a U-shaped building, characteristic of late Jacobean court architecture of the early seventeenth century. Winton House, for example, was remodelled to a U-plan at this time, though with more flamboyance.

Elliot identifies twenty-eight rooms in all. He begins

poster bed covered in green cloth, with matching curtains and valance with 'braid lace', three armchairs and stools, a pine table with matching tablecloth and two further feather beds. Thus there were three storeys on this side of the courtyard.

The central section including the tower joined the two wings. Here was the 'lettermeit hous', where the 'lower orders' and servants dined, with a pantry and cellar, and inner and outer bedchambers above. There were further bedrooms above, and on the ground floor a kitchen, little kitchen and 'wardrop'.

Another inventory compiled and signed by Thomas himself in 1635 included what he must have considered his most valuable possessions: silver plates, trenchers, salt cellars, spoons, forks, bowls, goblets and jugs for wine, candlesticks together with expensive furnishings, including a long turkey carpet and chairs and stools covered with velvet and damask. Special mention is made of 'ane bleu cloath bed lynit [lined] with taffitie, with riche lace and fringe, togidder with the chaires, stooles, and table cloath conforme thairto [matching] . . .'[40] His collection of tapestries was extensive. No mention is made of his paintings – at least two portraits were painted during his lifetime – nor his personal collection of books which remained intact at Tyninghame until they were acquired by the National Library of Scotland in the twentieth century.

Hugh Trevor-Roper wrote a short essay on the book collection, published privately in 1977.[41] He considered the collection unique as it had not been dispersed over the centuries and the books were all signed, including some that were annotated, indicating those that were read more carefully. There are some surprising inclusions and equally surprising omissions. There were more books on history, politics and political thought than any other subject, even than law, which was his profession. Some were in English, others in Latin, French and Italian. There were few books on religion, for which he appears to have had little interest. He owned a copy of the Geneva Bible and the *Institution*

of the Christian Religion by Calvin, but Trevor-Roper notes that neither was much used and observes that he was opposed to all forms of religious extremism: 'The only books of religious interest are those concerned with the movement for the reunion of the churches.' Although strong in France and England at the time this movement had little or no following in Scotland.

What is rather shocking is that this cultured, sophisticated and cosmopolitan politician had no books on Scotland, other than a few on entirely practical subjects. He owned books on the history of many other countries but none on the history of Scotland. Curiously, besides works of literature, classical and French and Italian, there were 'a disproportionate number of "books on courtesy"', the seventeenth-century equivalent of 'How to Survive at Court'. Whatever lessons they contained, Thomas not only survived but succeeded.

The mansion house at Tyninghame was now a well-appointed country seat. As for the township, which lay to the south and to the west, life in its scattered dwellings and hamlets cannot have changed very much. Other than the descriptions of the extent of the estate in the sasines quoted earlier, there are no descriptions of any garden ground or orchards, although they would have existed. Session and parish records name George Key as gardener in Tyninghame in 1616,[42] and Andrew Strong in 1636.[43] In Elliot's inventory 'four forms for the garden and tuo saitts', were kept in the bakehouse and brewhouse. Seats and garden benches would probably have been placed in the pleasure garden, which in the early seventeenth century would have been some form of decorative parterre, adjacent to the house. At Tyninghame, a formal parterre still exists to the west of the house. Marilyn Brown describes the gardens in Scotland, post the Union of 1603, as broadly the same style: 'there might be a walled garden or series of walled enclosures, terracing or water features, sundials, fountains, sculpture; and the

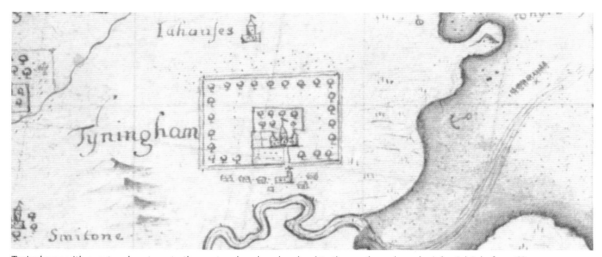

Tyninghame with quartered parterre to the west and enclosed orchard to the north, as drawn by John Adair before 1682 (Courtesy of the National Library of Scotland)

outlook from the garden remained important . . . Many of these gardens belonged to royal officials . . .'[44] The manuscript map of East Lothian by John Adair from before 1682 indicates that Tyninghame included many of these features by this date.

The enclosure with dotted lines to the south may indicate some form of terracing. A wide path leads from the house to the church of St Baldred, with scattered village houses and the River Tyne to the south. The whole is enclosed by a tree-lined boundary wall, but no extensive woodland is indicated. Although Adair used simplified pictograms to represent estates and buildings, the maps are remarkably accurate in establishing what was on the ground when he conducted his surveys. Given that the layout depicted by Adair closely fits the description of typical earlier gardens, it suggests that this was more or less the design of the garden enjoyed by the 1st Earl of Haddington.

Thomas made his will and drew up the two inventories just two years before his death in 1637. During his lifetime, as one of the most prominent and active members of the Scottish Cabinet of James VI, he showed a remarkable capacity for hard work. Whatever his achievement, it was not without making enemies.

Trevor-Roper quotes a contemporary epitaph for him:

> Here lies a Lord who, while he stood,
> Had matchless been, had he been good.

And yet in his testament, Thomas shows himself to be considerate to his fellow parishioners, to his servants and to those in need. When describing his funeral arrangements, he specifically asks that it should be a modest affair:

> I direct and entreite my said executor (Thomas Lord Binning) to commit my body to Christiane burial, in decent and modest maner, without pompe or superfluitie, and in place of grit charges bestowed by many at suche occasiounes upoune unnecessary shewes, that he give to the poore of the parochines quhair I shall die or be buried, a bountifull distributioun according to his conscience and discretioune: I farder ordane him to give sume ressonabill recompence to such of my old servand is as he knows to have beine faithfull to me, and stand in need . . .[45]

CHAPTER 4

Mothers and Daughters

After the death of Thomas, the 1st Earl of Haddington, four male members of the family succeeded him without coming close to the fame and achievements of their great ancestor. In 1685 another Thomas became the 6th Earl at the age of five. It was some years before he made his mark, but he was to become one of the leading eighteenth-century agricultural improvers in Scotland and wrote an important book on forestry. Of the women in the story, little has been written. Although Thomas always attributed his interest in planting to the influence of his wife Helen, both his mother, Margaret Leslie, Countess of Rothes, the eldest daughter of the Duke of Rothes, and his mother-in-law, Margaret, Lady Hope, were influential figures. All three women were well educated and literate which was not always the case for well-born women at that time. Undoubtedly they wrote letters but very few have survived, so to draw them from the shadows, the light must be cast by circumstantial evidence and the letters of others.

Ironically, the one female member of the family who did achieve fame in the seventeenth century, Lady Jean Hamilton, did so unknowingly. She was the fifth daughter of the 1st Earl of Haddington and was married to John Kennedy, the 6th Earl of Cassilis, when just only fourteen. He was also a minor although his exact birth date is uncertain. She was born in 1607 and died in 1642 but very little is known of her life; no portraits of her survive. However, in popular tradition, she is forever associated with the King of the Lowland gypsies, Johnny Faa, from Dunbar. The Border ballad, 'Johnnie Faa, the Gypsy Laddie', recounts the story of how she fell under the gypsies' spell:

> Yestreen I lay in a well-made bed,
> And my good lord beside me;
> This night I'll ly in a tenant's barn,
> Whatever shall betide me,[1]

But there was no going back. On discovering her disappearance, her husband saddled his horse to take his revenge. The gypsies were all caught and hanged. In several of the later nineteenth-century versions of 'The Gypsy Laddie,' the Earl of Cassilis's name appears, but why the story should have become associated with his wife is unclear.[2]

That so little is known about Jean Hamilton, when so much has been written about her husband, John Kennedy, is hardly surprising as the role of women in seventeenth-century Scotland was barely commented on by historians. In his monumental two-volume history, *The Memorials of the Earls of Haddington*, published in Edinburgh in 1889, the author Sir William Fraser rarely mentions the women in the main text.

Instead, wives are listed at the end of each chapter, with their dates and their children. They are notable because of their husbands, their fathers, their brothers or their progeny.

Helen Hope, wife of Thomas, the 6th Earl of Haddington, might be seen to be the one exception as, by her husband's own admission, it was she who first planted trees at Tyninghame and inspired him by her example. Her success is all the more remarkable as she began planting on a large scale when she was a young wife of twenty-three, with two children under four and, as far as we know, with no architect nor experienced hand to guide her. Nevertheless, Helen Hope, one of the great women gardeners of eighteenth-century Scotland, remains an enigmatic figure. Even her portrait, painted by the celebrated court painter Sir John de Medina in 1694, may not be entirely Helen.

John de Medina had eventually been persuaded to come to Scotland in 1694 by Helen's mother-in-law, the Countess of Rothes whose cousin, Susannah, was the wife of George, the 1st Earl of Melville, Secretary of State for Scotland until 1693.[3] He had had his portrait painted by Medina in London in 1691 and he commissioned a portrait of his wife. Medina was very reluctant to leave his lucrative London practice and travel to Scotland but the Countess of Rothes persisted and eventually a compromise was reached.

In order to stay the shortest time possible in Scotland, he agreed to travel with canvasses ready prepared, including a number with the draperies already painted, 'so that ther will be little to doe except add a head and a neck'![4] Once in Scotland he would only paint the faces and then return to London and finish them in his studio. He would then roll the finished canvases in twos and threes and send them back; the frames would be sent separately.

In her portrait, Helen is shown holding a stem of white flowers; that these are her hands with their elongated fingers and her shoulders with their pronounced slope is unlikely. She gazes confidently at the viewer, not at all perturbed by her loose silk taffeta dress and décolleté, in the still-fashionable style of Peter Lely's 'Windsor Beauties' of the 1660s. In 1694, the year this portrait was painted, Helen was seventeen, not yet married to her first cousin, Thomas Hamilton, and this painting marks her 'coming out'.

She was born in 1677 and died in Edinburgh, aged ninety-one, in 1768. What little we know derives in the main from what can be inferred from the history of the Hope family and from what her husband wrote about her in a letter to their grandson dated 22 December 1733, the year after the death of Lord Binning, their oldest son. (The letter was published in the second edition of Thomas's *A Treatise on the Manner of Raising Forest Trees &c.*, 1761).

Helen came from a very wealthy family who had made their money firstly through the propitious marriage of her grandfather, James Hope (1614–61), to the heiress Anne Foulis. He came into possession of the Foulis' valuable lead and silver workings in Lanarkshire which he developed into an even more profitable business, not only producing ore, but exporting it to Holland. His son, John (1650–82), Helen's father, educated as a young man in Leyden, became an enlightened and astute businessman who was equally successful in further developing the business. John married Lady Margaret Hamilton in 1668, the eldest daughter of Charles, 4th Earl of Haddington, who had been born at Tyninghame c.1650. The lead business prospered, and their increased wealth enabled him to purchase Niddry Castle in 1678, when Helen was one year old. He also bought the lands of Abercorn, now known as Hopetoun, probably with a view to building a fine country house for himself. In Edinburgh, they owned a very large house in the Cowgate, across the street from the one occupied by the Haddington family.

Opposite: Lady Helen Hope by Sir John Medina, 1694 (Courtesy of the Earl of Haddington)

Niddry Castle and its once-famous walled garden, West Lothian

The gardens at Niddry Castle included the great, three-acre walled garden, created by George, Lord Seton, the 3rd Earl of Winton. His family estates included Seton, Winton and Niddry, 'where gardens of considerable elaboration are known to have been established in the fifteenth and sixteenth century'.[5] George Seton took pride in his several gardens, continuing the restoration begun by his father after the destructions caused by English invasions of the 1540s, when Seton gardens were targeted.[6] He rebuilt Winton House and restored the gardens, adding a grand terrace and orchards. The palace at Seton was one of the most renowned in Scotland; Queen Mary, James VI and Charles I were all entertained there and delighted in the gardens, terraced walks and splendid interiors.

Accounts of the garden at Niddry Castle have not survived and it was probably never as grand as Winton or Seton though it shared their pedigree and high stan-

dards of horticulture. John Reid, who had been born at Niddry in 1655, was the author of the very first gardening book printed in Scotland and 'Published for the climate of Scotland': *The Scots Gard'ner*, 1683. Both John Reid's father and grandfather were gardeners at Niddry Castle. Here he was 'persuaded to learn the old but pleasant art of Gard'nery'.[7]

When Helen's father purchased Niddry Castle in 1678,[8] John Reid had moved on, but there is no reason to think that the 'gard'nery' would not have continued to meet the Seton family's high standards. This was the garden, with its high level of horticulture, that Helen Hope knew as a girl and here, perhaps, the seeds for her love of gardening were sown.

The family also owned a substantial Edinburgh town house in the Cowgate, built by Helen's great-grandfather. Helen's parents had ambitious intentions to rebuild it in the French style, and the plans are the work of Claude Comiers, found glued as lining paper

Hopetoun Chest, Newhailes, with Comiers' plans lining the drawers (Courtesy of Dr Joe Rock)

inside the drawers of a seventeenth-century chest, known as the Hopetoun Chest, in Newhailes House.[9] It is a very early example of the taste for French architecture and design that was developing in Scotland and England in the seventeenth century.

The ground-floor plans show a practical layout, with family rooms to the back and stables and kitchen at the front. Lady Margaret's bedroom is large, the same size as the saloon, though her husband's suite is almost half the size. All visitors to the house would have been aware of Lady Margaret's status.[10] Sir

Christopher Wren observed: 'The women [in Scotland], as they made here the Language and Fashions, and meddle with politics and philosophy, so they sway also in architecture.'[11]

In Scotland as in France women 'meddled' and held sway – and succeeded, though their achievements were not always recognised. Lady Margaret proved herself to be an extremely capable and enterprising businesswoman and ambitious mother who also laid the foundations of the Hope family landholdings in East Lothian.

Elevation de la Facade du de-dans de la cour
De l'Hostel D'Hopton, à Edimbourg
Suiuant le dessein de Mr Comier preuost de Ternant.
1680

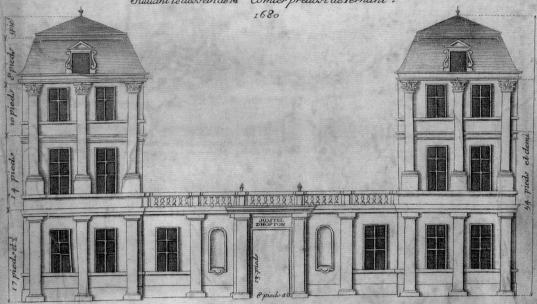

HOSTEL
D'HOPTON

Elevation de l'entree de l'Hostel d'Hopton à Edimbourg
Suiuant le dessein de Mr Comiers preuost de Ternant
1680

The house in the Cowgate, however, was never rebuilt to Comiers' plan. In 1682 tragedy struck. While accompanying the Duke of York (later James VII and II) on a journey to Scotland, John Hope drowned in the shipwreck of the *Gloucester*.[12] He was thirty-two; Helen was four or five years old and her brother Charles was only three.

Lady Margaret, now widowed, managed the family business and estates. During the years of her son's minority, the lead and silver enterprises continued to flourish, and they had income from their estates; when Charles came of age, he was one of the richest young men in Scotland. Rather than rebuild the house in the Cowgate, Lady Margaret set her sights on developing the land at Abercorn for her son. The family's wealth and status demanded ambitious designs: she approached the king's architect, Sir William Bruce, with whom she was acquainted. Comier's plans were put aside, eventually becoming lining paper in the chest which her daughter inherited.

Interestingly, among her many friends was Patrick Hume, created Lord Polwarth in 1690. When he became Chancellor in 1696, he and his wife Grisell regularly held dinners in the Abbey Apartments at Holyrood House, their official residence. On at least one occasion, in November 1696, Lady Margaret was invited together with her son Charles and her sister-in-law, the Countess of Rothes, who brought her younger sons, Thomas and Charles. Thomas, aged sixteen, came with his eighteen-year-old bride, Helen, Lady Margaret's daughter, whom he had married just a few months before. It was a real family party. Another guest was Sir William Bruce, the 'king's architect' and the most eminent Scottish architect of the day.[13] It is highly likely that planning for the Abercorn estate had already begun. Two years later, in 1698, Lady Margaret Hope signed the contract commissioning Bruce to design an imposing house at Abercorn for her son Charles, who was still a minor: Hopetoun House. Work began the following year.

Opposite: Elevation of proposed house by Comiers as seen from the Cowgate (Courtesy of Dr Joe Rock)

Above: Lady Margaret Hope by Sir John de Medina, 1694

Helen had grown up watching her mother successfully managing both the lead mining and exporting business, with warehouses at Leith, as well as the family estates. She must have witnessed the lengthy deliberations between William Bruce, his assistant Alexander Edward and her mother over the grand design for Hopetoun House. The seed for this ambitious project may have been sown by their father before his death, but it was her mother, Lady Margaret, who nurtured it from the beginning to completion.

As the older sister, Helen observed her younger brother Charles beginning to take an interest in the architecture of the house and the design of the policies. Charles eventually became one of the emerging class of 'gentleman architects' in Scottish high society at the turn of the century, and Hopetoun with its policies set the fashion. But it was his mother who set him in the right direction and who, for the second time, chose to follow the French style. For the garden, with its broad axial vistas ending in 'eye catchers' or termination points, demonstrated: 'an emerging "Scottish" approach to garden design during the late 17th century that was based partly on contemporary French models, and which incorporated far-reaching vistas on a monumental scale, as part of a new conception of the "country seat" in Scotland. In this regard Hopetoun was a trendsetter for later designed landscape development in Scotland.'[14]

At Hopetoun, Helen witnessed woodland design on a grand scale, for Bruce always set his houses firmly at the centre of their grounds – as at Kinross, Balcaskie and Thirlestane – with commanding views of avenues, parterres and including a separated walled garden for kitchen produce. It was a far cry from the garden of Niddry Castle where Helen had grown up, and from the barren landscape she was about to call home at Tyninghame.

The marriage of Helen to her first cousin, Thomas, 6th Earl of Haddington, took place in 1695; he was the son of her mother's brother, Charles. Helen was eighteen; Thomas was sixteen. The marriage was arranged by two ambitious women: Lady Margaret Hope and her brother's widow, Margaret Leslie, the Countess of Rothes. The husbands of both women had died in their early thirties, leaving them as widows with very young children.

Helen's aunt now became her mother-in-law. She seems a formidable woman in many respects and was the elder daughter of one of the most powerful men in Scotland, John, the Earl (and later Duke) of Rothes. A favourite of Charles II, he was rewarded with many high offices of state including Lord Chancellor of Scotland for life and president of the Privy Council of Scotland. Like many other landed gentry after the

Restoration he had constructed an imposing country-seat, at Leslie, completed in about 1672. This is where Helen's husband, Thomas, had been brought up, for although he had been born at Tyninghame where his parents were living in 1680, when the Duke of Rothes died in 1681 the Haddingtons moved almost immediately to Leslie, and Margaret claimed her inheritance.

Unusually for the time, the duke had provided for the earldom of Rothes to pass through the female line to his eldest daughter, Margaret. The arrangement was for her eldest son to inherit the Leslie estate and the second son to inherit Tyninghame. Margaret became the 8th Countess of Rothes (but not Duchess, as she had hoped). Together with her husband Charles, the 5th Earl of Haddington, she took on the active management of the extensive Leslie estates. Tyninghame was rather forgotten and the land was let to tenants who took little care of the hedges and ditches; there is no evidence for a tenant in the house. Charles died just four years later, and from then on, much as Lady Margaret Hope was doing, Lady Margaret, Countess of Rothes, managed both estates until her death in 1700.

The 'Palace of Rothes', as Daniel Defoe called the mansion at Leslie, was a far grander house than Tyninghame or Niddry Castle. A series of south-facing terraces, with fountains and statues, led down to the River Leven and woodland with rides and gardens extended on the further bank. Lengthy tree-lined avenues divided blocks of enclosed fields. This splendid garden is where she brought up her three sons and her daughter, and its management was no small undertaking.

In spite of her father's fame, Margaret Rothes is only known to us from the few portraits that survive and indirectly from correspondence. The way she persuaded John de Medina to come to Scotland indicates a determined and forceful character. It was 'quite a coup' as Medina's biographer, Rosalind Marshall, described.[15] It was the Countess who suggested that

Charles, 5th Earl of Haddington, and his wife Lady Margaret Leslie, later Countess of Rothes, by circle of John Wright (Courtesy of Clan Leslie Charitable Trust)

the minutes and accounts of the tutors (trustees) of Thomas, 6th Earl, for the years 1685–1702, were kept in a volume known as 'The Tutors' Book'. The entries confirm that the countess had a deep understanding of the practicalities of estate management.[16]

The same book provides the earliest written evidence that, firstly, plans for tree planting were under way and secondly, that there was already a tree nursery at Tyninghame in 1685, more than fifteen years before Helen and the 6th Earl began their planting. It confirms that Lady Rothes was the one making decisions concerning the garden.[17]

Very little is known about the early gardens of Scotland, secular or monastic. John Reid's book did not appear until 1683. Horticultural skills were passed

down by word of mouth from grandfather to father and to son, as in Reid's own family at Niddry. An estate such as Tyninghame would usually have had an orchard and a garden, for fruit and vegetables, known as a yard. The Tutors' Book provides the earliest written evidence of such a yard at Tyninghame, although the orchard itself is not mentioned. From an inventory prepared by William Lindsay, Earl of Crawford, in 1692, it is clear that Tyninghame had a significant selection of fruit: for example, among the forty pears he listed was 'the Qwince pear of Tininghame'.[18] It was one of the five gardens in the south of Scotland visited by Crawford where apricots were grown and also one of another five gardens able to provide the care and shelter needed for peaches and nectarines. Among the

Leslie House on *Map of Fife* by John Adair, 1694
(Courtesy of the National Library of Scotland)

when he marries Marion Cockburne.[20] On 10 December 1682 his name appears again, this time he is named as 'My Lord Haddington's Gardiner'. His name occurs in the Tutors' Book again in 1685 and on 30 December 1689 the death of a William Hunter was recorded in the parish records.[21]

There are no estate plans of this date but the simple design shown on John Adair's map of 1682 gives some indication of the layout and where the orchard might have been situated on the north side of the house (p. 34).

After the death of William Hunter, it seems a year passed before a replacement was found. The countess depended on her agent-cum-factor, sometimes called the chamberland, John Shirreff, to carry out the tutors' instructions. He was anxious to know what to do with the fruit and produce in the orchard and was ordered to establish what the profit from the fruit would be and having established the amount – 'the fruit of tinninghame according to the wheat measure there is of peass ten pecks and off aples thirty-five pecks'[22] – he was told let the new gardener know the figures and 'if he be not willing to bargain at those termes or about those terms . . .' my Lady will provide an other gairdner agsT (by) Martinmass . . .'[23] Although every other decision of the tutors was implemented by one of their number or by John Shirreff, it was always the Countess of Rothes who decided gardening matters.

The final reference to the garden in the Tutors' Book is to its boundary. On 12 March 1694 the instructions given to John Shirreff were: 'As to the park dyke at tinninghame John Shirriff is allowed to higher ye them ane Ell higher than they are and that all provisioned necessar to be made for that effort.' (An ell was roughly thirty-seven inches, just under one metre.) This was probably the area to the north of the house as shown on the Adair map as the township lay scattered to the south. It is not clear when the dyke was first built, as the enclosure of parks around the houses of landed gentry occurred all over Scotland and royal

others was Leslie where three different varieties of peaches were mentioned: 'the Pavie, the Rambouillon and the Newington'.[19] Which of these was growing at Tyninghame he does not record, but Lady Rothes might have been able to recognise them and she might even have been responsible for their introduction.

In seventeenth-century Scotland there was considerable variation between estates in terms of gardeners' contracts. At Tyninghame the gardener was entitled to the profit from the sale of excess fruit and vegetables; he also had the use of a little piece of ground south of the nursery and he had an acre of land for his cow. In return, in addition to the maintenance of the gardens he was expected to keep the hedges and drystone dykes in good order and keep a good stock of young trees and hedging in the nursery. The gardener in question was William Hunter, whose name first appears in the Tyninghame parish marriage records on 7 July 1680 deer parks had been enclosed since the Middle Ages. However the depiction by Adair of a single line of trees inside the wall indicates where tree planting had already begun at Tyninghame. Here, a higher wall was probably necessary to keep the deer out rather than keep them in.

Meeting in Edinburgh on 8 November 1695, the minutes report a significant event: Helen was now married to her first cousin, Thomas (still a minor), and he wanted to know what their allowance would be and where they would live. He set his hopes high:

> Mistris Helen Hope now countess of Hadinton his spouse and the said Earle cra(v)ing the advice of his said Curators anent the place of his residence ffor some tyme. And what might be yearly allowed ffor the expense off his board his lady and other attendants which the Earl represented would nott be under eight or nyne in number and ffour horses at least and what would be the curators reasonable advice anent what should be allowed him or his Lady for the . . . cloaths and other incidents of that nature besydes there yearly board.

His hopes were dashed as the tutors did not hesitate, and ' . . . all agreed in one mynde that it was not ffit for the Earl for some tyme to take up a family himself and the most proper way they would advise was That for some tyme he should live in family with the countess of Rothes, his mother, which the curators thought would both spare his money and let him understand the way off Liveing.'[24] A sum of 6,000 merks was allowed to Lady Rothes for their and their attendants' board and lodging.

The young couple cannot have been surprised to find they were told to live at Leslie. Although Helen was now eighteen, Thomas was sixteen and such arrangements were common in the eighteenth century. Within two years he was a father: Charles, their eldest son was born there in 1697. They remained at Leslie for four years until the death of the Countess of Rothes in 1700. During her years there, Helen would have observed her mother-in-law, a forceful woman who ably managed the gardens at both estates. On both sides of Helen's family, it was the women who were in charge; neither her own mother nor her mother-in-law remarried after the deaths of their husbands. When Margaret Leslie, 8th Countess of Rothes, died and her eldest son Charles inherited the estate, it was time for Helen and Thomas to move to Tyninghame. Once there, it was natural that Helen, rather than her husband, took the initiative, gardening and planting trees on an ambitious scale. She had the drive, the horticultural knowledge and there was no holding her back.

Thomas described Helen as 'a great lover of planting' and writes that 'she did what she could to engage me to it; but in vain. At last she asked leave to go about it; which she did; and I was much pleased with some little things that were both laid out and executed, though none of them are now to be seen: For, when the designs grew more extensive, we were forced to take away what was first done.'[25] Sadly, no gardener's accounts survive for their years at Tyninghame.

The only description of Helen's work is that written by her husband in 1733 and published in the 'Letter from the Right Honourable, the Earl of . . . to his grandson' that was in included in the book which was to make her husband's name as one of the foremost agricultural improvers in Scotland in the eighteenth century. In it, Helen is portrayed as the wife who set her husband on his path to fame. The initial steps in planting and designing the estate at Tyninghame were taken by Helen. Eventually, Thomas joined in and became hooked. He begins his book with the boast: 'Having been a Diligent Planter for Upwards of Thirty years, and having more thriving Trees of my own Raising, than I believe any one Man ever Planted in his Life Time, I have Vanity Enough to think my Experience may be of use to my friends . . .'[26]

Thomas 6th Earl of Hadinton.

CHAPTER 5

Husband and Wife

However common a thing it was for first cousins to marry in Scotland in the seventeenth and eighteenth centuries, it cannot have been an easy transition for a well-educated eighteen-year-old girl to settle down with her sixteen-year-old cousin, whose main interests were horses and dogs. The portrait of Thomas in a pre-painted suit of armour, was completed by Sir John de Medina in 1694. It shows a young man with a plump face, smooth complexion and rosy cheeks, framed by an elaborate wig of cascading curls. He looks rather complacent, arrogant even.

Helen also had to get used to the fact that her husband was not rich, certainly not as rich as her own family, and that life at Tyninghame would be a very different affair to the life she had known. Thomas was not destined to run a business as Helen's father had been; he was an aristocrat and although he later developed an interest in practical agricultural improvements, his early efforts were more geared toward saving money than to making any. Moreover, they arrived at Tyninghame in 1700 at the time of great hardship in the countryside as the famine, or dearth, continued. George Turnbull, who had become the minister for

the parish a few months before, noted in his diary on Christmas Day the previous December: 'This also was a sad year among the commons and tradesmen the dearth continuing and increasing.'[1]

The political and financial successes of the 1st Earl of Haddington set a high standard for his heirs, which they struggled to achieve. The Haddington family fortunes were far less robust when Thomas inherited his title. His father, Charles, the 5th Earl of Haddington, had died heavily in debt and one of the first duties of Thomas's trustees had been to put the estate in order. The trustees of his cousin, Charles Hope of Hopetoun, Helen's brother, made a friendly offer in 1691 and bought the Byres, originally acquired by the 1st Earl. Thomas's marriage to his cousin Helen four years later strengthened the existing close financial ties. His trustees also managed to restore to him the hereditary title of Keeper of Holyrood Park, a title that had been forfeited in 1681 when Thomas's father refused to sign the oath of allegiance acknowledging the divine right of the king. These years were the 'killing time' in Scotland when tensions between Covenanters and Charles II were at their most fraught and the king took more and more desperate measures to subdue the wave of Presbyterian support engulfing the country.

These same tensions had been faced by the 1st Earl of Haddington at the end of his career. From the time

Opposite: Portrait of Thomas, 6th Earl of Haddington, by Sir John de Medina, 1694 (Courtesy of the National Galleries of Scotland)

of his death in 1637, each of his subsequent heirs tried to be loyal to the king but were also attracted to the Presbyterian cause to a greater or lesser degree. It was a balancing act that became more and more difficult as the king clung to his supremacy, not just in ecclesiastical matters but increasingly in secular matters also. The minister at Tyninghame from 1610, and for the following fifty years, Rev. John Lauder, 'Mr John', was a staunch Presbyterian and Covenanter whose entries in the kirk session records for the earlier years show a concern for local rather than national problems. However, his entries from 1637 reveal the extent of the rift between king and country in this part of East Lothian. On 17 March 1637 he intimated to his congregation that there was to be a mustering at Beanston Moor (between Tyninghame and Haddington) on the following Thursday, 'especiallie all that had subscribed to the Covenant, and were to stand to it'.[2] The following spring Mr John rode into Edinburgh and signed the Covenant at Greyfriars Kirk. He brought a copy back to Tyninghame, where it was read and signed by all present.

Thomas, the 2nd Earl of Haddington, had also signed the National Covenant in 1638 (it hangs in Mellerstain); in 1640 when the Scots army under General Leslie crossed the border for a second time to meet Charles's army, the earl held supreme military command of south-east Scotland. The fighting came close to Tyninghame. In August, Mr John was summoned by the Dunbar presbytery to take his turn as chaplain for the East Lothian regiment and to join General Leslie. He accompanied them on horseback as they marched from Dunbar to Dunglass at night on 7 August and he camped with the men the following day by Langton, where he preached then returned home. The 2nd Earl stayed at Dunglass, to command Berwick, while the army marched south to Newcastle where they met little resistance. While celebrating the victory in England, a powder magazine exploded, destroying much of Dunglass Castle and killing

Thomas and several members of his family. He was buried at Tyninghame two days later.

His son, another Thomas, who had inherited as a minor, also became a Coventanter but then surprised his family by marrying Henrietta de Coligny, a Roman Catholic, whom he had met in France. The marriage ended after two years with the sudden death of Thomas and the earldom passed to his brother, John. He became the 4th Earl of Haddington only eight years after the death of his grandfather, the 1st Earl. His marriage contract to Lady Christian Lindsay was signed on the same day and at the same place as her sister Anne's contract to John, the Earl of Rothes, thus beginning the close liaison between the Earls of Haddington and the Leslies of Rothes.[3]

The 4th Earl was a supporter of Charles II and attended his coronation at Scone; he then survived the Commonwealth years by taking little part in government affairs but after the Restoration he became a privy councillor and took a more active role. Of his affairs at Tyninghame little is known other than his grandson Thomas's account: 'My grandfather came late to the estate. And the civil wars in the time of King Charles I did not permit him to stay at home (for being lame he could join neither side); but when they were over, he tried to raise some trees, which he planted around the house and gardens. There were indeed but two rows of them.'[4]

Enclosure had been encouraged by Parliament after the Restoration of Charles II in 1660. Between 1661 and 1700 there were four Acts which prepared the way for the departure from the open fields and runrigs of a communal system to a more self-contained system of single ownership and boundaries.[5] It was the grandfather of Thomas, the 6th Earl, who had begun to enclose the lands on his estate, but it was his father, Charles, who benefitted from the offered tax relief and who, in the 1670s, began the serious work of planting, draining and further enclosing his land for pasture and crops. His efforts might have had more lasting effect had the family not moved to Leslie in 1681 on the death of the Duke of Rothes.

After the early planting forays by his wife, Thomas admits 'but, being at last obliged to make some inclosures, for grazing my horses, I found the buying of hay very expensive; this made me wish to have enough of my own yet I did nothing of that kind for some years'.[6] The young man painted by Sir John de Medina and described by Sir William Fraser in his biography of the family hardly suggests an ideal husband. Since 1703 he had taken his place in Parliament; when the question of the Union between Scotland and England arose in 1705, Thomas voted for the Union. One of his opponents, George Lockhart of Carnwath, wrote of him, 'He much affected, and his talent lay, in a buffoon sort of wit and raillery; was hot, proud, vain and ambitious'.[7] Another contemporary paid him the dubious complement: '[he] has a genius, whenever he sees fit to apply himself'.[8]

His 'buffoon sort of wit' sometimes found expression in rather puerile, bawdy poems that he regularly sent to his friends for amusement. One of his closest friends and correspondents at this time was John Erskine, the 6th Earl of Mar, who was a leading figure for the Unionist cause at the turn of the century. He became Joint Secretary of State for Scotland with the 3rd Earl of Loudoun in 1705. Several letters that have survived in the Mar family archive cast more light on the gossip and social life the pair enjoyed in London than on the political cause they shared.[9]

Lord Haddington's role in the safe passage of the Treaty of Union was as a member of two of the subcommittees that calculated the amount of the 'Equivalent': the lump sum of £398,085 10s. 0d. that Scotland was to receive from England under the terms of the Act of Union. Apparently, he attended well, the committees acted diligently and took 'extraordinary pains', in the opinion of Patrick Earl of Marchmont.[10] But his barbed comments in a letter to Mar of 18 July concerning his fellow committee members show him to be as irascible as ever.[11]

In mid-October he replies to a letter from Mar, ending in typical fashion: 'I wish I could give you as hopeful ane account of this country as you gave me of the bath [Bath], but that I am sure you don't expect, for we hve nether singing, Dancing, or playing but for Prayers Go[d] ha[ve] mercy on old Scotland.'[12]

This close friendship soon became strained by the differences in their attitudes towards the Union. A final letter contains a premonition of the rift that was to emerge between them, and which led to them taking up arms against each other at the Battle of Sheriffmuir eight years later.[13] John Erskine, as Secretary of State for Scotland, was based in London for a period after 1707. During these years he became so disillusioned with the implementation of the Union and the continuation of the state of poverty in Scotland that after 1711 he campaigned for its repeal. He finally realised that his hopes in the Hanoverian dynasty were misplaced and he turned to the Jacobite cause when James VII and II, in exile in France, promised that he would repeal the Union in return for his support.[14]

Besides his parliamentary duties and his position as Secretary of State, the Earl of Mar was passionate about design – architectural as well as landscape and he was an able surveyor and draughtsman. Margaret Stewart, in her detailed account of his life and work, summed up his character: ' . . . we can deduce from his interests and writings that he preferred to be out of doors attending to his gardens rather than indoors. He loved congenial company . . .'[15] John Erskine had grown up at the Mar family seat at Alloa and in the early years of the eighteenth century he developed elaborate plans for the estate and town, including for its economic development. These were far more ambitious than any plans Helen and Thomas may have had for the garden at Tyninghame. In 1702, when Mar visited Tyninghame, garden plans for both were in very early stages; Helen had begun the 'little things' that her husband thought well executed and around this time Mar was also preparing the new layout for Alloa.

Thomas never mentions garden designs or tree planting in his letters to Mar, though he was well aware of the latter's ability and experience. Sometime before 1707, perhaps influenced by Mar, Thomas followed his wife's lead: 'I had given over my fondness for sport and began to like planting better than I had done; and I resolved to have a wilderness.'[16] He continues: 'though the first Marquis of Tweeddale, my Lord Rankeilor, Sir William Bruce, my father, with some others, had planted a good deal; yet I will be bold to say that planting was not well understood in this country, till this century began. I think it was the late Earl of Mar that first introduced the wilderness way of planting amongst us, and very much improved the taste of our Gentlemen, who very soon followed his example.'

The planting of Mar's own wilderness at Alloa was carried out by his gardener in 1706. By saying that the 'wilderness way' was 'introduced', Thomas implies that it came from elsewhere. It was a style that had its origins in France in the gardens created for Louis XVI by André Le Nôtre at Versailles. Neither Thomas nor Mar had been to France by this date, but Thomas was familiar with William Bruce's designs for his brother-in-law at Hopetoun House, and they visited each other regularly. Lord Rankeillor, mentioned above, was a cousin of Thomas' wife and her brother, and he also advised on the design of Hopetoun.[17] The landscape in particular shows a strong French influence, with its long avenues radiating from the house and a *jet d'eau* rising from a formal pool.

Bruce was assisted by Alexander Edward, a skilled draughtsman and cartographer, who also worked for the Earl of Mar. In 1701 he was commissioned by a group of Scottish landowners, including the Earl of Mar and Charles Hope, to conduct a Grand Tour to England, the Low Countries and France, and to collect material to illustrate the latest styles in architecture and landscaping, and the latest engineering works and

methods. He made sketches and notes of his own as well as buying plans of others. Thomas may have seen some of these items and drawings, many of which are in the Hopetoun archive. His friendship with John Erskine, Earl of Mar, was very close, and this may also be the reason why he credits him with the introduction of 'the wilderness way'. Historians may not agree with him on this point, but there was no doubt that as a landscape designer the Earl of Mar had few equals. His design for Alloa is on display in the Victoria & Albert Museum, Dundee, where it is the only example of Scottish garden design.

This style of seventeenth- and early eighteenth-century planting in Scotland, was formal, with geometric patterns of circles and straight rides or avenues, each originally with a 'termination point', or something to catch the eye and terminate the view. The Earl of Mar referred to these as 'vistos', Thomas Haddington refers to them as 'termination points'. They are 'eye-catchers' which also had a practical use as an aid to orientation: one straight ride can look very much like another in a wilderness. In this, the formal Scottish Historical Landscape style differed from the French in an important way: 'the vistas are directed towards pre-existing natural or historic features such as battle sites, monuments, even modern industrial developments.'[18] In France, terminating vistas in this manner was not a key feature. At Versailles, for example, the vistas end on the horizon, adding to the sense that Louis XIV's influence was endless.

At Tyninghame the scale was more modest. ' . . . I [Thomas] resolved to have a wilderness. I fixed upon some ground near my bowling-green; I laid it out in a centre with fourteen walks from it, the most of them having tolerable terminations; but as it was too little,

Opposite: Plan of Alloa after 1710: a Grande Allée leads through formal gardens and Wilderness to the harbour; to the east, avenues and vistas dissect the expansive Wilderness (Courtesy of the National Records of Scotland)

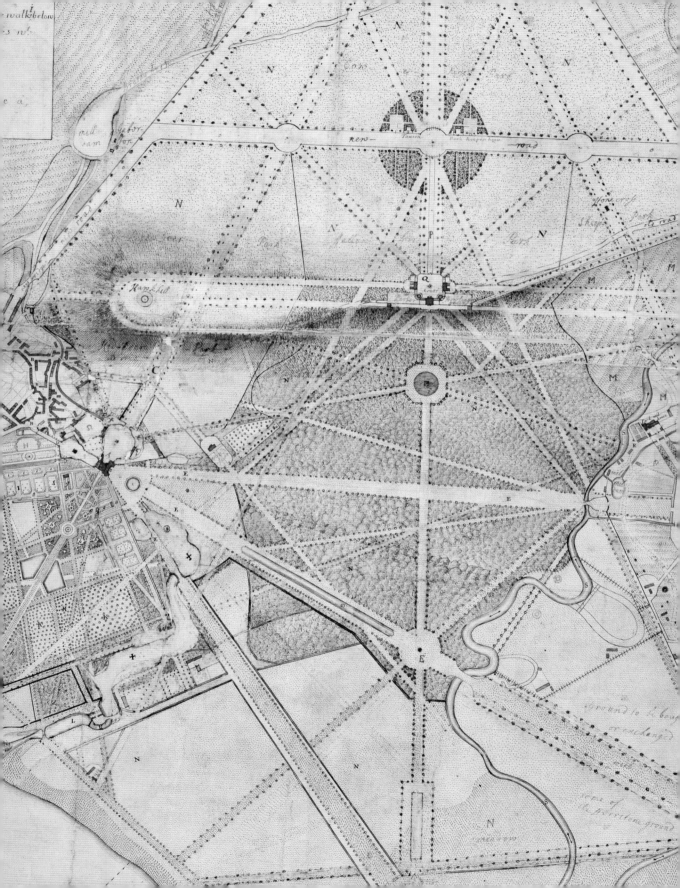

Tyninghame. Detail from General Roy's *Lowlands Military Survey of Scotland 1747–55* (British Library: Licensor SCRAN)

to the north-west of the kirk occupies the position of the minister's house and the house by the name Tyninghame was in fact a farmhouse. Its central position at the avenue intersection, may have mislead the cartographer. Bearing in mind that Roy's surveying teams often only sketched towns and estates by eye or copied from existing plans (only the more important landscape features such as roads, rivers and lochs were surveyed using compasses and traverses), his map cannot be relied on as an accurate picture of the estate in every detail. In other respects the survey is reasonably accurate.

Although the name 'Wilderness' is still shown on Ordnance Survey maps of the Tyninghame estate and describes the arboretum to the west of the house, the formal layout has disappeared. Where this style of planting has survived is in the Binning Wood, the great wood of some 300 acres began by Helen in 1707, the year of the Union. The story concerning the event is told by Thomas:

> There was a field of three hundred Scots acres . . . called the muir of Tynninghame . . . the ground of very little value, except some small part of it, for which one of my tenants paid a trifle of rent. This ground she [Helen] desired to inclose and plant; it seemed too great an attempt, and almost everybody advised her not to undertake it, as being impracticable; of which number, I confess, I was one; but she said, if I would agree to it, she made no doubt of getting it finished. I gave her free leave; the Gentleman and tenants had their loss made up to them and in 1707, she began to inclose it and called it Binning-wood.[20]

in some years I enlarged it greatly; and your father, who had an admirable taste, put it in the figure it is now in.'[19] The survey by General Roy is the first map to give us a good outline of the amount of enclosure and planting at Tyninghame. It also indicates a small area, with avenues leading from a centre, possibly the bowling green, surrounded by rectangular, enclosed fields.

Could this be their wilderness? Originally the avenues would have been bordered with hedges – holly, yew, box were favourites – but very few examples of this labour-intensive style survive today and, by 1755, the design had already changed. Roy's map is inaccurate in other details: notably it omits Tyninghame House itself and the Walled Garden. The house shown

Lord Binning is the hereditary title of the eldest son of the Earl of Haddington. Helen's son would have been ten years old at the time.

Having seen his wife's success, not to mention her

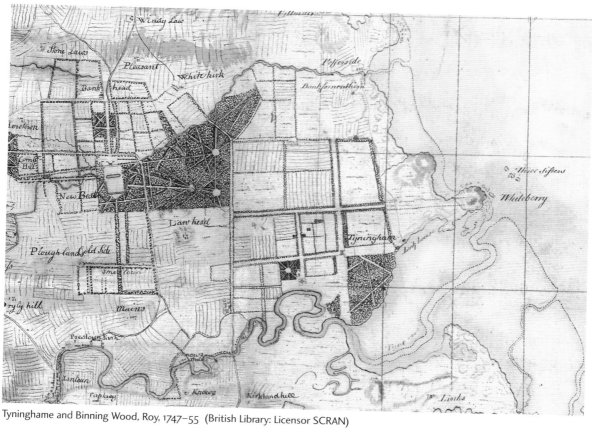

Tyninghame and Binning Wood, Roy, 1747–55 (British Library: Licensor SCRAN)

determination, Thomas began to take more interest and wanted to become involved in the design. The question was, whose idea was best? Having decided the wood needed a centre with 'walks from it, with the best terminations we could find', he chose one centre, and his wife chose another. 'I preferred my choice, she her's.' As it happened, Helen's younger brother, the Earl of Hopetoun, together with the Earl of Marchmont and Sir John Bruce (the son of the architect William Bruce), were all about to visit Tyninghame and 'we resolved to leave the determination of this controversy to them'. The one chosen by Helen, was nearest the house and the one by Thomas, a little further to the west. Alexander Hume, Lord Marchmont, evidently had drawing and surveying skills as he was

able to set up instruments – possibly a theodolite with a compass and a separate measuring chain – take down measurements and draw up plans. When they visited the muir and inspected the two circles, Lord Marchmont insisted on methodically taking the views and the walks from each circle and setting them on paper before any decision was taken. Sir John Bruce meanwhile wandered off and found an alternative circle, nearer Whitekirk, to the north of Helen's circle. Again, Marchmont insisted on the same procedure. When they got home, he set the three centres and the walks from each on paper. 'When this was shewn, it was agreed unanimously that all the three should be laid out on the ground; and the planting carried on by that plan. This was done, and stands to this day, with very

little variation; only that there are some serpentine walks, and some figures, laid down by your dear father, when he was but ten years old . . . I shall only say, that all who see it express themselves highly pleased with it.'[21]

The collaboration between this group of friends indicated the close family ties that continued between these four families: Haddington, Hopetoun, Marchmont and Bruce. The older and younger generations had been together at Abbey Apartments in 1696 as the guests of Patrick Hume where they very probably talked about the forthcoming plans for Hopetoun.[22] Now his son, Alexander, and William Bruce's son, John, together with Charles Hope were the guests of Thomas and Helen, invited to discuss (and in this case, implement) landscape design. It was a case of déjà vu.

The Binning Wood was felled between 1942 and 1945 to help the war effort, but was then replanted in the 1960s following the original design. Sadly, the termination points – which would probably have included the Bass Rock, North Berwick Law, Whitekirk, adjacent properties and natural features – are obscured by the belt of planting which encloses the wood, but aerial photographs convey the scale of the work Helen and her husband undertook and clearly show the avenues radiating from the three circles.

Some of the original planting has survived nearby: the veteran lime trees (interspersed with oaks) in the Limetree Walk on the other side of the A198 were spared the axe. They may not look old – the trunk of lime trees can grow thinner with age, not wider – but they are original. The walk originally linked the wood to the house.

At this junction five 'ways', or 'gaits' in old Scots, intersect. Generations of map makers have failed to recognise the meaning and the Ordnance Survey maps today label this 'Five Gates'.

Opposite: Aerial view of the Binning Wood
(Courtesy of Historic Environment Scotland)

In the final paragraphs of the letter to his grandson, Thomas admits to taking pleasure in planting and enclosing, and tells him that he invited some farmers from Dorsetshire to come and advise him as 'I did not like the husbandry practised in this country.' He divided the land and 'as I knew the coldness of the climate, and the bad effects the high winds had, I made strips of planting betwixt every inclosure, some forty, fifty or sixty feet broad, as I thought best. These look very well, and I hope will be a great shelter, and come to warm the ground.'[23]

These improvements probably took place from 1707 onwards; although actual dates are missing, the letter appears to deal with events and planting in a chronological sequence. The next project was the planting of a barren piece of ground near the house: 'Upon my going one year to London, I committed it to your father, who took it in hand, made it in walks, and now it is an exceeding pretty spot of ground; and as it every way differs from any thing about this place, it is liked by all that see it.'[24] As Thomas admits, several years passed before he enjoyed planting. His son, Charles, Lord Binning, on the other hand, followed in his mother's footsteps and evidently enjoyed gardening from a young age, no doubt encouraged by her. It was a love which stayed with him throughout his short life and which he developed later at Mellerstain, the family home of his wife Rachel Baillie, whom he married in 1717.

Notwithstanding her son's gardening prowess, Helen was still the main instigator of large-scale planting at Tyninghame. The last project described by her husband seemed even more hare-brained to him and their friends. She set her heart on planting on very poor sandy soil, what had, since the Middle Ages, been an extensive rabbit warren of some 400 acres (even larger than the Binning wood) by the seashore, to the east of the house. At the time, the rabbits had been partly cleared, and it was providing minimal grazing for some young cattle and sheep. 'A Gentleman, who had lived

Limetree Walk

some time at Hamburg, one day walking with your grandmother, said, That he had seen fine trees growing upon such a soil. She took the hint and planted about sixty or seventy acres of this warren. All who saw it thought that the time, labour and trees were thrown away; but, to their great amazement, they saw them prosper as well as in the best grounds.'[25] Once again, Helen's efforts were an example to her husband who had to admit, 'I cannot say but it answers very well. As I have a great deal more of such kind of land, I design to plant it all.' Some of the old Scots pines, oaks and sycamores planted here have survived in Fir Links Wood, Little Binning Wood and Links Wood, but large sections have been replanted.

Thomas's account reveals that the planting at Tyninghame developed in a piecemeal fashion rather than as the fulfilment of an overall design. When William Bruce laid out the grounds at Hopetoun, Kinross or Thirlestane, for example, he placed the house at the centre, with the avenues leading from it. This had been advice of John Reid in *The Scots Gard'ner*

(1683): 'Make all the buildings and Plantings ly fo [lie so] about the houfe, as that the Houfe may be the Centre; all the Walks, Trees and Hedges, running to the Houfe.'[26] However when Helen began planting trees, she began as a lover of planting rather than as a lover of design. She chose pieces of ground that were of little agricultural use to her husband, 'the muir of Tynninghame . . . the ground of very little value', as Thomas put it, rather than set out avenues across the fields to the north of the house, destroying enclosures newly planted by her husband. Again by choosing reclaimed rabbit warrens by the seaside, of little worth, she did not use any of the good land. 'The whole field was dead sand, with scarce any grass upon it; nor was it only so poor upon the surface but continued so some yards down.'[27] Roy's map clearly indicates the eighteenth-century layout, with its small geometric fields of six or seven acres, hedges, shelterbelts with straight tracks and avenues. The design lacks overall coherence, as the practicalities of enclosure, so dear to her husband's heart, took precedence. That the bones of this early eighteenth-century landscape survive in the Binning Wood, the field boundaries, avenues and roads today is partly due to the absence of pressure from industrial development and attendant housing (as at Alloa, for example, where most has been lost) but it is also a measure of the success of a design where expediency and economy took precedence over aesthetics.

Thomas wrote down his thoughts on planting in 1733, the year after the death of his son, and when he himself was nearing the end of his own life. His tone is business-like and in the accompanying letter to his grandson, the tone is calm, even reflective. He also acknowledges the contribution of his old friend, the Earl of Mar. In the years after the Union, and again after the death of Queen Anne in 1714, the mood in the country was very unsettled. On 5 August 1714, Thomas took part in the proclamation in Edinburgh of the Hanoverian king, George I. As far as the exiled Mar was concerned, the years after the Union saw the whittling away of the financial concessions for Scotland that he had fought hard to obtain; he, and others, felt they had been betrayed by the British government. Sometime in the same year, the 'Old Pretender', James VIII and III, wrote to Mar giving him 'express & repeated orders' to lead a rising whenever required, and the authority to call a parliament in Edinburgh following a restoration.[28]

Helen observed the gulf between the two old friends widen. She, too, was deeply concerned about Scotland's predicament. Despite being a well-educated woman, she was not necessarily expected to take an interest in politics, but she did. Only a handful of her letters survive – though none to her husband. Given her passion for gardening and her limited travels (she may not have visited London before this date), it is perhaps surprising that two of her surviving letters are about matters of State. Both are to the Duke of Montrose, her husband's cousin, who had taken over as Secretary of State for Scotland from the Earl of Mar on 24 September 1714.

Montrose did not last long in the position which he lost the following year in the struggle between factions vying for the king's favour. Helen wrote to him shortly afterwards. Her handwriting is steady and flowing but her spelling is often phonetic and her phrasing awkward. The letter is dated 6 August 1715 and in it she shows perspicacity and a real concern for her country:

> . . .when I consither what a general satisfaction there was amongst al the Good piple [people] in the country at your being med Secretary in hopes that your ames should be higher than most of our own grit mens ar, & now al thes expectations must be sunk for a trayfel [trifle]. . . .our King is to be pityed a strangour amongst us, who can not knou men so weal at 1st as he may do afterwards, & I make no doubt but the gread and ambition of som may com to discover it self, & made them wearied of, but I rather wish ther oun faults wer discovered, then [than] that ther intrest shal be resed [raised] by the roving [destruction] of yours.[29]

And then she adds in a postscript: 'I doubt not you hear from bettour hands the preperations of our Highlanders & the los we ar at by having no govement to derect what we shal do.'

Jacobite unrest, fuelled by the disappointments following the Union, had found a new leader. The Earl of Mar raised the Jacobite standard in Braemar the following month, on 6 September 1715. By the time he moved to attack Stirling Castle in November, his army had reduced to around 7,000 men. This was still more than double the number of the Duke of Argyll, who had some 3,000 men for the Government side, including Thomas, 6th Earl of Haddington, and his son, Lord Binning, who would have been seventeen or eighteen. The Battle of Sheriffmuir took place on 13 November 1715, was chaotic, bloody and the result inconclusive. Despite their superior numbers, the Jacobite army could not press home their advantage and retreated to Perth. Although both sides claimed victory, this marked the beginning of the end of the uprising for the Jacobites.

The Earl of Haddington had his horse shot from under him and he was wounded in the shoulder; Lord Binning survived unscathed but cannot have been unmoved by the butchery he witnessed. It had been a fierce battle, as recorded in many ballads, but if Thomas ever wrote about it, his letters have not survived. In spite of taking up arms against each other, the two friends did eventually make contact after Mar was exiled. He left Scotland with James VIII in December 1715 and died in Aix-la-Chapelle (Aachen) in 1732. His last letter to Thomas, written some time in 1731, is not about politics or women, but about Tyninghame with suggestions for improving the 'beautys about the place',[30] a subject which was always dear to them both.

It must have been an awful time for Helen, not knowing the fate of her son and her husband while differing accounts of the battle circulated. Father and son spent a few days at Stirling Castle before returning. Helen's second letter to Montrose gives us a rare insight into her private life and her feelings. It was written two weeks after the Battle of Sheriffmuir, on 28 November. Having apologised for encroaching on his time, she continues: 'when you consither hou retired I now live, & wer I not obliged to som of my frends that is at the pains to wrait [write] to me I should have an ode laiff [life] just now'.[31] She sounds cut off and lonely at Tyninghame. Her husband, who had been in London prior to the battle, might not yet have returned home by this date and Helen is evidently shaken by recent events:

> . . . the misery the Jacobites his broght this
> nation to, is but what ther pricapels leds them
> to, but the slounes [slowness] of our relief is
> what evary body must observe, & make differ-
> ent reflections according as they ar affected, the

Jacobites improves it against the government, the enamies to the Unyeon lods [Lords] it with it, as a mark that the English wil always conteme us, the discontented repais & the Kings best frends dus not knou what to say, I shal always valou my self for being the number of the last, & therfor dus earnestly desair to knou from your Grace what ansuer I shal make.

Helen is torn between her loyalty to the king and despair at what she sees as his lack of support for Scotland in the face of Jacobite strength. She compares the relatively small number of troops sent to Scotland (to fight at Sheriffmuir) with the speedy relief sent to Lancashire at the Battle of Preston, which took place at the same time as the Battle of Sheriffmuir, where the Jacobite army was quickly defeated by the Hanoverian forces: '& if because we ar Poor or remote, therfor we ar contemned I'm soor [sure] it's not right, nather in the sight of God or indifferent [impartial] Judges'. Unwilling to have 'a harch thoght of our King', she tentatively lays the blame 'at the dore of a Whigish Ministry' before finishing the letter: 'if you think it to deap a point for me to inquair after, or to rais on for you to ansuer, I shal belive your Grace's silence proseds rather from that, then the mistaking of me, who I'm soor his a deap concern for both my King & country besaid my being'. She signs off: 'Your Grace's most Humble servant H Hadinton.'[32]

Helen's observations are acute, and she is up-to-date in her information but her suggestion that politics may be 'too deep a point for her to enquire after' also shows her acknowledgement that the duke (and by implication, society), might not consider it a woman's place to write about such matters. Her confident hand and the few crossings out suggest that she wrote frequently but, sadly, only three of her letters have come to light, the third to a friend about her health. Her husband's letters fared better, although none to his wife survive.

CHAPTER 6

Fathers and Sons

Under Queen Anne, Thomas had not received any recognition – official or honorary – but perhaps in acknowledgement of his support for the House of Hanover, and in particular after his part in the Battle of Sheriffmuir, he was rewarded with the Order of the Thistle and appointed Sheriff of Haddingtonshire on the death of the Marquis of Tweeddale. He was now thirty-six years of age and, as a representative peer, his reputation was cemented as an establishment figure. He was re-elected by his fellow peers in 1722 and 1727.

The informal portrait of Thomas by William Aikman, probably painted just before 1719, shows him with a ruddy complexion, clean shaven with close cropped hair and without a wig.

He is wearing a tilted, black, narrow-brimmed hat, a plain jacket and unbuttoned waistcoat. His shirt has a small, rumpled collar with a long black narrow tie or ribbon. He almost looks as if he is dressed for work in his tree nursery. He has the same plumpness of face as in his earlier portraits, but his figure has filled out in the intervening years. Thomas would have been about forty. Aikman painted many portraits of aristocrats in fashionable wigs and elaborate costumes but invariably with a pared down elegance and a sharpness of obser-vation.[1] Occasionally, as in this portrait of the 6th Earl, the informality of the pose and his almost sardonic expression, suggest a frankness and honesty of gaze

from the sitter and the artist alike. Of all the portraits of Thomas, this is the one which best conveys the down-to-earth character of the man.

A month after his wife's letter, Thomas also had reason to write to his cousin the Duke of Montrose. He was concerned about the future of his son Charles,

A down-to-earth portrait of the 6th Earl of Haddington in middle age, by William Aikman, *c.*1719 (Courtesy of the Earl of Haddington)

Lord Binning, 'to make him fit to serve'. His son's education at Glasgow University was coming to an end; it had been chosen by Thomas as 'the place where he could get least harm'. On 4 January 1716 he continues, 'as I now have no project of ever having any thing myself by my refusing to serve in parliament, so I shall doe what I can to send him abroad this spring, but as I never had the advantage of being abroad myself, so I wil need the advice of my friends that have been'.[2] Thomas had studied at Glasgow himself and his younger son, John, may still have been there at this date.

Binning's prowess at the Battle of Sheriffmuir had been honoured in 1718 with the commission of Knight Marischal of Scotland for life, but his experience on the battlefield left him with little appetite for a career in the army, which, Thomas assured Montrose, gave him a good deal of joy. In his account of the life of the 6th Earl, William Fraser makes no mention of the refusal to serve in Parliament which is made plain in this letter. But three days later the Earl had been persuaded to change his mind and began another shorter letter saying he had decided to stand after all. The letter was finished politely by Lord Binning on the reverse. He apologised on his father's behalf for 'he is so wearied with letters at present'. Binning, who was eighteen or nineteen, made no mention of any future career plans of his own except to reveal that he was aware his marriage was being discussed: 'Give my humble service to my Lady Dutches . . . I return to her Grace most hearty thanks for the care she is about my marriage, but I shall take her advice in doing for my self. adieu.' Already in Charles a streak of independence was apparent and perhaps by then he had set his sights on his future wife, Rachel Baillie, the daughter of Lady Grisell Hume and George Baillie of Jerviswood and Mellerstain. He married Rachel Baillie, or Rachy as she was known, in August 1717.

The arranging of the match took place between Thomas and Grisell, who was keen to see her daughter, now aged twenty, off her hands. The fact that Binning was a year younger was of no account to Grisell. More important were her daughter's feelings and the correspondence between Rachy and Binning indicated their keenness for each other. The wedding, which marked a union between families who had been friends for at least three generations, was reported in the *Weekly Journal or Saturday's Post* of 14 September 1717: 'Last Sunday the Duke of Montrose came here [Edinburgh] from the West to be present at the Wedding betwixt the L. Binning, eldest Son to the Earl of Haddington, and Mrs Bailie, Daughter to one of the Lords of the Treasury, which was celebrated last Night with an Entertainment and Ball, and a great deal of the best Company in this Kingdom.'[3]

Opposite: Charles Hamilton, Lord Binning, 1697–1732, Knight Marischal of Scotland (Courtesy of the National Galleries of Scotland)

Above: Rachel, Lady Binning, by Maria Verelst, 1725 (Courtesy of the Earl of Haddington)

Lady Grisell was a meticulous keeper of accounts throughout her married life and an edited version of this valuable insight into eighteenth-century domesticity was published in 1911 as her *Household Book*.[4] Her remarkable story is the subject of a recent biography by Lesley Abernethy which sheds new light on the day-to-day life of Lord Binning and his family. Correspondence from Grisell indicates that Binning did indeed travel abroad as his father wished – to Holland, from where he sent the Baillies fifty-seven pounds of ham, and to Paris, from where he wrote to Rachy.[5] There is, however, no record of any letters or gifts to Tyninghame.

Both sets of parents had reason to believe that this would be a mutually advantageous and successful marriage; in addition, a shared passion for planting their estates strengthened a gardening friendship and plant exchange that was to last most of their lives. In spite of this, Lady Grisell had some reservations about her daughter's father-in-law: if the 6th Earl worked hard on his estate and was often away in London on parliamentary business, when he was home in Scotland, he continued to drink hard, sometimes staying out in the tavern till the early hours, as she observed in a letter to her husband on 1 November 1717.[6]

George Baillie and his wife lived at this time in the peel tower at Mellerstain, although nothing remains of this today as in 1725 William Adam was commissioned to build a replacement. Grisell had already begun planting the estate in the 1690s and ordered trees in their thousands.[7] She must have been delighted to welcome Charles, Lord Binning, into the family as he had had a fine introduction to planting from both his parents and had himself played a part in designing the Binning Wood and the Wilderness at Tyninghame. In their turn, Helen and Thomas were happy to share their expertise in the development of the grounds and walled garden at Mellerstain.

In his writing, Thomas never makes any references to the gardeners at Tyninghame. Their names only

The Gardeners' Arms, Market Street, Haddington, c.1900, prior to alteration (Courtesy of East Lothian Council)

appear in the Tutors' Book and in parish records. Another source is the Ancient Fraternity of Free Gardeners of East Lothian, founded in Haddington in 1676. Their preferred meeting place came to be in rooms in The Gardeners' Arms, a public house in Market Street.

This was one of the oldest of such societies in Scotland, later than Glasgow (1605) but earlier than Aberdeen city (1716) and Edinburgh (1722). Part tradesmen's guild and part benevolent society, their members were originally practising gardeners, but they gradually expanded to allow other tradesmen to join, reflecting their increasing importance. William Hunter, gardener at Tyninghame when Lady Rothes was supervising garden affairs, was a member in 1694 when he bought birch and onion seed. James Tait, who was gardener to the 6th Earl from 1715, was a member from 1721 until his death, after which his widow received occasional payments of between three and five shillings between 1740 and 1761.[8]

Where gardeners were allowed to run their own business, as was the case in Tyninghame, the more enterprising among them advertised in the *Edinburgh Evening Courant*. William Miller, gardener at the abbey of Holyroodhouse, John Baillie from Haddington and James Tait all advertised between 1721 and 1723. On 26 December 1721, and for two weeks following, James Tait advertised the sale of trees, fruit trees, 'Flower-roots, all sorts of Flowering Shrubs, all sorts of Garden Tools, . . . all sorts of Grass Seeds, Hope Cloves [a kind of clover] – Saint Foyn and Ray [Rye] Grass, to be sold at very reasonable rates.'[9] Notably, he is the only one advertising herbaceous ornamental plants and flowering shrubs.

James Tait was also the only gardener advertising the sale of grass seeds at this time. Landowners in East Lothian, or Scotland, were yet to be convinced of the benefits of sowing a field with a named variety of grass seed in a fallow year. This 'improvement', of sowing grass or clover for a fallow year between crops and for pasture, was one of Thomas's favourite themes. He devotes several pages to this in his book, explaining that he had learned of it from a farmer from Dorsetshire whom he had invited up to stay with his family in Tyninghame, in the hope that 'he would put the People here on a better Way of Husbandry and teach them to make their Fences better'.[10] However, the new method of rotation did not go down well, 'the Whole Country (who are ever Angry at New things) were against me'.[11]

In the summer of 1723, the same newspaper, *The Edinburgh Evening Courant*, announced the first meeting of the Society for Improving in the Knowledge of Agriculture, at Gray's House in Hope Park, Edinburgh. The Scottish society was the first of the European agricultural societies; Thomas became a leading member, taking pride in his agrarian improvements, of which sowing grass for a fallow year was but one. Others included planting strips of trees as shelter belts, hedges with ditches for enclosure and, famously, his methods for raising trees. He was one of the earliest Scottish 'Improvers', ploughing a lonely furrow, or so it seemed to him.

It is difficult to date when he first began crop rotation, sowing clover or rye grass, but the advertisement in the *Edinburgh Evening Courant* suggests that it was prior to 1723. In a letter to his son from around 1730 he complains about his neighbours who were still 'wedded to the old ways' and who dismissed the ideas of Jethro Tull, the English agriculturalist, for example, without proper understanding. His son must have been well used to hearing his father's frustration with fellow landowners, who read and talked about improvements without ever putting them into practice.

While Thomas also queried some of Jethro Tull's improvements, he respected his practical experience. He had little time for writers who merely copied what had gone before or for those 'who have writ like Philosophers. These entertain rather than instruct their Readers, while some like Quacks and Chymests, promise a great Deal, but perform nothing. I shall advance nothing, but what I can shew, neither shall I take up Time with talking of the soil that is proper for Planting, since I never met with any, but some Tree or other would grow on . . .'[12]

The Earl of Haddington's Treatise on Forest Trees was not published as a book during his lifetime. He probably wrote it around 1730 as a collection of notes for his brother and other family and friends. Twenty-five years went by before it came into print in 1756. It was included in a compendium of horticulture, a kind of bumper edition of six gardening items, including John Reid's *The Scots Gard'ner*. It was a small format, 'duodecimo' (sixteen centimetres) – the size of a

A veteran oak tree growing by the old drive, below the obelisk

modern paperback – printed in four volumes of differing lengths which could be bound separately or together. Five years later it was published again, bound in boards and priced at 1s. 8d.[13] This was much cheaper than the previous edition. There was evidently a demand for a handy sized, moderately priced, practical guide from one whose fame had grown as one of East Lothian's agricultural improvers. The second edition, which appeared when Helen was in her early eighties, included corrections and the *Letter from the Right Honourable, the Earl of . . . to his grandson.* The manuscript in Thomas's hand (on which both editions were based) was found at Mellerstain in 1949. What is appealing about Thomas's writing is the straightforward way he sets down the information; his tone is conversational without being unnecessarily verbose.

Thomas's reputation as a tree planter stems from the fact that he wrote this careful account of his practices both of raising trees and with directions for planting on a large scale, including for profit. Many other Scottish landowners were planting trees as the seventeenth century gathered pace – and this increased after the Union. Among the neighbours in East Lothian and nearby, planting was going on at Biel, New Hailes, Newbattle, Newbyth, Ormiston, Oxenfoord, Saltoun, Whittingehame and Yester (Gifford).

The book has four chapters: the first covers broadleaf trees, the second aquatics (trees which grow in wet or waterlogged soils), then evergreens and, finally, a chapter on fences and grass. Beginning with the oak, one of his favourite trees, he finds they 'succeed on a variety of soils.'[14]

He describes the making of the seed bed, the sowing of the acorns, the weeding and after two years, the method of transplanting and setting out *in situ*. He was ahead of his time. Modern forestry follows his example of close planting using a nursery 'crop' which is subsequently thinned. The author goes on to give careful directions on pruning, leaving one upright stem and taking care to form a tree that will have enough branches to draw up the sap but not to let the tree get top heavy, for it will be blown over.[15]

Following this pattern, he then describes his methods for growing other broadleaf trees together with his personal assessments. He recommends beech for fine hedges in the Wilderness, as well as for avenues, walks and groves. Elm, ash and walnut are all described together with the Spanish or sweet chestnut (*Castanea sativa*), whose nuts he gets from France, Spain and Portugal and which grow very high.

Among other trees, he notes the sycamore, hornbeam and laburnum. Lime tree seed was hard to come by and all those raised by Thomas were layered. He was very opposed to any kind of artifice and particularly disliked limes clipped into pyramids or pleached.

The first tree that features in the section on acquatics, is the birch. It can 'Thrive in what ever Soil . . . no Tree is more sought after by the Country people than this, both for their Houses, Ploughs, and other utensils of Husbandry', not to mention a further use 'By Tapping them in the Spring they Extract a Liquor, which after Fermentation becomes a Spirituous Delicious Wholesome Wine.'[16] Of the alder, or aller in Scots, Thomas complains he has wasted more money on these than any other. Among willows he favours what he calls the Huntingtown willow, or the white willow (*Salix alba*) 'a good fuel when dry'. Today willow is grown to fuel power stations. When it comes to dwarf willows, the kinds used for basket and hoop making (for barrels and pails for example), he is luke-warm; 'As for making baskets we have so few of that trade, that there is little Demand for these rods.'[17]

Sweet chestnut, one of the tallest trees in the Wilderness planted by Thomas, 6th Earl of Haddington

The Scots pine, or 'fir' as he calls it, takes pride of place among evergreens. 'I believe I have Raised and Planted out more of this Kind of Tree, than ever one man did.' He planted many thousands every year for thirty years, and devotes more words to raising and planting this tree than any other. It is only to be raised from seed, gathered from the cone 'or Clog as it is called here'. What follows is a detailed account, involving trial and error. When it comes to planting out the two-year-old saplings, he gives instructions to dip the roots in a tub of earth and water mixed to a 'the thickness of a pap' before placing them in a basket for transport.

The evergreen oaks (*Quercus ilex*) and cork trees (*Quercus suber*) he planted were still too small for him to say whether they would grow tall enough for ship's

Scots pine on the edge of the old warren at Mosshouse Point

timber, as he had been told. Were he to see the evergreen oaks at Tyninghame today he would find them impressive; the cork trees did not survive. The cedar of Lebanon was introduced into Britain in the mid seventeenth century, but the seed was hard to come by and Thomas had no success in obtaining any, but he rightly guessed that the tree would do well in parts of Scotland, as it eventually did in Tyninghame. There are a few survivors in the Wilderness and one veteran on the north lawn.

Thomas always disliked the fashion for clipped trees. He vowed never to put an evergreen in any other shape but its own, unless in a hedge. '[I] have Reduced my Pyramids [of holly and yew] and hope to make them come to their Natural Shapes.'[18] He makes no mention here of the holly hedges that he planted, which were still one of the glories of Tyninghame 200 years later. He briefly mentions other evergreens: laurel, Portuguese laurel, privet, box, laurustinus (*Viburnum tinus*) which, although usually bushes, he intends to try to grow as trees; larch, though not a true evergreen, he rates a pretty tree, unlike junipers, which he dismisses.

Before leaving the subject of trees, he addresses the subject of the wilderness, which he has seen undergoing a transition during his lifetime, even though 'they have not long been introduced into this country and the Way they were at first laid out was, there was a Center, Straight Walks from it, Ending on as good Views as could be had'. He then takes a swipe at people engaged in the business 'to lay out Ground for Gentlemen, [they] are in my Opinion, very unfit for it. They are too formal, and Stiff, besides they make Every thing so Busy that they croud the ground too much.' Perhaps this explains why the grounds around Tyninghame House were never divided by broad avenues reaching out from the house, with the intervening spaces subdivided into smaller, decorative gardens.

The final chapter is devoted to fences, by which he means hedging on banks with ditches on either side, and it contains detailed instructions for the different types he has tried, together with their measurements. The book ends with a section on the merits of sowing clover and grass seed. Thomas was convinced by his trials and saw red clover sown after barley yield a crop for hay and another for seed while giving good pasture, all in a single year.

Charles, Lord Binning, had been Thomas and

Helen's greatest disciple; his early interest in tree plant-ing and laying out paths had begun at Tyninghame, but was to have free reign at Mellerstain after his marriage. A letter from Lady Grisell Baillie to her husband the month after their daughter Rachel's wedding to Binning in September 1717, described how impressed he was with the landscape setting of the house, and how he envisaged terraces, sloping banks 'waterworks and ponds'.[19]

As the eldest son, Charles would have expected to inherit Tyninghame in due course but in the year of his marriage his father was not yet forty and that prospect was a distant one. He and Rachel lived some time with the Baillies in their London home and for three years at the manor house at East Barnet. He began to write poetry and enjoyed literary company. He wrote a ballad about Sheriffmuir, but little else has survived. Rachel, his wife, was an accomplished musi-cian as were her mother and sister. Five years later he became Member of Parliament for St Germans in Cornwall (1722–7).

But it was Mellerstain that had captured his heart and, in 1725, when William Adam was paid ten guineas for the plans of a new house to replace the Tower, the correspondence was addressed to Lord Binning.

To the factor, Captain Turnbull, Charles gave detailed planting instructions of the tree species together with planting distance, thickening planting in some places and opening up walks in others. The planting distances are close: between two feet and two-and-a-half feet, even closer than his father recom-mends in his *Treatise*. And he adds 'as long as one tree is more than three foot from another, I shall never have hopes of seeing it thrive'.[20] Sadly Charles, Lord Binning, never did see them mature as his life was blighted by tuberculosis; in 1731 his health deteriorated and the Baillie family decided that his best hope was to spend time in a warm climate. They moved to Naples with the older children and stayed there for sixteen months. The younger children stayed behind with their grand-

parents at Tyninghame. Even a week before his death he was sending instructions for work to continue at Mellerstain.

Charles died on 27 December 1732. Five of their eight children survived and, at their father's dying request, their education was committed to the care of Rachel's parents, George and Grisell Baillie, who had cared for him with such concern. Losing their eldest son was a severe blow for Thomas and Helen, who had not been able to accompany him to Italy. Thus Thomas's eldest grandson, also Thomas, became heir to Tyninghame aged eleven. Although the Hadding-tons were on good terms with the Baillies and contin-ued to send trees and planting advice to Mellerstain, there was a sense of distance that was growing between them and their grandchildren. When the family even-tually returned to Mellerstain from Italy, they were keen to carry out the uncompleted plans that Charles had left for the grounds and walled garden there. This was one area where Lady Grisell and Mr Baillie deferred to Helen and Thomas, who could both be relied on for practical help which they readily gave. Helen's advice was sought in settling a dispute with William Boutcher of Comely Garden Nursery, as she had sound knowledge of fruit trees and was already acquainted with the nursery.[21] Woodland planting continued apace at Mellerstain, in accordance with Binning's dying wishes. In an account dated 31 January 1733 nearly 100,000 trees were planted, including over 60,000 firs and 7,200 hollies from Tyninghame. Thomas's claim to have raised more firs than any one man does not seem far-fetched.

Thomas's own health at this time continued to wane. He retired in 1734 under Walpole, 'disgusted by the venality that was practised'.[22] Not long after the death of his son, he felt the need to write to his grand-son, Thomas, now his heir, to tell him something of the story of Tyninghame which his father had known so well. This was the *Letter from the Right Honourable, the Earl of . . . to his grandson*, that was eventually printed in the second edition of his book and in which he pays tribute to his wife.

Helen then received a double blow: as she was recovering from the death of her eldest son, she lost her husband barely two years later. Thomas died in October or November 1735 and was buried at Tyninghame. However difficult life had been with Thomas, his affection for her and their companionship had endured. Now Helen faced huge disruptions in her life. Young Thomas, the grandson who was heir to Tyninghame was to be educated with his brothers and sisters by his mother and her parents. It was increasingly unlikely that Helen would see much of her son's children as they grew up, and this proved to be the case. They already spent much of the year in their London house and now proposed to take a house in Oxford, where the eldest boys would get the best education. Helen's dismay can be inferred from a letter written by Lady Grisell to her husband at this time. This reaction from Helen, who as far as we know, rarely left Scotland, is understandable. She must also have wondered what fate would befall the planting and the estate to which she and Thomas had given so much of their lives. The woodlands had been the fulfilment of her dreams but instead of staying on, she flitted. She may have had no choice. Helen, the Dowager Lady Haddington, was probably expected to move out of the house which now belonged to her grandson. As her daughter-in-law's family were educating him in England, the house would again stand empty for many years.

Barely six months after the death of her husband an advertisement appeared in *The Caledonian Mercury* on 3 and 10 May 1736: 'Roup at Tyninghame to sell all sorts of household furniture, viz. Beds, Hangings, Feather beds, Blankets, Tapestry, Pictures, Plate, China, Table and Bed linens, all sorts of Kitchen, Brewing, and Dairy utensils, Peuther and Brass Ware: As also, a Coach, Chariot, and Chaise.' The sale began at 10 a.m. on 11 May and goods could be seen for eight days previously. Printed inventories were to be had from James

Hope ws and at the sale. It seems clear from the amount of goods to be auctioned that the house would barely be habitable once it was over.

Helen died in Edinburgh on 19 April 1768, when she was ninety-one. She probably lived with her younger son John, an Edinburgh lawyer, but she must also have spent time with her daughter Christian who had married Sir James Dalrymple and lived at New Hailes, near Musselburgh. Christian had sixteen children and died just two years after her mother. In Helen's will, her 'goods and gear after mentioned' included some silver plate valued at £355 19s. 7d. and books valued at £2. An account book at New Hailes for 1771 has an entry: 'a black cabinet bought at my grandmother's sale, £29 19s 4d'.[23] The purchaser was David Dalrymple, Lord Hailes. This was the cabinet lined with the architectural plans for her parents' house in the Cowgate, the house that was never built.

When the house had been cleared after the roup in June 1736, Helen possibly took Thomas's manuscript with her to Edinburgh. When she was in her early eighties a second edition of Thomas's *Treatise on Forest Trees* appeared. It included corrections to the former edition together with the *Letter from the Right Honourable, the Earl of . . . to his grandson*. A comparison between the two printed editions of her husband's book and the Mellerstain manuscript indicates the hand of someone with intimate knowledge of the text and the terrain, and this could only have been the Dowager Countess of Haddington.[24]

But for her husband's *Letter*, Helen's great love of planting would have remained overshadowed, for he makes no mention of her in the text; but for Helen, Thomas would have had nothing to write about and without his wife his writing might never have been published.

Many of the trees they planted at Tyninghame are still there today and the bones of the landscape they designed together – field boundaries, avenues and woodland – have survived.

CHAPTER 7

The Old and the New

Helen's departure to Edinburgh from Tyninghame followed the pattern for widows among the Scottish nobility in the eighteenth century. Their lives changed the moment their husbands died. Their marriage contracts had been drawn up with this eventuality in mind and their income came from rents that they had been assigned. Accommodation could be provided in the form of a dower house or shared apartments in the family home. If the heir was still a minor, she might remain longer there, with tutors appointed to supervise finances and education until he reached his majority. It remains a matter of conjecture whether Helen was offered a home in Tyninghame as might have been expected or whether, in the light of the apparent cooling of relations with the Mellerstain family, she chose to join her eldest surviving son, John, in Edinburgh. Nothing more is known of her life until her death was recorded thirty-six years later. Widows, even more than wives, vanished from the records. Once Helen had left and the house was cleared, it was left to the minister, the grieve and the factor to look after their respective charges until the new heir came of age.

At Mellerstain, Thomas, the 7th Earl of Haddington, was always called 'Tamie' by Grisell when he was a boy. He is portrayed by Aikman with his brother John, who died in 1730 when he was only four years

old. This portrait must have been painted around the time of John's death. The black servant was called Judy; what looks in the portrait like a wide silver torque around her neck was probably a steel collar which would have had both her name and the Baillie name engraved on it, as this was the norm. There is no evidence that she was ill-treated, on the contrary, but the collar restricted her freedom. (There is no record in Grisell's account book of any purchase price, which suggests that she and another black slave, Cyrus, were gifts.)[1] She may even have been at Tyninghame with the younger children, Charlie and Rachel, when their parents and the rest of the family went to Naples in 1731.

The Baillie entourage left Mellerstain for England in October 1736. They were a large party: George and Grisell with their daughters Rachy and Grisie, and Rachy's children, little Grisie, Tamie, George, Charles, Rachel and their governor, plus footmen and other servants. Ostensibly their destination was Oxford but there were illnesses and diversions en route and it was not until the end of April the following year that the family finally arrived. Finding suitable lodging for seventeen was not an easy task and Grisell grumbled about the poor accommodation they had to accept.

The time in Oxford does not appear to have been particularly agreeable. There was none of the social life

of Bath or London and the expenses for the young boys' education were considerable. It had been agreed that Rachel, his mother, would pay for Tamie's education, and the Baillie family would pay for George, his younger brother, who would one day inherit Mellerstain. For example, an elaborate student gown, 'requiring 8 yards of green damask, 10½ yards of gold galoun [braid], 10 dozen buttons and 5 dozen tassels, costing in all over 33 pounds' was bought for George.[2] There were also tuition fees, special dinners and hall fees together with a bridle, saddle, saddle cloth trimmed with lace and a whip which George needed for the horse he rode while he was there. As always, these expenses were entered by Grisell into her account book. Tamie's expenses have not survived but, as the seventeen-year-old Earl of Haddington, his aristocratic position cannot have demanded any less than his fourteen-year-old younger brother. While they were there, George Baillie, then aged seventy-four, died unexpectedly in August 1738 and his body was sent back to Mellerstain for burial. The family remained in Oxford for four years. Letters from both mother and daughter to family in Scotland reveal how little they were enjoying their stay.[3] There were no plans for Thomas, Lord Haddington, to return to Tyninghame.

Thomas was nineteen and his brother, George, sixteen when they set off for their Grand Tour in April 1740. Their devoted grandmother, Grisell, now seventy-five, had compiled a detailed notebook for them, containing information about the best routes, superior inns, things to see, prices of goods and services, and how to avoid being robbed. It amounted to 120 pages. They were accompanied by Mr John Williamson as tutor-cum-guardian and together they spent several years travelling on the Continent, including spells in Rome and Geneva.[4] When they finally returned to Scotland in 1744, Thomas visited Tyning-

hame but he did not stay long; his grandmother thought London society a preferable environment for her grandchildren. Once again, the Baillie family and servants headed south. The journey took thirteen days. Besides Grisell and her two daughters, five grandchildren, eight servants and fourteen horses went by road, while another six servants and the baggage went by sea.[5] His grandmother doted on Thomas and he appears to have thrown himself into society life in London with abandon.[6]

Thomas was in no hurry to wed, and was thirty when he married Mary Holt, the widow of Gresham Lloyd, in Tyninghame in 1750. Surprisingly little is known of his life considering that he held his title for fifty-nine years, longer than any predecessor or successor. He did not seek public office for himself but as he voted in the elections for representative peers, he evidently visited Scotland at least every few years. He may not have chosen Tyninghame as his main residence, at least not until later in his life when he appeared as one of the notable figures of Edinburgh society in 1785, caricatured by John Kay, the Scottish engraver. His eldest son, Charles, Lord Binning, was born in 1753 but was not baptised at Tyninghame, nor was his next son, Thomas, who sadly died in London when he was sixteen.

During these long absences, work on the estate must have carried on as before with the gardener, Thomas Thomson and others reporting to the grieve, and the grieve reporting to the factor. John Hamilton, the younger brother of the 6th Earl, was at the church at Tyninghame to witness the baptisms of two of his three children in the early 1730s.[7] As Helen was now living with John in Edinburgh, her links with Tyninghame, even her influence, may have continued, but the church records never mention her visits.

Although she and her husband will always be remembered for their planting rather than their building, it was during their tenure at Tyninghame that the old village gradually disappeared and the new village

Opposite: Portrait of Thomas and his brother John, with Judy, by William Aikman, 1728 (Courtesy of the Earl of Haddington)

slowly took shape along the roadside to the west of the house. There is no evidence in surviving papers that any residents were 'cleared' nor that Tyninghame was a planned village as is often claimed. Its appearance as 'the very model of an estate village'[8] is deceptive. With its factor's house, sawmill, Widow's Row, cottages and village hall it may convey that impression but, as Joy Dodd's research has shown, it evolved piecemeal.[9] In the old 'toun', when tenants or owners got into difficulties, their land reverted to the earl or he bought it back. This allowed the 6th Earl to begin building new houses for tenants in the early years of the eighteenth century. These were sited further away, by the road, thus uncluttering the views across the river from the house.

While Helen and Thomas lived at Tyninghame, the drive to the house would probably have been along the shared 'Hard Gait' or 'High Gait', which Thomas had famously hedged with holly. This was a straight track which led to the church from the nearest road (now the A198) from North Berwick and Whitekirk to the old Edinburgh road to Dunbar, Berwick and London (now the A199). This was the gait that had 'aye been', and to which Mr John frequently refers in the kirk session records.

Thomas's friend, the Earl of Mar, had written to him in 1731 from Aix-la-Chapelle suggesting that he alter the landscape design to 'answer' to the house. Although he had been away from Scotland since 1715, Mar had remembered that Tyninghame, for all its merits, lacked a cohesive design centred on the house. The aspect to the south, to the river, the salt flats and the distant Lammermuir Hills was delightful but was spoilt by the clutter of cottages and glebe land:

> Tininghame is a fine situation and the house is in the right place . . . The old house is now so well repair'd and so convenient that it were follie to think of making a new one, but all the policie to be made to answer to it, so that the views from it may be as fine as they would be from a new house . . . One of the greatest beautys about the place, and which ought to be most studdied to improve is the Saltgrass meadows on the south side. A canal through them opposite to the middle of this front would be a very fine and agreeable prospect from the house . . . .[10]

Here Mar is envisaging a canal, or a long straight body of water, on the further side of the Tyne, in the formal style which still dominated landscape design on the Continent and in Scotland. The river is tidal at this point and the 'Saltgrass meadows' were, and are, often flooded at spring tides and after heavy rain or snow. The difficulties of achieving this feat of engineering were not negligible, and he added, 'but if that cannot easily be compassed, it would be nixt best to have a nice smooth flatt meadow in the middle, the larger the better, with a canal around it on the four sides, and all the old tracks of the river and broken parts of the meadows filled up and smoothed'. Even this plan would have involved costly engineering and was unlikely to have succeeded or appealed to his friend. But Mar had not finished:

> The church to be taken from where it now is and to be placed in the new village; a pavilion to be made over the burial place of the family, and another answering to it on the other side of the gravel walk to be from the house and court to the meadows, for a summer house. That which is now cornland besouth the church, with the church yard to be smoothed and laid into grass so far as can be seen from the house on both sides.[11]

Mar's letter established two further facts otherwise unrecorded. He remembered the house as 'now so well repair'd and so convenient', indicating that at least improvements here had taken place when Helen and Thomas were in residence and he refers to the New Village, or New Tyninghame as it was known. It is possible that Thomas had written to Mar in his exile, knowing his friend's interest in town and village planning, describing the developments and building that was taking place. However, his grandson, the 7th Earl, having spent most of his life in England and abroad, had other ideas for the estate. The plans of this older generation held no appeal.

Soon after Thomas, the 7th Earl, came of age, although he was still not living there, some things at Tyninghame had begun to change and a new order appeared. The minister's three cows and horse had, since 1711, been allowed to pasture in the earl's park because the minister did not have enough land of his own. Pasture for his animals was not the only thing the minister lacked – a house was another. For almost eighty years, the minister or the Dunbar presbytery complained about the state of the manse. As early as 1665, a visitation had reported that the manse was ruinous. They were still considering the matter in July 1711 when the earl was urged to build him a new house.[12]

As a stopgap, it was suggested that rather than repair the ruinous manse, the earl should repair another house he owned, known as Lady Trabroun's House, that stood somewhere between the main house and the Walled Garden, and is shown on Forrest's map of 1799. With eleven hearths[13] it was both spacious and in a better state than the manse, so the Rev. and Mrs Turnbull settled there, as did the successor Rev. George Buchanan. Much tree planting had taken place in the Wilderness around Lady Trabroun's House so it did not intrude on the view from the house, as had the old manse.

The 7th Earl's ideas for the estate never included building a new manse, on the contrary, he wanted to remove it; and not just the manse, but the kirk of St Baldred also. The opportunity for change arose in 1760 when the minister, George Buchanan, died on 28 April. It is not known when the idea of merging the parish of Tyninghame with that of the adjacent parish of Whitekirk was first mooted but it is evident, even from the Earl of Mar's ideas, that this plan must have had a long gestation period. The 7th Earl was a relative 'outsider', so it was perhaps not surprising that he was the one who cut the ties with the past. He formally approached Thomas Miller, Lord Advocate, for his legal opinion as the Crown needed to approve any such merger. In his reply, the Lord Advocate wrote: 'I think your scheme for removing the Kirk and uniting the two parishes is a very natural one as being so necessary for your own conveniency & the improvement of your Estate & not hurtful or inconvenient to others.'[14]

Whatever the reasons given for uniting the parishes, once in effect, it heralded the greatest single change to the estate in its history. The kirk of St Baldred's would no longer be the centre of parish life, moreover, the link between the house, once the bishop's castle, and the church was severed. The sense of veneration for the holy site had dissipated since the Reformation although the memory of St Baldred lingered on, his name still marking the landscape and its maps.

The Lord Advocate touched on two points which indicated the real intentions of the earl: improvement and convenience. When the earl formally approached the presbytery of Dunbar for approval later that year,[15] he noted that there were few inhabitants in the parish and the stipend no more than 1,000 merks. As the neighbouring parish of Whitekirk was also very small, with an equally small stipend (900 merks in this case), an annexation of the two 'will be of prejudice to no person whatsoever so it will be a benefit to the Memorialist by leaving him at liberty to beautifie and improve the seat of the family and the adjacent fields'. The benefit to the minister of the two merged parishes would be the greater stipend of 1,900 merks and more glebe land (or the financial equivalent).

There was one further beneficiary to be taken into consideration: the New College of St Andrews. They saw this merger as an opportunity to increase their income and set one condition: they increased their teind (tythe) by 200 merks. This was the case that the 7th Earl put before the presbytery, and, though undated, must have been towards the end of 1760. Accompanying the document are valuations of the glebe lands and of the minister's old garden, and a plan, surveyed by Robert Ainslie, dated 9 December 1760.[16] Interestingly, one of the witnesses was Alexander Morrison, a plasterer from Edinburgh. This is the only indication of any serious refurbishing of the interior of Tyninghame House by the 7th Earl.

In the following April, the Dunbar presbytery met to finalise the union of the two parishes. The Lords of Session and Lords of Plantation and Valuation had allowed the merger of the parishes and for the incumbent minister at Whitekirk, Mr John Clunie, to receive the stipends for both parishes together with glebe lands, pasturages and gardens of both. As there was not enough land available at Whitekirk to increase the acreage, it was accepted that this would be converted into rent, paid by the earl to the minister, in addition to the stipend. As the minister was to live at Whitekirk, there was no longer a reason to build a manse at Tyninghame, instead, the earl offered ten shillings and agreed to bear the expenses of altering the church at Whitekirk to accommodate the larger congregation. The presbytery agreed and the merger took place later that year and was recorded in the Whitekirk session minutes for 30 August 1761.[17]

The union of the two parishes and the consequent abandoning of the old kirk of St Baldred has overshadowed the fact that there had been a gradual decline of the original township which became known as Old Tyninghame. The township itself was not 'cleared' on this date, on the contrary, it seems that residents lived in their houses until they died or became infirm; their children moved away and only when old houses

became empty were these taken down. One of the last to leave was James Watt, still living in Old Tyninghame when his wife died in 1743 and he may still have been there in 1760. As new houses of stone and mortar became available in New Tyninghame, although a few were taken by local families, more were taken by incomers. From 1709, when the first mention is made of New Tyninghame in the baptismal records, until 1712 'eighteen families are mentioned as living in the new village, of which fifteen were incomers'.[18]

Tyninghame is unusual in having two sources for parish records besides the usual ones for baptisms, marriages and deaths. The first are the records of the Tyninghame kirk session from 1615 until 1761, much of them written in homely detail by John Lauder. The second is *The Diary of the Rev. George Turnbull*,[19] minister at Tyninghame from 1699 until 1731, although his diary stops in 1704. Between them they incidentally record the life of the township in the seventeenth and early eighteenth centuries, by which time Tyninghame had developed into an agricultural and fishing community. Besides fishermen, farmers, tenant farmers and their hinds (labourers), the inhabitants included: shepherd, gardener, mason, tailor, weaver, keeper of ale house, wright, locksmith, tasker (thresher of corn), miller, tinker, blacksmith, wright at the sawmill, maltman, cooper, carpenter, carrier, flesher (butcher), bellman, boatman and a nurse (to bairns).

The earl's household had included: falconer to the Earl of Haddington (1646), porter, servant, cook, grieve, baillie or chamberlain, master of horses (1725) and coachman. New occupations occurred in the middle of the eighteen century, such as, in 1749, surgeon 'just now in this parish', and a shoemaker in New Tyninghame in 1750.

Strangers attracted attention. Those passing through were occasionally soldiers but more often

Opposite: Plan of the glebe and minister's garden at Tyninghame by Robert Ainslie, 1760 (Courtesy of the Earl of Haddington)

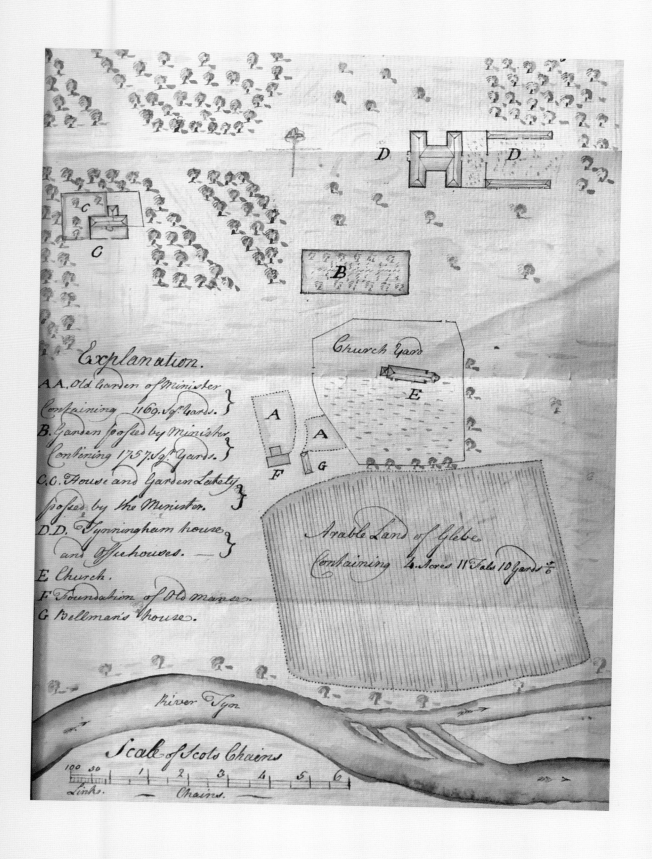

Explanation.

A.A. Old Garden of Minister
Containing 1169 Sqr Yards.

B. Garden posses by Minister
Containing 1757 Sqr Yards.

C.C. House and Garden Lately
posses by the Minister.

D.D. Tynningham house
and Offeehouses. ———

E. Church.

F. Foundation of Old manse.

G. Bellman's house.

D   D

C

B

Church Yard

E

A   A

F   G

Arable Land of Glebe
Containing 4 Acres 11 Fals 10 Yards ⅜

River Tyn

Scale of Scots Chains

100 50   1   2   3   4   5   6

Links.   Chains.

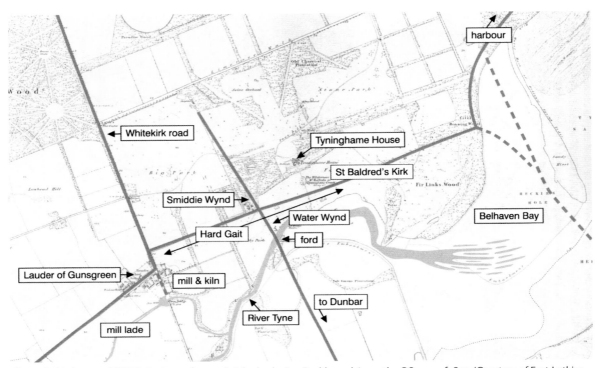

The probable layout of Old Tyninghame, from a sketch plan by Joy Dodd, overlain on the OS map of 1855 (Courtesy of East Lothian Antiquarian and Field Naturalists' Society)

beggars or 'cripples', sometimes wearing their blue gowns or badges that authorised their right to ask for alms. Vagrants were frequently escorted, or in the case of cripples, carried, over the parish boundary. In 1701 the session appointed William Purves as constable 'to go through the parish thrice a week & expel the vagrant beggars and if any be found begging through his fault the expence to be defrayed from his wage'.[20] The session had enough difficulty caring for 'our aine poore' without taking on further burdens.

Tyninghame's Anglian Northumbrian heritage was manifest in its settlement pattern: church, great house and smaller houses, loosely clustered along the High Gait or Hard Gait as it was known. Other East Lothian villages show a similar nucleated pattern, sometimes with houses around a village green as at Stenton and Dirleton. In this it differed from the layout of the fermtouns or kirktouns in other parts of Scotland,

where loose clusters of houses were apparently less orderly although based on the units that two or three plough teams could cultivate.[21] In the parish of Tyninghame, there were also outlying settlements or hamlets where most of the farmers were tenants of the estate. These parcels of land were referred to as 'shotts' in an estate book of 1608 belonging to the Lauders of the Bass,[22] and included long vanished place names. Other names have survived: Bromhill, Brounrig and Haflat (Halflands), for example. The hamlets that featured in Mr John's kirk session records are the fishing communities at Scougall, Pefferside, Ravensheuch and Fisherhouses along the shore north of the Tyne; further inland were Lochhouses and Muttonhole; Knowes, with its mill by the Tyne, and to the east: Easter and Wester Gateside, Kirklandhill and Belpots, near Belhaven.

The old village, or toun, consisted of three main lanes or 'gaits': the Hard Gait which led to the church

The former Hard Gait, with a few holly trees, remnants of the eighteenth-century holly hedges

and main house from the Whitekirk road (A198); the Water Wynd which led down to the ford across the River Tyne; and the Smiddy Wynd which must have led north from the Hard Gait, possibly at the point the Water Wynd led to the river from the Hard Gait. There would also have been a lane or track leading to the corn mill, by the mill lane and also a well-trodden path from the centre of the village to the sea, where there was a small rocky harbour to the north of Whitberry Point. Another track would probably have led from the village to the anchorage on the riverbank, downstream from the church. From these records, Joy Dodd has traced a possible street pattern.[23]

Some vestiges of these old ways survive but as they no longer lead to significant destinations, they have been by-passed or swept aside to facilitate access by car, rather than horse drawn transport or on foot. The 6th Earl planted deep holly hedges along both sides of

the Hard Gait. They became famous in the nineteenth century but gradually declined and the hedges were grubbed out in the 1960s.

The old track to the ford across the river, named Smiddy Ford in the nineteenth-century Ordnance Survey maps, may have dated from monastic times. From the middle of the sixteenth century, the only bridge across the Tyne was at East Linton, three miles to the west. (The existing bridge on the A198 was built in 1778.)

In September 1637, Magnus Clerk took the initiative and approached the elders with a plan to buy a boat to be used as a ferry – the stepping-stones were useless at very high tides or after stormy weather. The elders agreed, £7 7s. was collected and he was appointed boatman with instructions to buy a boat. The ferry was probably somewhere near the Whitekirk Road. Besides ferrying general traffic across the river, to and from church on Sundays (but forbidden during services), the boatman also ferried children from the south side of the river to and from the school. One of the early houses in New Tyninghame, built on the Whitekirk Road by the 6th Earl, was for the boatman, George Kilpatrick: the entry for the baptism of his daughter Agnes on 19 May 1713 records his dwelling as the 'new boathouse'. The boatman's house and garden (yard) were rent free, the cost being shared by the earl and the kirk session.

The ancient burial ground that surrounded the church was enclosed by a stone dyke or wall, and Robert Ainslie's plan indicates two gates giving access to the kirk. The earl and his household would enter by the north gate and the village folk by the east. In the seventeenth century access was by wooden stiles over the walls and stepping stones were put down to make a 'causey' through the mud.

Most of the houses in the old toun were to the west of the church. Their construction methods were very rudimentary: timber-framed houses with rubble stone for the lower courses of the walls and a roof thatched with turf (divots), broom, reeds, heather or whatever was available. They were low, with a single hearth, earthen floors and very small windows with shutters but no glass. Only larger houses had glazed windows and were slated or properly thatched. 'Pre-improvement cottages in the Scottish countryside were by and large bio-degradable.'[24] Perhaps it is not surprising that no aerial photographs give any indication of their whereabouts. Very occasionally, a hard frost melting in morning light may show a faint imprint of bygone houses in the park, to the left of the farm gate by the present Head Gardener's House. At Mellerstain in 1702, a 'cot-house' was built for four shillings and others are mentioned in Lady Grisell's *Household Book*, costing five shillings, eleven shillings and a penny, and fourteen shillings and fourpence. A pair of gloves for Grisell cost one pound two shillings.[25]

A metal farm gate (p. 79) now stands where once

the Water Wynd and the Smiddy Wynds crossed the Hard Gait. The outline of the old road leading to the kirk has also vanished under the parkland, but the section leading from the old to the new village can still be seen in the slight change of level in the slope of the ploughed field, between the Walled Garden and the line of trees to the west.

Not far from this crossroads, which was the centre of the toun, stood the stocks and 'jougs' where the beleaguered minister disciplined his erring flock. Their sins ranged from slandering to fornication; from playing golf or football to working on their rigs or fishing for herring or netting solan geese (gannets) on the Sabbath; from fighting and 'flyting' (abusing, quarrelling) or getting drunk to stealing. There were also those who were chastised for what they did not do: not attending church, not baptising their children or not attending communion. For these transgressions, if deemed guilty, the punishments invariably included a fine and ranged from spending time before the congregation on the penitent's pillar or stool in the kirk ('Sitt on the pillar in linen claithes'), or in the jougs outside the church door or in the stocks by the crossroad.

A far more serious crime was witchcraft, which usually involved the presbytery at Dunbar, senior Church members and the judiciary in Edinburgh. Mr John first mentions this in 1629 when he was called to Edinburgh to assist the Minister of Dunbar in the trial of a woman suspected of witchcraft, but he gives no details. In the 1630s there were cases of malicious gossip, where witchcraft was mentioned as the cause of an illness and a stillborn calf but Mr John did not take the accusations further. The quarrelling women who frequently appeared before the minister (when their sharp tongues got the better of them, they invoked the devil), were always investigated thoroughly before the charges of witchcraft were dropped. The call from the now triumphant Covenanters in the 1640s was for moral regeneration and the rooting out of immorality in all its forms.[26]

The Water Wynd leading to the old ford

The General Assembly passed Acts in 1640, 1644, 1645 and 1649 calling on presbyteries and kirk sessions to search out witches and destroy them thus setting off new bursts of investigations. However, when the trials of witches in neighbouring parishes increased between 1649 and 1650, the entries to the session records changed and make sobering reading: '17 September 1649 Janet Nicolson execut and brunt [burned] at Hails for witchcraft.'[27] Intimations from the pulpit followed in October and November asking the congregation to search diligently for witchcraft and if they had anything to say against Agnes Angus from Stenton or Agnes Raleigh from East Barnes, who were both under suspicion. 'On Monday, the witches at Whittingehame brunt, being three in number.' Three

more were accused in December – and again Tyninghame parishioners were invited from the pulpit to give evidence: 'Patrick Yorston and Christian Yorston, in Wittinghame, if any in this parish either knew or have any delations [denouncement] against both or either of them, that they show it to the kirk session.'[28] The perception of witchcraft was now rife.

On 6 January the minister noted that some of 'our pepell confronted with some witches from Prestonkirk parish', as if this were a normal occurrence. He had become caught up in the febrile atmosphere of the time and the better judgement he had showed in previous years deserted him. The following week he urged the elders to search for the witches at Prestonkirk before adding: 'Upon Tysday ane man in Whittinghame brunt for witchcraft, upon Wednesday, the 23 January, six people at Staintone parish brunt.' Searchers for witches were invited to the parish.[29] In the meantime, and with no prior intimation, Agnes Kirkland and David Steward (sometimes spelt Stewart) from the parish were apprehended and imprisoned. This presented a problem as Tyninghame did not have a prison; the smiddy may have been used (there was a precedent in August 1633) and the elders drew up a roll of all the parish, from which six people were to keep regular watch. The next week Mr John was ordered to Dunbar where ten witches were burned. 'Persecution was as epidemic in an area as it was in time . . .',[30] and Tyninghame was engulfed by the wave that spread out across East Lothian.

The parishioners had to wait until the end of the month before the commission arrived, following which an assize court was established and on '9 [April 1650] Agnes Kirkland and David Stewart were execut.' It was rare in Scotland for those found guilty to be burned alive; usually they were strangled at the stake before their bodies were burned. The kirk records contain no mention of Agnes Kirkland, other than her execution, suggesting that she was an incomer with no family. David Steward(t) 'from this syd of Peffer' is recorded in 1643 as the father of a son, David, who died of the pox aged five years.[31] No mention is made of a mortcloth, which indicated he was poor. He had a daughter, Agnes, who was baptised on 16 October 1646 when his occupation is given as 'piper'. The mother was not named in either record nor were there any witnesses. Agnes Kirkland was probably an older woman, possibly the unnamed mother of David Steward's children; he was a poor piper and they were both vulnerable.

The episode demonstrates the dominant role that the kirk and the minister played in village life. Even the church building was used as the 'schoolroom' for village boys, as was the case at Whitekirk and Prestonkirk, but it was not always a satisfactory arrangement. The pupils occupied the western end of the building and the poorly paid schoolmaster not only had to contend with unruly boys but sometimes pigeons! An entry in February 1634 asked for the 'dowis' (pigeons) to be banished as they soiled the seats and a house was needed for the school, 'becaus the bairnes abusit the kirk by playing in the same and breaking the seittis and glass windows'.[32] The windows and roof were repaired but the pigeons returned so Alexander Storie was paid six shillings to buy gunpowder to shoot them.

Schoolmasters came and went every few years. In 1675 a visitation observed that children were still being taught in the kirk 'for want of a school'. This changed after the Education Act of 1696, as each congregation was ordered to provide a suitable house for a school and an annual salary for a schoolmaster to be paid for by the minister, proprietors (heritors) and their tenants. The situation was rectified around the time that the Rev. George Turnbull arrived in December 1699 to fill the vacancy that had lasted almost five years since the death of the previous minister, Rev. Thomas Edward. The session minutes for this year note that a room was found and 'furnished with a desk for the master, three long forms, a writing table with a forme on each syde for the use of the schollars, a new half doore, and a little glass-window to the outer doore for greater light to the schoole'.[33] This does not suggest that a new school was built, rather than an existing building was given a new use, but its exact position is unknown.

Early in 1649, a newcomer arrived 'quha learns the Lassis in the toune to red'. She was Margeret Geddes, from Teviotdale, but originally from Ireland and besides reading she was also teaching them to sew. The elders demanded a reference from her previous employer or threatened to send her away – without testimonials, single women attracted attention.[34] In the absence of a welfare state, when parishes were responsible for their poor and sick, any incomers were viewed with suspicion. No further references to school-

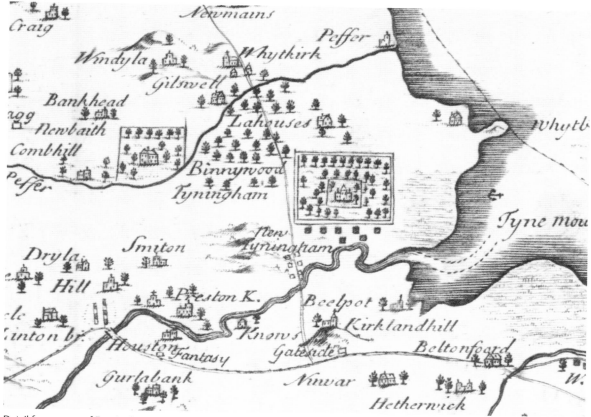

Detail from a map of East Lothian, printed 1736 and surveyed by John Adair (Courtesy of the National Library of Scotland)

ing for girls occur for the next fifty years; it is possible that it continued, but in an informal and undocumented way.

Under the Rev. Turnbull, education for older girls is put on a more formal footing. In May 1712, 'The session thinking it verie convenient that a womens school be keepit at the Knowes ground for teaching lassies to sew white seame & other things proper for young girls (who are first to be keepit at the publick school until they can read the Bible) they are content to give ten pounds scots to a discrete woman, whom the session shall be pleased with together with the ordinair quarter payed for her encouragement.'[35]

The kirk session also records paying a schoolmistress for a women's school at Westergateside in 1715. It may also have taken boys, as in December 1712 William Nicholson was described as keeping the school. This was not the public school, now in the hands of the schoolmaster Robert Bisset (who also kept the session records) and it was closed. However, girls' education continued, and 'a woman school be keepit in the Knowes ground for lasses & grounding young ones and allows the fee given to Wm Nicolson to be given to an honest woman'. Mistress Blair continued as schoolmistress at Westergateside and was still paid by the session in 1715. The elders were full of good intentions regarding the education of young women in the parish but further evidence of its implementation is sadly lacking.

One of the first things Rev. Turnbull had under-

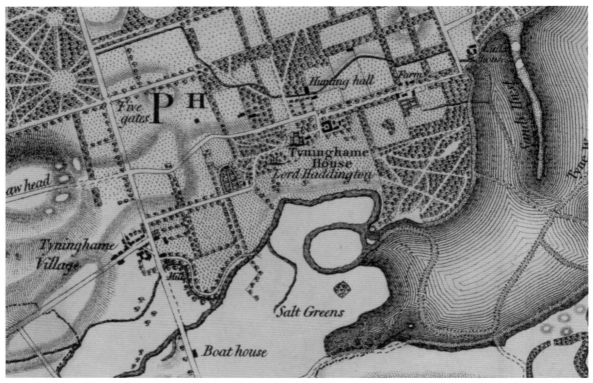

Tyninghame, detail from William Forrest's map of Haddingtonshire, 1799 (Courtesy of the National Library of Scotland)

taken when he arrived at Tyninghame, was to make sure that every household had a bible. He had noticed that the very poor could not afford books for their children at school and that some of the elderly, who wanted to read the bible, could not afford them. Accordingly, 'three dozen of bybles, three dozen of confessions of faith, with some dozen of Proverbs & Catechisms to be distribute by the Minister to the parishioners as he shall see cause'. Learning to read in the village school was a solemn business.

Most residents of Old Tyninghame had either left by the 1750s or they had died and incomers had arrived to settle in New Tyninghame; the ties that had bound this community were inevitably loosened. The bakehouse, which was enlarged later and became the village hall, is dated 1708 on a lintel inside. In 1715 five houses were built for the 'poor and widows'. The kirk records refer to these as 'the Hospital', which eventually became known as Widow's Row, at the west end of Main Street. Another five houses were added in 1720. The woods planted by Helen and Thomas were producing enough wood by 1752 to warrant a sawmill and when fourteen fir trees were supplied from the estate for the purpose and six 'spars' of cherry and elm were supplied to the sawmiller, his house was built the following year. ('Spars' referred to timber which could be used for rafters, door frames, window frames and furniture.)

Gradually, the new village took shape as smiddy, ale and porter house, malt house and a schoolhouse were added. Farm workers' cottages clustered around the Mains, indicating an early eighteenth-century rather than late eighteenth-century construction when 'a trend started to separate the farmhouse and the farm

Decorated stones from the twelfth-century kirk embedded in a gable wall

workers' cottages from the steading, a situation which reflected the growing differentiation between the farmer and his workforce'.[36] By 1799, when William Forrest's map of Haddingtonshire was published, the village is shown on the north and south sides of the main street. Lady Trabroun's House, used as the manse, can just be seen to the west of Tyninghame House.

It also shows the new bridge over the Tyne, recently completed. According to the entries for the combined parishes of Whitekirk and Tyninghame in the *Statistical Account of Scotland 1796*, the population of the latter in 1755 was recorded as 599.[37]

Forrest's map shows the way the landscape had changed around Tyninghame House: St Baldred's Kirk is not shown; there are no signs of the Old Toun; parkland dotted with clumps of trees surrounds the house;

a new drive adds drama to the approach as it sweeps in to the north of the old Hard Gait, across the Big Park, along the side of the Wilderness where the mile-long avenue stretches to the sea, until the trees finally give way to reveal the house. To the south, the view to the distant Lammermuir Hills is unimpeded, save for a picturesque ruin: the twin arches of the old kirk. The improvements envisaged by the 7th Earl appear complete.

The gravestones were taken from the churchyard and the ground levelled; building stone was taken from the kirk and used elsewhere on the estate – some decorated stones found their way into the walls of the Stables House. The final burial that took place at Tyninghame was that of its last minister, George Buchanan, on 28 April 1760. The best mortcloth was used and the bell was tolled.

CHAPTER 8

Walled Garden and Woodland

The changes to the landscape and the buildings in the second half of the eighteenth century at Tyninghame were not recorded. Apart from Thomas, the 6th Earl, neither his grandson, the 7th Earl (1735–94), nor great-grandson, the 8th Earl (1794–1830) wrote descriptions of their building work or embellishments to the gardens or policies. And yet the second half of the eighteenth century was a time of the greatest change to the landscape of Scotland. The enclosure of the old rigs with boundary hedges or stone dykes, and the introduction of shelter belts of the kind that the 6th Earl, and to a lesser extent his father, had championed were now accelerating. The smaller 'ferm touns' were disappearing throughout East Lothian and beyond, just as Old Tyninghame had disappeared, and were replaced by single tenant farms with handsome new farmhouses and steadings. Instead of their scattered jumble of dwellings, a more orderly pattern emerged. As agricultural improvements gathered pace, they were mirrored by those in horticulture which, in turn, were reflected in changes to the design of gardens and to walled kitchen gardens in particular.

As the eighteenth century progressed, the taste for formal gardens waned, and the trend for a 'natural', informal landscape around the house increased. Gardens in the Lothians were among the first to show the new style in Scotland: one of the first in the early 1750s was Sir Thomas Hay who employed Mr Bowie, a landscape designer, to reconfigure his garden at Alderston 'in a natural way'. And he went on to recommend his services to his cousin and neighbour, the Marquess of Tweeddale at Yester, as Mr Bowie was 'the only person that I have met with in this part of the world that has a good fancy in laying out ground in a natural way'.[1] When Amisfield House, near Haddington, was built in 1755, the grounds were laid out with avenues and 'with a wood on each side, and the lawns with clumps and single trees . . . and a most beautiful kitchen garden by the river'.[2] This kitchen garden, prone to flooding, was replaced between 1782 and 1788 by a larger, stone-walled garden, further away from the river.

The earliest map indicating a walled garden at Tyninghame is William Forrest's map of Haddington-shire in 1799 (p. 82). It shows an enclosure at some distance from the house, on the western edge of the Wilderness. The holly hedges that the 6th Earl had planted along the Hard Gait were now substantial and would have partially screened the garden wall, as would the trees in the Wilderness. The garden has a curved wall at the northern end, a perimeter path and central axial path running roughly north–south and a cross-path bisecting this, running east–west. Two more lateral paths bisected these quarters, dividing the garden into eight compartments. This layout was a standard design.

The grandest walled kitchen gardens comprised several acres – nine acres at Blair Castle and eight at Amisfield for example – the garden at Tyninghame is four acres. It is about 170 metres from the centre of the curved wall to the south wall and 105 metres wide. The southern wall stands a little way back from what had been the Hard Gait, the lane into the old village and the kirk. The site of the original kitchen garden, within the orchard, had been much closer to the house, integrated in the overall design (p. 34).

Together, the change in taste in garden design and the improvements in horticulture called for the relocation of the old walled gardens and orchards; they were removed and rebuilt further away from the house, often hidden by tree planting. This was happening all over Scotland, at Blair Castle and at Taymouth Castle fine, large, new walled gardens were built away from the houses in the 1750s. In East Lothian, Forrest's map shows walled gardens at Leuchie, Seacliff, Newbyth, Broxmouth, Gilmerton, Archerfield, Alderston, Amisfield and Yester, all now at a distance from the house.

At Tyninghame, it is possible that there was already a larger, stone-walled garden on this site which existed from the early eighteenth century, until the brick walled garden replaced it in the 1760s. There are very few references to a walled garden in estate papers, none in the first half of the eighteenth century, but there are signs on the ground: an old gateway stands in isolation on the Hard Gait and the foundations of a wall with another entrance on the western side can still be seen.

Evidence of Helen's knowledge of fruit trees and walled garden layout, together with her business acquaintance in the 1730s with William Boutcher of Comely Garden Nursery, add weight to the supposition that an earlier stone walled garden was relocated here from the vicinity of the house much earlier than had been thought. There is an entry in the 'Timber and Pruning Book' for 23 January 1755, for 200 fir spars for the espalier trees in the garden, suggesting that a lot of fruit trees were about to be planted.[3] Planting for the Walled Garden may have begun even before the new brick walls were built, as the old ones still provided shelter . . .

The present garden has several features which are uncommon, if not unique. The first is the curved northern wall, the inside of which was south facing thus providing the best aspect for growing fruit. The most usual shape was a rectangle, but there was experimentation with different shapes, sometimes dictated by the lie of the ground. The undulating walled garden at Brechin Castle in Angus is unique and is thought to date from 1777.[4] Sir John Clerk had a roughly semi-circular walled garden (1730) at Penicuik House and in his other house at Mavisbank, Midlothian, the original brick-lined walled garden (1739) was oval but so designed that it would have appeared circular when viewed from the house. In East Lothian the original walled garden at Amisfield may have been hexagonal or circular.

Another unusual feature at Tyninghame are the twin free-standing walls, on either side of the central path, about thirty metres to the south of the curved wall. An estate plan of 1859 shows the walls, with a greenhouse on the wall to the east of the central path, but not on the wall to the west, although there are signs of its former existence on the ground – a sunken water tank and lime washed wall – indicating that there were once a pair of matching hothouses here.

The heated greenhouses in the Edinburgh Botanical Gardens that stood on Leith Walk from 1763 to the early 1820s were also situated on free-standing walls, but there are very few of this design in Scotland.[5] Walls within perimeter walls were built in order to extend the area for training fruit,[6] though this was perhaps more common in the nineteenth century, as

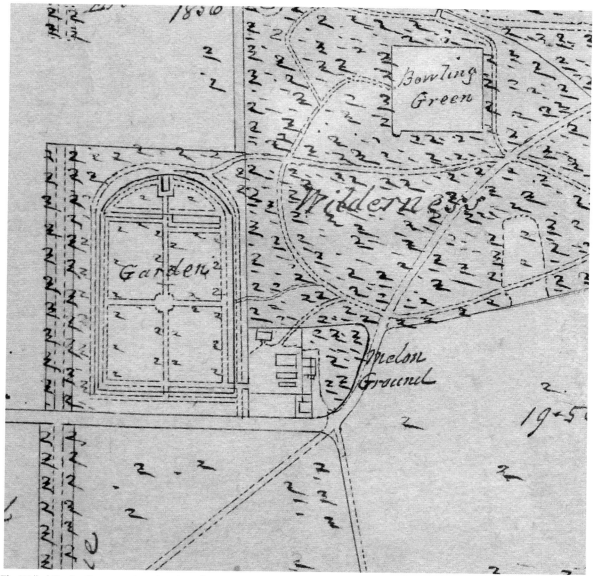

The Walled Garden from an estate plan drawn by Mathew Stobie in 1859 (Courtesy of the Earl of Haddington)

at Luffness or at Chatsworth in Derbyshire, than the eighteenth. It was usually the perimeter walls that were heated.

A mid eighteenth-century date has traditionally been accepted for the construction of the Walled Garden at Tyninghame. Writing in *Country Life* in

1989, Marcus Binney noted the date of 1763 carved in a stone near two rusticated doorways on either side of the conservatory. Two years later, again in *Country Life*, he mentioned a brick inscribed RW 1761 found by Kit Martin, the architect who bought and oversaw the conversion of Tyninghame House and outbuildings in

1989.[7] Neither of these doorways nor the inscriptions are visible today. However, on the outside of the south wall by the west corner, there is a brick with the date 1759 firmly carved in its surface. The numbers are uneven, in contrast with the beautifully incised Roman numerals above. Several series of these latter bricks are found throughout the garden (see later). The dates suggest the garden wall may have taken four years to build, from c.1759 to c.1763.

Care and thought were given to the entrances to the expensive new garden and its layout. Just as the main house had a 'grand' entrance for visitors and a modest entrance for the servants, so the design of doorways into walled gardens indicated clearly which were for the owners and their guests, and which were for the gardeners and tradesmen. Visitors to the garden from the house would approach either through the Wilderness, from the east, or from the Hard Gait to the south, and these are the finest entrances.

The entrance from the east opened to the central cross-path, flanked with espaliered apple trees, leading to a central fountain. The doorway has a typical mid eighteenth-century design: a rounded dressed stone archway with a Gibbs surround – larger 'blocks' which protrude, alternating with smaller ones. The Victorian wrought iron gate, dated 1893, has a simplicity which accords with the period of the masonry. At some point in the twentieth century, for reasons unknown, it replaced an earlier gate of a more classical design. An edition of *Country Life*, August 1902, included photographs of both the interior and exterior gateway walls, with a small statue of a seated lion on a corbel surmounting the archway on each side; they were known as the 'Florentine lions'. Only one of these has survived and is now on the inside wall.[8]

The other significant entrance is the gate in the south wall, which gives the longest, most impressive

view of the whole length of the garden, terminating in the Camellia House, or conservatory. The brickwork in the wall widens to accommodate the masonry of a doorway from an earlier house, built into the garden wall. The house in question may have been that of Lady Trabroun, the one used as the manse (p. 82) and demolished sometime after the merger of the parishes.

A wrought iron gate replaced a wooden door at some point in the twentieth century. On entering the garden through this gate, the whole length of the garden was revealed. In the centre, where the two main paths intersect, is a sixteenth- or seventeenth-century Flemish fountain. This was a garden intended to delight and impress. The 7th Earl would have been keen to show off the trained fruit trees, the soft fruit bushes, the range of vegetables and the hothouses with tropical fruits, tender plants and vines. (Melons and cucumbers, which were grown on smelly hotbeds heated by dung or rotting tanners' bark, were placed outside the walls, among the frame beds and gardeners' sheds and usually hidden from view.)

The gardeners used more humble entrances: the wooden door on the west wall or one of two other doorways flanking the Camellia House that are now part of the Walled Garden House. An entrance wide enough for carts was built at the southern end of the east wall giving access to the working area with frames and hotbeds. It gradually increased in size during the nineteenth century to accommodate a bothy, potting shed and free-standing greenhouses, and was the site of the Head Gardener's House. In Forrest's map of 1799, two buildings are clearly shown (p. 82).

Gardeners' bothies were usually situated on the north side of the north wall, the least favoured aspect for fruit growing. At Tyninghame, some were originally situated here, as shown on Forrest's map, but the house which was added to the Walled Garden in 1989 has since taken their place. The wide entrance at the north end of the west wall, by the garage, was probably a nineteenth- or early twentieth-century addition, when

Opposite: Inscription 1759 on a brick in the south wall contrasting with the carefully incised Roman numerals XIV above

wider access was needed from the road for more modern machinery.

The perimeter path was laid roughly four metres in from the wall, following a rule of thumb that the width of the border between the path and the wall should be the same as the height of the wall. It would originally have been bordered with fruit trees on dwarf stock, either espaliered, or cup or vase shape. Some very old apple trees along the path in the south-east corner survive; they may not be the original planting but they exemplify the typical design.

The Walled Garden is the only brick structure in the estate. The clay would have been sourced locally and the bricks may have been made on site or nearby. They are handmade: nine inches long, two-and-a-half inches high and four inches wide, a typical size for eighteenth-century Scottish bricks. The width of bricks has hardly varied over the centuries; between four and four-and-a-half inches is what can be comfortably held and laid with one hand. The length and thickness could vary more. The coping is also brick, specially shaped for the purpose. Although brick was far more expensive than stone it was preferred in Scotland for walled gardens, both for its heat retentive properties and for the comparative ease of fixing timber frames or wires to the mortar joints.

The Walled Garden at Tyninghame would have been one of the earliest in East Lothian to be constructed away from the house and with brick. This choice was in accordance with the advice given by John Reid in *The Scots Gard'ner*: 'as for Walls, Brick is best, next is Stone and Lime; 4 ells [12'4"/3.8 metres] is low enough, 5 or 6 if you please'.[9] The long, curved north wall at Tyninghame increased both the length and exposure to sunshine.

The walls are roughly the height recommended by Reid but the curved north wall is a little higher in places. This was normal as it needed to protect the garden from the north winds and also to accommodate any tall fruit trees trained on its south-facing side. One

Opposite: The gateway to the Wilderness, with the 'Florentine lion', viewed from inside the garden

Above: A seventeenth-century stone doorway from Lady Trabroun's House in the south wall with the date 1666

short section to the east is much lower; it was rebuilt at some time with bricks of a later date.

Hotbeds, as described by John Reid, were made by first digging a pit four feet deep then filling it with horse manure and covering this with four inches of sifted compost. This was then covered either with sticks arching over it or with frames with glass panels, and finally covering with mats which could be lifted according to the weather. The rotting manure generated the heat and the glass or matting retained it. This was the

The curved south-facing wall with fan-trained fruit trees and the orchard

way pineapples were successfully raised, for example. Variations on this technique have continued to evolve; in the eighteenth and early nineteenth centuries it was used on a larger scale for growing melons as well as cucumbers. Tanner's bark was sometimes substituted for dung as it retained its heat longer than horse manure. It could be re-activated by adding fresh tan and the hotbeds kept going for several months at a time. It took great skill to maintain the correct temperature for the appropriate plants by controlling the heat in this fashion. Seventeen cartloads of oak bark (waste tanners' bark) at ten pence per cartload were bought during the year 1792.

Tyninghame had both hothouses (glasshouses) and hotbeds: a bill for '2 slots for hotbeds and cleaning ye hothouss dor lock 10d' was submitted to the factor, John Wauchope, by the gardener James Taylor in February 1781.[10] 'Because a constant supply of fresh stable manure was required for a frameyard, it reeked of dung . . . Then there was the aesthetic problem of the frameyard's appearance . . . even the best of frameyards was a squalid mess.'[11] The result was that these yards were usually sited within the kitchen garden complex, but outside the walls; at Tyninghame the area thus designated was to the south-east, where the Head Gardener's House was eventually situated.

The need for heat and shelter was one reason why walled gardens proliferated in the north of England and in Scotland where the cooler climate and stronger winds made them a necessity. As well as hotbeds, heated walls became a feature of kitchen gardens in the eighteenth century, particularly in the north. For these, the wall needed to be at least two feet thick in order to accommodate the internal flues. Moveable glass casements, that could be opened or closed, were positioned against the wall to protect the fruit. The source of heat could be a small fireplace embedded low down at the back of the wall, or there might be a stove in a shed, known as a 'fire house'.[12] The hot air circulated inside the wall as it zigzagged upwards through the narrow, serpentine flues to a chimney at the top.

A coal stove, with a flue pipe connecting to the wall, would normally be the source of heat for a hothouse. They were also known as stove houses and usually situated against perimeter walls; free-standing walls were more likely to be 'hot walls' (without a permanent glazed structure against them). Unusually, at Tyninghame, these free-standing heated walls were probably always planned as part of hothouses constructed a little later than the outside walls; at least one hothouse was in use before 1781, when the bill was received to clean the hothouse lock. 'Small coals' for the stoves in the hothouses were brought by cartload from Penston colliery near Macmerry.

The date of the original construction of these two eighteenth-century hothouses can probably be pinned down to the years between 1763 and 1785. The western wall may have lost its lean-to hothouse, but the opening at the base of the brickwork at the eastern end reveals where the pipe from the stove joined the flue in the wall. The stone footings of the original hothouse are clearly visible.

A typical stove or furnace for a hothouse of the

The original flue at the foot of a heated wall

period was a small brick furnace, 'some twenty inches deep and sixteen inches square inside . . . They were built well below floor level so that the house received the maximum benefit from the lowest flues . . .'[13] The stoves were kept in good working order by James Hannan, a local mason who did much of the building at Tyninghame House and in the village. He cleaned the flues and mended the 'furness in the garden' at the end of November 1791.

The reputation of the hothouses at Tyninghame must have spread locally – a particular claim to fame was the plantain, a Musa cultivar like the banana, grown by Thomas Thomson, son of the previous head gardener, at the end of the century. R. P. Brotherston, head gardener at Tyninghame from 1874 until 1923, made the claim that plantains and bananas had been fruited in Tyninghame in the hothouse in 1789: 'Thus it has been recorded that Thomas Thomson fruited the Plantain in the Pine Stove [hothouse] at Tyninghame in 1789, and the Banana, and the latter was so seldom fruited . . .'[14]

The 7th Earl must have been delighted. Although he had not shared his father's and grandparents' passion for gardening and planting, he had always been keen to 'to beautifie and improve the seat of the family', as he had written in the memorial to the presbytery in Dunbar. Walled gardens, or kitchen gardens, were often purely functional spaces but larger, grander gardens like Tyninghame invariably combined or disguised functionality with ornament: the walled garden at Amisfield has neo-classical pavilions in each corner, one of which was adapted for use as a doocot; the Pineapple House at Dunmore sits above the gardeners' stone bothies. At Tyninghame, the decorative elements are on a smaller scale: the cast-iron neoclassical chimney pots, for example, possibly designed by Robert Adam.

Instead of plain, utilitarian chimney pots, these are elegant neo-classical Grecian urns with covers masquerading as finials. The circular vents are positioned at the side, rather than the top. At Dunmore, the Pineapple House is flanked by similar shaped chimneys; today they are the only surviving vestiges of the former hothouses below, originally intended for pineapples.

The Tyninghame 'chimney urns' may have been acquired very shortly after 1785, the year in which the 7th Earl of Haddington married his second wife, Anne Gascoigne, daughter of Charles Gascoigne, manager of the Carron Company. The speed with which he remarried, just six months after the death of his first wife, Mary Holt, caused something of a furore among his friends and family, particularly as the bride's father was known to be in financial difficulties. The earl himself had some concerns about the implications for his own financial position and he consulted both his friend David Dalrymple, Lord Hailes, and his lawyer. In a letter to the lawyer, Lord Hailes recounted his advice: ' . . . he should tell her beforehand that he meant to treat Mr G.(ascoigne) with all the respect and friendship due to a father-in-law, but that he was resolved on no account whatever to be engaged in money transactions with him, less or more.'[15] He then went on to admit there was no point in opposing the marriage of the earl as he was 'much in love'. Lord Binning was very opposed to his father's second marriage, which was not surprising considering the bride-to-be was seven years younger than he was, but it went ahead. They were married in Edinburgh on 8 March 1786. The earl was sixty-six and Anne Gascoigne twenty-six.

Charles, Anne's father, became a partner in the Carron Company in 1765 and in 1769 he took over as manager and is credited with improving many of their techniques; nevertheless, the company's fortunes waxed and waned. In spite of this, their work – cannons, engine parts, fireplaces, utensils and stoves – was in demand both at home and abroad and, in 1786, at the invitation of Catherine the Great, he left Scotland for Russia to supervise an installation of an iron foundry at Kronstadt. He remained there for the rest of his life. Perhaps the chimney urns were a wedding present to his daughter before he left . . .

The design was either by Robert Adam, or William and Henry Haworth, and they were made about 1780.[16] The Haworth brothers worked closely with the Adam brothers (John Adam was a partner at Carron from 1763), both making the patterns – the replicas used for casting – and designing in the Adam style. They were skilled woodcarvers and were invited to Falkirk to adapt their skills to designing and making the patterns for cast iron, by then a burgeoning indus-

Cast-iron chimney pot with vent, made by the Carron Company, on a previously heated wall

try.[17] The urns were originally the upper parts of pedestal stoves intended for neo-classical interiors, including for houses designed by Adam. There is an example in the Victoria & Albert Museum and another at Temple Newsam House, Leeds.

In Scotland they were occasionally used in gardens – Forgandenny House in Perthshire has a pair on the entrance pillars and two were recently removed for safekeeping from the entrance to the grave plot in Larbert Churchyard of Sir Michael Bruce of Stenhouse. (Bruce's land had been bought by the Carron Company.) In their original condition, the vents in the urns made them ideal for re-use as chimneys, as in the Walled Garden at Tyninghame. There is no record of

any pedestal stoves in the house at Tyninghame so the most likely explanation is that the urns, without the stoves, were always intended as either decorative or functioning chimneys for the Walled Garden. Their date may indicate that the freestanding hothouse walls were built in the mid-1780s, after the earlier hothouse on the north wall. When the 7th Earl died in 1794, his dowager countess moved away: she went to Russia to join her father and married James Dalrymple in St Petersburg two years later. Her stepson, Charles, was forty-one when he succeeded his father as the 8th Earl of Haddington. He had married Lady Sophia Hope, daughter of the 2nd Earl of Hopetoun, renewing the bond between the families that had existed for over a hundred years.

Whether it was Thomas, the 7th Earl, or his son who installed the beautiful fountain in the roundel on the central axis of the garden is uncertain. According to Sir Timothy Clifford, it is probably seventeenth-century Flemish. It sits on a tiered square plinth with four horses at the top, their forequarters emerging from the coils of a serpent, as if they are about to leap over the scalloped tazza, or basin, below. Two are mounted bareback by smiling putti. Water spouts into the tazza, from where it drips down to the pool. The tazza and its cargo are held aloft by a grimacing Atlas-like putto, with water dripping from the basin forming a watery curtain around him. In many walled kitchen gardens, a functional 'dipping' pool was placed at the centre. Whether that was the case or not here, the fountain is an accomplished piece and an effective focus when visitors entered through the main doorways.

The long view which unfurled when entering the Walled Garden from the south had plenty of drama with the fountain, well-tended beds on either side and

Left: Pedestal stove with urn, made at the Carron Ironworks in the 1780s (Courtesy of the Victoria & Albert Museum)

Opposite: Marble Fountain with putti and sea horses

The Walled Garden. OS 6″ to the mile map of Haddingtonshire, 1854 (Courtesy of the National Library of Scotland)

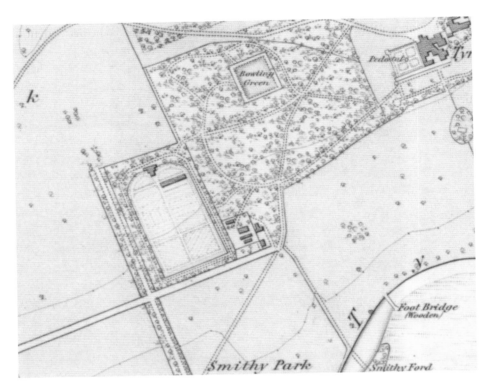

the distant glazed Camellia House, framed by the elegant urns on the hothouses. The photographs in *Country Life* (pp. 152–3) also show painted lead figures on plinths, punctuating the view. They are English, dating from the late eighteenth or early nineteenth century and are no longer in the garden.

The conservatory, known as the Camellia House, stood against the curved north wall. The OS map of Haddingtonshire of 1854 shows a substantial T-shaped building projecting from the wall with gardeners' bothies, the 'back sheds', behind. Its T-shape suggests it might not have had a fully glazed roof, more of a garden pavilion or possibly an orangery, so its temperature would have been cooler than the other hothouses. At least two, if not three, of the buildings shown outside the wall, to the south-east, were glasshouses added in the nineteenth century.

The original glasshouses that stood against the free-standing heated walls have been replaced by slightly wider structures which date from the nineteenth century and have been modernised in the twentieth.

The Camellia House, as its name suggests, must have contained camellias at one time. When these were introduced into the British Isles in the mid eighteenth century, they were thought to need protection to ensure flowers and so they were placed in orangeries or glasshouses. The present building was designed by Mackenzie and Moncur, and possibly gained its name in the nineteenth century when camellias became more widely available. It is a combination of cast iron and timber, with two of the cast-iron roof beams stamped Foundry and the third, Dunbar; the pillars, staging supports and the mechanism for opening the roof lights are also cast iron, presumably from the same Dunbar foundry which was operational from the 1820s.

Together these indications of eighteenth-century horticulture reveal a thriving kitchen garden where large quantities of vegetables could be grown, and fruit coaxed into productivity by the latest heating methods.

The head gardener from 1751 to 1760 was Thomas Thomson. One of his sons, also Thomas, eventually became a gardener at Tyninghame and was credited with getting the plantain to fruit in 1789. He was on the payroll in 1791 but nothing is known of Thomas Junior's immediate successor as head gardener until 1780, when James Taylor presented his half-yearly account to the factor, John Wauchope WS, on 4 June 1781. His 'own half years' wage due' was ten pounds; each of his four gardeners' wage was one pound, together with five shillings and threepence for 'kitchen money', plus three and a quarter bolls of oatmeal. Among the other invoices handed to Mr Wauchope between 1791 and 1793 by Mathew Stobie, the estate factor, were regular payments to 'journiemen Gardners and women employed in the Garden' – the former were paid quarterly, the latter at five pence per day.

As to what exactly was being grown, only one list has survived: the yearly account from Peter Roughead, seedsman at Haddington, paid on 6 June 1781.[18] It came to £24 7s. 3½d.

The vegetables listed included five different types of pea, four kinds of cabbage, five sorts of bean, two kinds of spinach, radishes, carrots, turnip, onion and shallots, cauliflower, mustard and cress, white and green cos lettuce, asparagus, celery, curled and broad endive and best London flag leek.

As well as seeds, Roughead supplied standard fruit trees. 'Two Riding Trained Peach Trees' at three shillings each were ordered in October 1780, then 'Two Riding Cherrie Trees' in March the following year, but with no indication of the variety.

'Riding trees', also known as 'riders' or 'fillers', were temporary plants used to fill the upper spaces on the wall while the permanent, dwarf trees grew to their full size.[19] The riders, planted against the wall, were bought as standards – a single upright stem or trunk with a well-branched crown. The lateral branches would be cut back as the permanent trees filled the space and after some years, the riders, two peach trees and two cherries in this case, could be removed if necessary.

Fruit trees were trained against both the inside and outside walls of the Garden. The elegantly numbered bricks may attest to this, as does the mortar, peppered with holes where nails were driven to hold the timber frames or wires to which branches of the fruit trees were fixed in position. These bricks marked with Roman numerals, some at a lower level some higher, are spaced along the walls throughout the garden. Gardeners had to be familiar with roman numerals as they were traditionally used on wooden tallies, or number sticks; their straight lines easy to carve or mark.[20] Numbers at the lower level are usually twenty-four feet apart and those at the higher level appear in alternate spaces, with their own numbering sequence. They may have marked the positions of the original fruit trees: the numbers at the lower level for the dwarf varieties that would be fan-trained and the bricks higher on the wall marked the spaces for the 'riders'. Considerable forethought went into their preparation as the numbers had to be incised in the bricks before they were fired. In his *Encyclopaedia of Gardening*, Loudon makes no mention of this system of numbering. Was it unique to Tyninghame?

In the more favoured climate in East Lothian, as the Earl of Crawford had discovered in 1692, both 'the Qwince pear of Tininghame' and apricots were growing. With the addition of two hothouses against the heated walls, successful fruiting could be assured, and the variety of tender plants grown, including grapes, could be extended. 'From the 1770s separate hothouses – "graperies" or vineries – began to be built for the benefit of the dessert grape. The vines were still planted outside, entering the house through holes in the low parapet walls which supported the glazed sashes above, where they were trained and bore their fruit . . .'[21] Even if vines were planted within the hothouse, their roots extended outside the wall (as is

The Right Hon:ble The Earl of Hadinton

1780   Bo:t of Peter Roughead Seedsman Hadd:n

Date	Item	Rate	£	s	d
June 23	To 1 Shovel			2	6
July 3	To 500 Yards Bounds	@ 4/8	1		10
	½ Peck Charlton Pease —			2	
Aug:t 4	To 1 lib Spinnage 1/4 & 1 Oz Colliflower 2/6			3	10
	.. 2 German Steel Scyths for Garden	@ 3/		6	
	1 D:o D:o for Farm			3	
Sept:r 4	To 1 Oz Early Cabbage —				6
Oct:r 20	To 6 Doz:n Matts	@ 3/		18	
	.. 6 Doz:r D:o	@ 4/.		4	
	.. 6 Large D:o	@ 6 each		3	
	.. ½ Peck Early framing Pease			4	
	.. ½ Peck Early Charlton D:o			2	
	.. 2 Riding Trained Peach Trees —	@ 3/.		6	
	.. 1 Bagg 1/6 & 1 Hay Knife 2/6			4	
Nov:r 25	To ½ Peck framing Pease —			4	
	.. 8 Yards Bounds & 2ee Shelot 2/8			3	4
Dec:r 1	To 400 Yards Bounds —	@ 4/8		16	8
	.. 2 lib White Mustard 1/. 2 lib Cress @ 2/. 4/.			5	
	9 To ½ Peck framing Pease —			4	
	.. ½ Peck Mazigan Beans			1	4
1781 28	To 6 Best large English Spades ⅌ M:r Leed @ 4/.		1	4	
Jan:ry 12	To 1 Doz:r Best Bass Matts —	@ 1/3 Each		15	
	.. 1 Forpet framing Pease —			2	
	.. ½ lib Early short Top Radish —			1	
	.. ½ lib Salmond D:o 1/. 1 lib Round Spinnage 1/4 —			2	4
	.. 115 Yards Bounds	@ 4/8		4	9½
	29 To 1 Best pruning Knife —			1	6
Feb:y 3	To 2 Oz Horn Carrot —				6
	17 To 1 lib Onion 2/6 & ½ lib Early Dutch Turnip 1/. —			3	6
	.. ½ lib Early Stone Turnip —			1	3
	.. 2 Oz Parsnip 4/ & 2 Oz Orange Carrot 4/ —				8
	.. 1 Oz White & Green Coss Lettuce —			2	6
	.. ½ Oz Cabbage D:o 1/. ½ Oz Solid Cellery 1/.			2	
	.. 4 pruning Knives 4/. 1 Best D:o 2/6 &			5	6
	.. 4 Oz Best Conden ...			3	10
March 1	To 1 Oz Colliflower 2/6 & 4 Oz Asparagus 1/4 @ 1/3 &		1	2	6
	3 To 18 Bass Matts —				

still the case at Tyninghame) as they do not need the protection of glass. Vines can stand wet and several degrees of frost during the winter but when growth starts, any drop in temperature below 10°C will be detrimental. During the winter, when the vines are leafless, the space within the hothouse was (and is) used for forcing other plants – strawberries, French beans and bulbs for the house, for example. The upright heated brick wall could be used for peaches, nectarines, cherries or figs.

Already in 1743, the sale of wood was contributing to the income of the estate. The 'Timber and Pruning Book',[22] kept by David Robertson, shows the sales of 'spars' (lengths of cut timber), trees and cartloads of prunings for the years 1743 to 1755. A contemporary 'Factor's Book' shows the sum of £34 14s. 7d. from sales of timber at the end of 1743.[23] The most frequent sales were for cartloads of prunings at 1s. 8d. per load.

The prunings, sold mainly for firewood but also for thatching, would have come from thinning the extensive plantations. Willow was prized locally for tool handles, sieves, hoops and even for carts.[24] However, in this part of East Lothian, where most extensive native woodland had disappeared well before the eighteenth century, the traditional skills associated with forests – coppicing, chair and stool making, basket making, sieve making, willow weaving and other coppice crafts – had all but disappeared. When the 6th Earl wrote about the uses of willow, he noted that he had had little success making a profit by growing willow for hoops or for baskets. On the other hand, there was a regular demand, usually in the spring, for hoops for barrels, which were extensively used for transporting foodstuffs as well as for wine and beer. These orders were typically between eleven and fourteen shillings.

When timber was sent for his lordship's own use – in the garden, for repairs to the house, for building the malt barn, for the sawmill – the value was noted but no charge was made.

From entries in the Timber Book, the Tyninghame sawmill can be dated to 1752; a house was added the following year as well as the malt barn and malt kiln. Entries concerning the garden are few: '12 ash (trees) for my Lord's rose' on 8 March 1754, and another forty-two the next year when a shed was also built in the garden. Water was also being piped to the garden: 22 January 1755, 'Stobs to the pieps [pipes] in the garden, 2 cartloads of prunings'. It was a busy time for the gardeners as the next day 200 spars of fir were sent 'for the espalier Trees in the garden'. Extensive garden work coincided with building substantial kennels at the other end of the estate to the north-east of the house, where the stables were situated nearby. 'Fir for the ruoff [roof] to nu Dog houss' and a 'Fir for real [rail] about dogs yard' in May and June that same year.

The timber sales noted in the Timber Book were the thinnings from the woodland planted at the beginning of the century rather than from coppicing. The most numerous sales were fir (*Pinus sylvestris*). Sales of fir were followed in descending order by ash, alder, willow, birch and, very occasionally, elm. There were no named sales of oak or beech, which took longer to mature. Fir outnumbered them all by a factor of ten. Besides cut timber, trees were sometimes supplied as young plants in the winter: Birch 'sidlings', holly, maple (sycamore), yew, whin (gorse) and hazel were all sold as well as several thousand hawthorns for hedging.

The emphasis during these years appears to have been on thinning the woodland trees, which were then sold, rather than raising large quantities of nursery stock for sale. For example, holly saplings that the 6th Earl had raised by the tens of thousands, were being sold a few hundred at a time and at a halfpenny each, and not every year. The woodlands and Wilderness were maturing. William Boutcher was impressed when he visited Tyninghame by 'the clearest evidence of the incomparable beauty, lasting strength and magnifi-

Opposite: Account of Peter Roughead, seedsman, Haddington, 6 June 1781 (Courtesy of the Earl of Haddington)

Late eighteenth-century watercolour of Tyninghame House, by an anonymous artist (Courtesy of the Earl of Haddington)

cence of holly hedges . . . These hedges were planted by the late Earl of Haddington, the greatest, most knowing and most successful planter of his time, and who, to all appearances, from a very poor and unpromising soil, exposed to, and close upon the great German ocean, has raised very extensive and flourishing plantations of the most valuable Forest-trees.'[25] He closed by addressing some comments to the 7th Earl, whom he hoped would allow the hedges to grow taller, up to twenty or thirty feet in height as, 'at present I think are not lofty in proportion to their thickness and strength'.

Thomas may or may not have followed this advice. He was Earl of Haddington for fifty-nine years, from 1735 to 1794, though was very little involved in public or political life. His younger brother George had inherited the house at Mellerstain, begun by William Adam and completed by his more famous son, Robert, in 1778. Tyninghame House must have seemed rather old-fashioned when compared to Robert Adam's masterpiece with its beautifully proportioned, light-filled rooms with the finest wallpaper and stunning plasterwork. Moreover, the grounds, envisaged by their late father, were now maturing and provided a fine setting. The 7th Earl may have been spurred on by his brother's building work; the development of the parkland and the fine Walled Garden are evidence of his improvements.

Although he may have altered, he did not radically change the house. The only testimony to the appearance of the estate is an anonymous watercolour painting from the late eighteenth century. A view from the path to the Mosshouse at the Point showing the wooded setting of the house with naturalistic clumps of trees in the parkland and the arches of the medieval church, now a picturesque ruin.

CHAPTER 9

Private Passions and Public Disturbances

The watercolour of the mansion house in its park, beyond the bend of the River Tyne with Highland cattle grazing on both banks amid clumps of trees, adheres to a stereotypical 'sylvan scene' of the late eighteenth century. Besides the mansion house and Lady Trabroun's House, other buildings are seen to the right of the picture. Nearest the main house is a building, or cluster of service buildings, and further right are the stables. These are all shown on William Forrest's map (p. 82).

The estate plan of 1859 shows the headland clearly named 'Mosshouse Point'; a central path terminates in a small circular clearing with an oval structure in the centre. Mosshouses, or fog-houses as they were often

Mosshouse Point overlooking Hedderwick Bay

Above: A fog-house at Ballachmyle, Ayrshire (Courtesy of Willie McClure, www.ayrshirehistory.com)

Opposite: Portrait of the 8th Earl of Haddington, by Sir Joshua Reynolds, 1777 (© wikiart.org)

known in Scotland – 'fog' being a Scots word for moss – were a form of 'sit-outery', constructed in a rustic style with a rough timber frame, often thatched with heather and lined with moss of different colours, hence the name.[1] Careful consideration was given to their position on the estate. It was a 'room with a view', placed by a river, on a hillside or in a glen, where it could reward a pleasant walk and from where a dramatic view unfurled. None of the owners of Tyninghame had shown any desire to embellish their estate with fashionable neo-classical temples, viewing pavilions, hermitages or grottoes. Though the mosshouse shared some features with the latter: both were constructed with rough, natural materials and usually overlooked a dramatic landscape. The mosshouse that once stood on the rise that juts into the estuary took advantage of the extensive views that its position afforded: across the water to the salt greens and fields, with the Lammermuir Hills on the horizon to the south, the low massif of Traprain Law rising in the distance to the west and the sand spit and waves of the ocean beyond to the east.

The most famous description of a fog-house is that by Dorothy Wordsworth, when she and her brother William, together with their friend Samuel Taylor Coleridge, visited Bonnington and the Falls of Clyde in 1803:

> We came to a pleasure-house, of which the little girl had the key; she said it was called the Fog-house, because it was lined with 'fog,' namely moss. On the outside it resembled some of the huts in the prints belonging to Captain Cook's Voyages, and within was like a hay-stack scooped out. It was circular, with a dome-like roof, a seat all round fixed to the wall, and a table in the middle, – seat, wall, roof and table all covered with moss in the neatest manner possible . . . We afterwards found that huts of the same kind were common in the pleasure-grounds of Scotland; but we never saw any that were so beautifully wrought as this.[2]

There is no surviving description of the one on Mosshouse Point, but it would have been in this vein.

The 'huts', 'common in the pleasure grounds of Scotland', that Dorothy referred to, could also be found in the Penicuik estate (Midlothian), at Craighall Rattray (Perthshire), Invercauld (Aberdeenshire) and Ballochmyle (Ayrshire), and were still being included in garden designs late into the nineteenth century. One was designed for Saltoun Hall (East Lothian) by John Hay in 1879.[3] The mosshouse existed at Tyninghame by 1811 as it is recorded in that year in a curious notebook of sundry 'Measurements', including some trees, a Shetland cow ('length from the rump to the root of her horns 5ft 8 inches') together with various paths: 'From the Gate in the Shrubbery under the Drawing Room Window, by the gravel walk to the Moss House at the point it measures 1,294 yds . . .'[4] The first four pages of the notebook have been torn out and it is unsigned. By 1811, Charles, the 8th Earl, who had acceded to the title in 1794, had been living at Tyninghame for seventeen years and his son, another Thomas, Lord Binning,

would have been thirty-one. However, as the notebook also contained 'Lord Ducie's Gout Tincture', among other remedies, it probably belonged to the father rather than the son.

Charles had married Lady Sophia Hope in 1779; their marriage followed the example of their great-grandparents and great-great-grandparents, and strengthened the ties between the Hamilton and the Hope families once again.

Thomas, Lord Binning, born in 1780, was their only son. In August 1794 the 8th Earl was rebuilding and improving Tyninghame, continuing work undertaken in the last year of the 7th Earl's life. In a letter sent to his factor and friend, Mr Wauchope, quoted by Sir William Fraser, he says, 'As to Baxter's plan, tho' I like it in general, yet there are many things to alter, and particularly in the Library part, so his section will be to change with the rest. I shall not be in haste, but of that hereafter. In the mean time let us hope that this Paris event has more than secured the building of my offices.'[5] The 'Paris event' was a reference to the recent execution of 'Robespierre and all his faction', from which the earl hoped to draw some comfort. It was a vain hope; the fall of Robespierre was followed by a further period of instability until the Revolution was finally ended by the rise of Napoleon in 1799.

The alterations to Tyninghame referred to in the letter of 1794, must have gone ahead. The Baxter in question was John Baxter, the Edinburgh architect, whose father, another John, had been the master mason responsible for repairing Rosslyn Chapel in 1736 for Sir John St Clair. Baxter had travelled widely in Italy as a young man and having taken over his father's firm, he found work all over Scotland. Very often his commissions were alterations to existing houses, as at Tyninghame; among his designs are the Merchant Company Hall in Hunter Square, Edin-

burgh, as well as the bridge over the River Tay at Kenmore.[6] He died in 1798. The full extent of Baxter's work at Tyninghame is unknown. The work on the library wing, adjacent to the original great hall on the first floor, may have included an extension of this section of the house and the addition of new windows but later remodelling by the architect William Burn has obscured the extent of Baxter's work. The firm may also have been responsible for building the clock tower to the east of the house, on the end of the laundry building.

The maker of the clock was William Veitch of Haddington, the first clockmaker to be admitted as a freeman in the Incorporation of Hammermen of Haddington, on 30 August 1758. He had been admitted as a member of the masonic Lodge of St David, in Edinburgh in April 1754.[7] The 8th Earl was also a freemason, having been initiated into the Canongate Kilwinning Lodge in 1768 when he was still Lord Binning.[8] He eventually became Deputy Grand Master of the Grand Lodge of Scotland under Lord Napier from 1788 to 1790. The masonic connection may be significant. The windows of the new library overlooked the parterre, where a special item was added to the garden sometime around 1800: an almost exact copy of one of the pair of identical seventeenth-century octagonal sundials at Newbattle Abbey, Dalkeith.

The originals are over three metres tall, free-standing and date from 1635. They were moved in the nineteenth century from their original locations and today one is in store and the other stands at the rear of the house. When they were described in the first definitive study of ancient Scottish sundials by Thomas Ross, he placed them in a special category of 'Dials of Exceptional Design'.[9] They have five sections: an octagonal base, on top of which are four winged sphinxes, or chimera. The Tyninghame 'sphinxes' are more decorous than their Newbattle counterparts as their breasts are modestly covered by an extra swirl of acanthus leaf, while on the originals, more flesh is exposed. They also

have furry legs, more like the lion's body they are supposed to represent.

The figures support an eight-panelled 'drum' with a fluted base. Each panel has two tiers; twelve of the tiers have bronze gnomons (the part that casts the shadow) and the other four have motifs and initials for William, Earl of Lothian, and his wife Annie, for whom the dials were built. At Tyninghame, the gnomons and dials, which would have to have been attached *in situ* in order to point north to the Pole Star, were never added; the upper tiers only are decorated with coats of arms and emblems for the 8th Earl of Haddington. Above this section are four male heads 'with scrolled beards . . . ; surmounted by 4 balls and an obelisk decorated with carved foliage; a ball and needle finial above'.[10] It is very grand. However, appearances can be deceptive; this description tells only part of the story.

The absence of gnomons and dials on the Tyninghame copy may not be as great a loss as it might seem because the structure itself, like an obelisk, can also tell the time approximately as it casts its shadow on the pattern of lawn and pathways at its feet. The other reason why the dials are less important than might first appear is because the carvings on Scottish sundials, including the dials themselves, often have a symbolic, as well as a literal meaning. In 1987, when Andrew Somerville updated the list of Scottish sundials with descriptions that Thomas Ross had produced in 1890, he came to the conclusion that neither small nor multi-faceted dials were very good at telling the time. Whereas large horizontal dials could be accurate to a minute or two, multiple dials – some could have over eighty facets! – were inconvenient to read and much less accurate.[11] Why then create them? And why so many? Scotland has more seventeenth- and eigh-

teenth-century sundials than any other country – a total of approximately 330.

Somerville gives three reasons: when these sundials were created, more stable government led to more mansion houses with pleasure gardens; when being built, Calvinist philosophy of the period demanded function rather than decoration for its own sake and finally, 'interest in science was increasing, along with the Renaissance interest in re-discovering the esoteric knowledge of the ancients'.[12] Moreover, freemasonry, which may have had its origins in sixteenth-century Scotland, was at the time widely believed to be the repository of this ancient knowledge. A sundial, placed at the centre of a parterre as at Tyninghame, besides showing the skill of the stonemason and providing a decorative centrepiece for the garden, told the time and illustrated some of the eternal truths held dear by the Brotherhood of Freemasons. When the Newbattle sundial and its Tyninghame copy are reviewed in this light, the carvings take on additional significance.

From its octagonal base to the elongated pyramid at the top, it is richly decorated with symbols with masonic overtones, including winged sphinxes and heads sprouting leaves like green men. The winged sphinxes at Newbattle were the earliest representations of a sphinx in Scotland, though possibly copied from an Italian sculpture rather than an Egyptian original.[13]

In choosing a copy of a Newbattle sundial for his parterre the 8th Earl was joining the Romantic search for artistic inspiration in Scotland's past. Among his literary friends with antiquarian interests, Walter Scott may have even been the one who influenced the decision to acquire the sundial. His own house and garden at Abbotsford were crammed with antiquarian relics including armorial bearings and sixteenth- and seventeenth-century pieces of architecture. Moreover, Scott was a fellow member of the Canongate Kilwinning Lodge. The sundial provided a fitting centrepiece for the garden, admired as an intriguing historical artefact by visitors, but whose discreet symbolism would be

Opposite: The Tyninghame copy of a sundial at Newbattle, casting its shadow at midday on 19 July 2020

Detail of sphinx-like figures with acanthus leaves

only appreciated by the 8th Earl's masonic Brothers and his successors. The 11th Earl was Grand Master of the Grand Lodge of Scotland from 1892 to 1893.

When Charles died in March 1828, the brief obituary that appeared in *The Gentleman's Magazine* noted: 'The Earl was greatly addicted to agriculture, and much improved and embellished his patrimonial possessions. On his estate at Tynninghame, he planted upwards of 1000 acres of timber, which flourishes almost to the sea-beach.'[14] Although his biographer Sir William Fraser never mentioned the 8th Earl's love of planting, there are occasional glimpses of what evidently was something of a passion. In another letter to his agent, John Wauchope, in August 1805, he wrote: 'We had much rain for an hour this morning early, since that, too hot to walk. I, however, have watered some young trees, and am in a stew. Invasion seems the word. The learned seem to expect that Nelson will fall in with the fleets.'[15] That the earl took it upon himself to water young trees during a heatwave is a measure of his interest and understanding. He was as concerned that the gardeners might not have done enough watering as he was about Nelson's possible success. Orders for seed continued to be sent to Peter Roughead in Haddington – ryegrass, red and white clover, and turnip, for example – while seeds for trees were ordered from Mathew Stobo at Dicksons in Edinburgh. One pound of Scotch fir (*Pinus sylvstris*) seed at three shillings and one pound of larch (*Larix decidua*) seed at five shillings were ordered in April 1791.[16]

Larch had been introduced to Scotland in 1738 when five small trees were brought from the Alps as a present for the Duke of Athol. One is still standing, known as the 'Parent Larch' of the many millions now growing on the hillsides in Perthshire. The 6th Earl had been familiar with it, calling it 'a pretty tree' in his *Treatise on Forest Trees*, but he did not include any instructions on raising it. That was left to the 8th Earl, who, although not radically changing the layout established by his great-grandfather, filled out and extended the woodlands begun by Helen.

Horticulture at Tyninghame continued on a significant scale. From George Gordon at Morrison's Haven, the old harbour by Preston Grange, 116 'Garden potts' were ordered. Nets 'for the use of the garden' were ordered and an entry of 'slatework, glass for the garden etc James Bennies' indicated that repair work was ongoing in August 1792. William McNab (1780–1848) served part of his apprenticeship here in 1799. His talents were recognised early, as after only fourteen months, he was recommended for a position at the Royal Botanic Garden at Kew. He eventually returned to Edinburgh in 1810 as a gardener at the Royal Botanic Garden, then still at Leith Walk, becoming Regius Keeper in 1820 and overseeing the move to Inverleith.

The 8th Earl appears to have been only marginally interested in politics until the ripples of insecurity which the French Revolution had stirred in Scotland turned to waves in East Lothian by 1798. There was a genuine fear of invasion which was not unfounded: various naval attacks had been attempted on the Irish and Welsh coasts during the previous two years. General Napoleon Bonaparte, whose forces far outnumbered those in the British Isles, had been given command of the 'Army of England' and French troops were being assembled along the Channel coast. In partial response to this, the Militia Act of 1797 gave the Lords Lieutenant in Scotland the authority to raise county militias, as in England. Charles, 8th Earl of Haddington, was appointed Deputy Lieutenant by the Marquis of Tweeddale, Lord Lieutenant of East Lothian, on 22 February 1797.[17] The Act was seen as conscription and was opposed throughout Scotland, including parts of East Lothian. What became known as the Tranent Massacre took place on 24 August the same year. On that day the High Street was lined with local people chanting and banging drums; during the recruitment a formal letter opposing the Militia Act was presented, signed by thirty men, mostly potters from Prestonpans. In the last of its four clauses the men stated simply: 'Although we may be overpowered in effecting the said resolution [repeal of the Act], and dragged from our parents, friends and employment, to be made soldiers of, you can infer from this what we trust can be reposed in us if ever we are called upon to disperse our fellow-countrymen, or to oppose a foreign foe.'[18] It was rejected; in the turmoil that followed afterwards eleven people – men, women and children – were killed. Mr David Anderson of St Germains was the Deputy Lieutenant in charge. Lord Haddington does not appear to have been involved.

The following year, the three Deputy Lieutenants

were authorised to replace the Marquis of Tweeddale, who was in poor health, and to organise the defences along the coast of East Lothian. Lord Haddington was to be convenor; the other two were Mr Buchan Hepburn of Smeaton and Mr David Anderson. In 1798 Britain was still at war with France and in May of that year, the Secretary of State for War, Henry Dundas, 1st Viscount Melville, drew up a plan of action which was sent to all lieutenants across the country. His report was adopted and circulated in the county together with a letter from the Lord Lieutenant and his deputies. The letter, dated 28 May 1798, was a rousing wake-up call in which the enemy, the French, were described as 'traitors who had betrayed their own country . . . [this enemy] have declared in their impudent and malignant wrath, that they will accept no terms of peace, and that nothing short of our utter ruin and extermination can satiate their unprovoked and unprincipled resentment against us.' The call to action was unequivocal: 'Our religion, our laws, our King, our country, our own existence and that of our families, and, in short, everything we can call dear to us, is at stake . . . and thus being trained and prepared, we shall like our forefathers, meet our unprincipled, boasting and insulting foe, firm and undaunted; and let us teach them, *Nemo me impune lacessit*.'[19]

These ringing cadences could not be further from the utterances of the potters from Prestonpans. Charles Haddington can have been under no illusions about the difficulties ahead when he accepted the position of Lord Lieutenant on the death of Lord Tweeddale in 1804, a position he was to retain until 1823. During these years he oversaw and implemented the conversion of East Lothian volunteer regiments into militias. They were called on to deal with civil unrest on many subsequent occasions, in particular in the years after the introduction of the Corn Laws in 1815, which maintained high food prices, and later as the desire for parliamentary reform took hold, leading to the Scottish Reform Act of 1832.

Charles regularly voted in the elections for the Scottish representative peers but his own tenure was short: from 1807 to 1812. After that date he did not put his name forward for re-election. Politics, it seems, was never his passion, he was more interested in local affairs. He supported both the 'Edinburgh Asylum for the Relief of the Indigent and Industrious Blind', founded in 1793 (later the Royal Blind School) and also the project to establish the Edinburgh Lunatic Asylum, which opened in 1813. His correspondence reveals a wide circle of friends including politicians and many literary figures: George Chalmers, Sir Thomas Dick Lauder and Walter Scott, who was a frequent guest at Tyninghame.

The Earls of Haddington had been hereditary Keepers of Holyrood Park since 1680.[20] Sections of the park were let out for grazing which brought in a steady income; there was also occasional quarrying not to mention the honour of the title and invitations to Holyrood. The duties of the Keeper were not onerous; they included keeping the dykes secure and their scattered tenants' houses in good repair. In 1814, the 8th Earl was approached by the Aesculapian Club, a medical dining club in Edinburgh founded by Dr Andrew Duncan, who was also a founder member of the Royal Caledonian Horticultural Society. Their members wished to extend the walks, plant alpines to beautify Arthur's Seat and to place an iron garden seat near the summit. In his letter Dr Duncan wrote: ' . . . without doing the smallest injury to your Lordship's tenants we may be able to render Arthur's Seat one of the most interesting hills in Europe for the student both of botany and mineralogy'.[21] He received short shrift from the Earl, who stated that already he had had to reduce the rent for Hill Park because of the intrusion of people with no right, and that no man who understood grazing would want to be his tenant; their request was totally out of the question.

Quarrying in the park had taken place for centuries – the stone for Holyrood Palace was quarried here in the sixteenth century. Successive earls had leased the Salisbury Crags quarries intermittently during the eighteenth century but in the early nineteenth century, as Edinburgh expanded, the demand for stone chippings for road metal increased. Not only were the stones extracted to pave the new streets of Edinburgh, but of London and other cities as well. More and more quarrying took place, chipping away at Salisbury Crags and the Camstone Quarry to the east, in full view of the citizens of Edinburgh who became more and more incensed.

Letters and articles appeared in the newspapers in Edinburgh and further afield. 'Edinburgh equals any, if it do not surpass, every other city in Europe for its picturesque and striking appearance . . . Deface or destroy the Crags themselves, and you remove nearly all that gave fascination, enchantment and sublimity to what every observer saw or felt in their vicinity. And yet, is not this work of destruction going on daily, without reprehension or remonstrance?'[22] On 18 October 1818, *The Scotsman* printed a correction to a previous report that quarrying at Salisbury Crags had stopped; in fact it was 'continuing more vigorously than ever . . . it would surprise anyone to see the quantity of rock that had been removed within a short time'. *The Caledonian Mercury* printed a similar message. The same year instructions were given to the Crown solicitor to prepare a case for the Crown lawyers.

Four years later the case had still not been resolved and accusations in the press continued. When part of St Anthony's Chapel collapsed in April 1823, *The Scotsman* went on the attack: 'Were it the duty of the Keeper of the King's park to preserve, as it seems to be his prerogative to destroy, the public might confidently expect that some fraction of the profits derived from the quarry on Salisbury Crags would be expended in upholding the Chapel.'[23] The same paper reported in July that the long-litigated case at the Court of Session brought against the Keeper of Holyrood Park, was

refused. The Earl of Haddington could continue to take stone away from the park.

Edinburgh magistrates (the town council) were initially seen as responsible for creating the demand for road metal. In October 1823 they refused to purchase further stone from the Salisbury Crags quarries and instead turned to the newly opened quarry at Ratho. The problem was that stone there was more expensive – nine shillings per cubic yard as compared to five shillings and ninepence from quarries at Salisbury Crags. It was not surprising that orders continued, as did the complaints. Even King George III was petitioned.

The king's involvement apparently had an effect and the amount of quarrying diminished, but it was not a legal decision. An appeal was made to the House of Lords to overturn the original decision by the Court of Session which had allowed the earls of Haddington to continue quarrying, and the matter was finally settled in September 1831. The Lord Chancellor ruled to reverse the earlier decision. The *London Evening Standard* reported, 'the tremendous smash of the rocks, called Salisbury Crags . . . made of late years . . . as a result of quarrying', would now cease. 'His Lordship dismissed the evidence as not relevant and concluded there was no ground in law nor in fact.'[24] The 8th Earl died on 17 March 1828, probably aware of the king's disapproval but ignorant of the Lord Chancellor's decision. It fell to his son, Thomas, to try to defend his family's rights to the title and income of Hereditary Keeper of Holyrood Park. It was fifteen years before an agreement on compensation was reached with the Commissioners of Woods and Forests, who acted on behalf of the Crown. Finally, a bill was passed confirming the terms by which the Earls of Haddington would surrender their title of Hereditary Keeper. On 22 July 1843, the *Caledonian Mercury* reported that £30,654 1s. 8d. was paid into a trust fund for Charles Baillie and George William Hope of Luffness, heirs to the 9th Earl, who had no children.[25]

CHAPTER 10

The Architect and the Owner

Thomas became the 9th Earl in 1828 and, as the family finances were in sound order, he lost no time in engaging the eminent Scottish architect, William Burn, to give the estate a facelift. His plan was to remodel Tyninghame House, the offices, outbuildings, lodges and parts of the garden. For this the earl may have used the quarry at Wester Broomhouse on the southern edge of the estate, one of the sources of the particularly deep-pink sandstone found at the eastern end of the Lammermuirs. It is Upper Old Red Sandstone, about four million years old. This was supplemented with pale grey sandstone for chimneys, windows and door surrounds which came from Angus, shipped from Dundee.[1]

Thomas was forty-nine when he began this extensive building programme, and had already developed a successful political career. He had studied first at Edinburgh University, then at Christ Church College, Oxford, before becoming Conservative Member of Parliament for St Germans in Cornwall (one of the rotten boroughs abolished in 1832) at the age of twenty-two. That same year, 1802, he married Maria Parker, the daughter of the Earl of Macclesfield. He went on to serve as a Tory MP for over twenty years, representing five further constituencies, including two more in Cornwall, Yarmouth in the Isle of Wight and Cockermouth in Cumbria. (Scottish peers could not stand for election in Scotland to the House of Commons.) He became a privy councillor in 1814 and was elevated to the House of Lords by the prime minister, George Canning, as Baron Melrose of Tyninghame in 1827. The 9th Earl was a serious politician and he was rewarded with high office; he was not as jovial, nor as corpulent, as his father by all accounts but he was a kindly, thoughtful friend and employer and a devoted husband.

He supported all the attempts for Catholic emancipation but was not so enthusiastic about the extension of the right to vote proposed in the first Reform Act, which he opposed. He served for a few months as Viceroy of Ireland (November 1834–April 1835), during Robert Peel's short-lived minority government, long enough for Haddington Road in Dublin to be named after him but not long enough for locals to remember the reason. When the Tories regained power in 1841, the earl was offered the prestigious position of Viceroy of India which, to the surprise of many of his friends, he refused on grounds of his health. Instead he was offered the position of First Lord of the Admiralty, which he held until 1846 when he became Lord Privy Seal. When Prime Minister Robert Peel finally

Opposite: William Burn's perspective drawing of Tyninghame House from the north-west, 1829 (Courtesy of RIBA)

succeeded in repealing the Corn Laws in 1846, he was strongly supported by the 9th Earl, who had always favoured free trade, to the dismay of many of his friends and colleagues.

Members of the family always maintain that each of the successive Earls of Haddington had either altered or extended the house. On 24 October 1828 William Burn spent two days at Tyninghame, examining the building in advance of preparing the drawings for its transformation. He sent his bill the following April for six guineas. Two of his clerks spent five days taking measurements and making plans.[2] It is clear from the floor plans that Burn prepared that he did not enlarge the house very much (p. 32). It was, by then, a sprawling, uneven H-shape with additional offices on the east side, forming a small courtyard with separate outbuildings (laundry, larders, servants accommodation) and further to the east, a separate stable courtyard with associated outbuildings. Burn spent a further two days at Tyninghame the following July, and in October he sent his invoice for his visits and travelling expenses including 'to various plans of additions and alterations, with complete working drawings and specifications, superintendence and details of all the finishings, 5 per cent of contract say £10,000 – £500.00'. Some £450 of this was paid in cash.[3] Among the earliest drawings the earl received were two perspective drawings of the house, one of the view of the main entrance (the north façade) and the other of the view from the south.

The existing rambling vernacular building, large and very plain, to judge from the glimpse afforded by the watercolour (p. 102) was to be replaced by Burn's emphatic embrace of what was to become the new Scots baronial fashion. Tyninghame was his first complete remodelling of a mansion house in the style for which he became famous and of which he was a pioneer. It was a re-invention of the traditional late Scottish sixteenth-century mansion house – with bells and whistles.

William Burn, son of the architect Robert Burn,

was born in Edinburgh in 1789 and sent to London as a pupil of Sir Robert Smirke, the architect of the Theatre Royal Covent Garden and the British Museum, who was patronised by the Tory establishment.[4] Burn returned to Scotland and began his own business in 1812. Scottish Victorian architecture of the period was characterised by a variety of architectural styles and Burn proved himself a master of them all. Given his training as a pupil of Smirke, it is not surprising that most of his earliest buildings in Scotland were neo-classical in style: North Leith Parish Church, Edinburgh (1812); the Assembly Rooms and Customs House, Greenock (1812 and 1817). Other buildings were in the more specific Greek Revival vein, as in John Watson's School, now the Gallery of Modern Art, Edinburgh (1825). Neo-gothic buildings included St John's Episcopal Church, Princes Street, Edinburgh (1817) and the New Abbey Church, Dunfermline (1818). He included a castellated style in his enlargement of Saltoun Hall (1818) and to this he added the Jacobean manor house, which 'by about 1825 Burn had made . . . his speciality'.[5] He was a prolific architect with a large number of country house clients; by 1830, his was the largest practice in Scotland. In October 1828, when he visited Tyninghame, he was ready to pull together the distinctive elements of the baronial style that had appeared intermittently from as early as 1820, as at Luffness House, owned by the Earl's cousin, Lieutenant General Sir Alexander Hope.[6]

A central role in the revival of interest in Scotland's past in the nineteenth century was played by Walter Scott, primarily as the author of historical novels such as *Waverley*, *The Heart of Midlothian* and *The Bride of Lammermoor*, but also through his house and gardens at Abbotsford, completed in 1824. The house that Scott and his team of advisers developed at Abbotsford was described in the Ordnance Survey *Object Name Book* for 1859 as 'magnificent in the extreme, a perfect romance in stone and lime, it partakes largely of the Gothic and Baronial Style of architecture while it presents examples of the beauties of every style, combined and united in the truest taste . . .'[7] Others described it differently. Miles Glendinning and Aonghus Mackechnie, in their study of 'Scotch Baronial' quote J. C. Loudon, who was more critical: 'Sir Walter's taste was antiquarian rather than artistic . . . The house is a curious piece of patchwork.'[8]

Scott, friend of the 8th Earl, had been a frequent visitor to Tyninghame; he was also a friend of William Burn and had introduced him to the Duke of Buccleuch, who employed him on several projects both at Dalkeith Palace (1828 and 1830) and on his estate at Drumlanrig (1830). As the favoured architect of Tory politicians, William Burn was the obvious choice for Thomas, Baron Melrose, 9th Earl of Haddington, and was a friend of the Duke of Buccleuch who had himself represented six Tory constituencies.

Tyninghame House, altered and increased in size by successive generations, would not have lent itself easily to the kind of neo-classical transformation Burn had originally developed. In 1828, it was a typical Scots baronial mansion, with a mixture of sixteenth-, seventeenth- and some eighteenth-century modifications. The roof line was uneven: the west wing was the tallest with four storeys, the east wing had three storeys and some linking sections in the middle of the house had only one or two. One section was a single storey 'add-on'. The sandstone rubble walls, originally harled (tiny fragments remain in corners by towers high up on the south front), had dressed quoins (corner stones). Some chimneys were tall. Tyninghame presented Burn with the opportunity to gather all the elements of the old baronial style together with his original Tudor and Jacobean variations – as employed at Luffness and at Lauriston Castle for example – in a single house. By emphasising the traditional, vernacular elements of the existing architecture and embellishing the house with more of these, Burn was creating his own, eclectic, revival of the old baronial style. The seventeenth-century models for his inspiration were all to be found in East Lothian or Edinburgh.

The harling disappeared as most of the house was refaced with dressed sandstone; on the west and on some of the façades on the eastern side the old masonry was left, conveying antiquity (genuine in this case). All have ashlar quoins, some of which pre-date Burn who did not believe in unnecessary expense and left what was sound. The uneven roof line was broken further by tall diamond-set chimneys and additional circular towers, including several which projected with corbels at first floor level. All were given what Colin McWilliam described as, 'swept-in candle-snuffer roofs', typical of the revival.[9]

The 'diamond-set' chimneys, favoured by Walter Scott at Abbotsford, that Burn had used at Lauriston the year before (1828), and frequently repeated, had seventeenth-century precedents at Luffness, once owned by the 1st Earl of Haddington,[10] and Moray House in Edinburgh. The bartizans, or corbeled turrets placed in angles or on corners, echo those he introduced at Pinkie (1825) but the swept-in roofs more closely resemble the ones he added at Lauriston. These clearly anticipate the lines at Tyninghame. As at Lauriston, most of the smaller turrets added are 'blind'; their slit windows are blacked out and conceal a rubble-filled interior. Their function is purely to enforce the baronial aesthetic.

The other towers breaking the roof line include the three earliest towers. The tower with the turnpike stair in the western corner of the south courtyard by the principal entrance at the time of the 1st Earl (door moved by Burn), the courtyard tower to the east and the tower on the west wing were all probably added in the seventeenth or early eighteenth century. These were given new roofs; the west wing tower, the tallest, became the grandest with the addition of purely decorative checker-set corbels below its tiles, which recall

Overleaf: Burn's perspective drawing to show the house from the south (Courtesy of RIBA)

the defensive 'machicolation' on castle battlements from which missiles were once dropped on the enemy below (p. 123).

Another decorative but very functional tower, with a flat roof, was also added to the west side of the court-yard. It housed the new water closets and bathrooms for the west wing. In all, Burn added five new turrets and one new tower; it could have been pure coinci-dence but the 9th Earl now had nine turrets. All the gables were crow-stepped; plain steps on the east side of the east wing, part of which were the servants' quar-ters, but on the main façades these were treated in a more elaborate fashion: the 'tread' having a squared edge and the 'riser' curving inwards in a double scallop or 'ovolo', 'in a Heriot's manner'.[11] This became a typical feature of many of Burn's later houses.

Crow-stepped gables and corbelled turrets had their origins in medieval Scottish castles or fortified houses and Burn became adept at transforming them to suit his clients' needs. To these quintessentially Scottish elements Burn added windows that were more Tudor or Jacobean in character. Successive owners at Tyning-hame had enlarged the original windows and added more. (The window tax for the house in the middle of the eighteenth century was for 142 windows, but this total included some outlying 'offices'). The watercolour (p. 102) shows the typical asymmetry of windows in the house of a Scottish laird. The painting only gives a glimpse of the house as it was, before Burn introduced extensive ranges of floor-to-ceiling windows in all the public rooms, but it is enough to show the enormous difference that so many new and large windows would have made to the interior as well as to its exterior appearance. The Tudor or Jacobean style windows that Burn designed, including bay windows, had stone mullions (vertical) and transoms (horizontal). This combination, that became a hallmark of new Scottish, or 'Scotch', baronial, appeared in William Burn's work in the 1820s: 'Burn varied and recombined these ideas in a new way that pointed to significant elements of the

future Scotch Baronial, including new features that enhanced modern domestic comfort . . .'[12]

Bay windows were not typically Scottish: Pinkie House in Musselburgh, now Loretto School, had a bay window, built for Alexander Seton in the seventeenth century. Colin McWilliam described it as a 'revolution-ary import from England and thus an architectural token of the Union of the Crowns'.[13] The 9th Earl and his wife were all in favour of them – four different styles of bay windows were added (five, if the windows on the end of the west wing extension are included). The single common feature was the Jacobean strapwork parapets with cannon ball finials and the flat roofs. The dormer window heads, projecting above the eaves, were given gables with crow steps or a scroll design with heraldic finials taken from the coat of arms of the Earls of Haddington.

Burn also added an elegant flourish – a long balcony with balustrades which wrapped around the west wing at first floor level and swept round to the south, terminating in a flight of steps which led to the terrace, garden and church beyond. Sadly, the stonework of the balcony deteriorated, and it was taken down in the 1950s. A balcony of this size must have seemed a very novel feature in its day though it too had its origins in Scottish architecture of the seven-teenth century. The balcony at Moray House which projects over the Canongate in Edinburgh is supported on curvilinear brackets and could be a precedent for the short balcony introduced by Burn at Luffness and the longer one at Lauriston. At Tyninghame, the cantilevered balcony was taken to extremes and became a full-blown terrace, 12 feet wide and over 130 feet long (pp. 118–19). It certainly impressed the Earl

Opposite top: Blind turret on the east wing with 'candle-snuffer' roof

Opposite bottom: Crow-stepped gable, enriched 'in a Heriot's manner'

Opposite: Diamond-set chimneys, turrets, bay window with Jacobean strapwork parapet and a section of cantilevered balcony on the east wing

Above: Dormer window heads with heraldic finials: a coronet, a rose and a cinquefoil. The turret has decorative checker-set corbels

of Lauderdale, a friend of Thomas who wrote to him in March 1832; 'I went over to see Tyninghame; there is only a small part of the balcony erected, but even that . . . convinces me that though I have all along maintained strong opinions in its favour, it will exceed even my expectations.'[14] The long balcony originally envisaged on the east wing, a counter balance to that on the west, with another set of steps to the garden, was never built. It was replaced with a shorter balcony, with supporting brackets with identical decoration that exactly replicated the balcony brackets at Moray

House. It is an example of Burn's extraordinary attention to historical detail and a poignant reminder of what has been lost.

It was this interest in accurate architectural detail of Scottish historic buildings that led Burn to persuade Robert William Billings to produce *The Baronial and Ecclesiastical Antiquities of Scotland*, published between 1845 and 1852, 'which became a vital source book for the Scottish Baronial style'.[15] The other balconies on some windows on the larger stair turrets were purely decorative, more suited to the imagined heroes and

Right: Replica of Moray
House balcony bracket

Opposite: Panel frames with
the coat of arms of the 9th
Earl of Haddington

heroines of Walter Scott's novels and poems than for
any practical use. But they added to the romantic appeal,
with strapwork detail rather than heavy balusters.

Burn altered the footprint of the house very little
– he extended the west wing to the south, added a corridor to the east wing but otherwise left what was there.
He remodelled the whole house from top to bottom
and from every angle. His asymmetrical transformation of the façades did not mean that they lacked
balance – on the contrary, blank windows were
constructed on the north and west fronts where an
empty wall would have broken a regular pattern and
he cleverly balanced the size of the west wing with the

additional details on the other, lower sections of the
house, 'clearly designed for romantic outline and
dynamic mass . . .'[16] The string courses with which Burn
'tied' the house together, he would have known from
Holyroodhouse, Heriot's Hospital (School) and also
at Luffness, where he added another. He did not need
to travel to the Highlands to find the characteristic
architectural details which became his hallmarks. No
doubt his clients, even the aristocratic ones, were flat-
tered by the architectural associations that their houses
had acquired as well as easing their conscience when
it came to paying the bill.

Following traditional practice, Burn added the

equally significant, personal detail: three armorial stamps of the Earls of Haddington on the north front, by the main entrance. The largest central panel frame has a quartered shield, supported by two 'talbots' – white hunting hounds, now extinct – and includes the earl's coronet as a crest and the motto on a ribbon below: *Praesto et persisto* – 'I stand in front and I stand firm'.

Above and on each side are two smaller panels with shields, one with three *fraises* (strawberry flowers) with five petals or 'cinquefoils' for the house of Hamilton, divided by a chevron and the other, with three roses divided by a 'fess wavy' or wavy band, with a border

of eight thistles. The thistles are for Hamilton of Byres and the roses are for Melrose – the 1st Earl of Haddington had been the 1st Earl of Melrose and the 9th Earl was created 1st Baron Melrose in 1827. Crowning the north front, on the central window head pediment are the initials 'h Mh'. Perhaps, in the tradition of Scottish marriage stones usually carved on or over the lintel, these initials commemorate the marriage of Thomas Hamilton, 9th Earl of Haddington, to Maria Parker, the only surviving daughter of the Earl of Macclesfield.

Having finished the exterior of the main house, Burn then went on to transform the outbuildings and an entrance gateway. The latter takes the form of an

Gateway incorporating part of a ruined cottage. The archway is understated. The visitor, arriving in his or her carriage, having driven for nearly a mile through parkland and wilderness, would have been surprised when the splendid house was finally revealed.

imposing asymmetric castle wall: the rusticated, coursed stonework appears to disintegrate into the rubble wall of an old cottage on the north side. Together, the archway and plain wooden gates announce the presence of an ancient family seat.

The remodelling of the exterior had effected a fashionable transformation of a plain old Scottish baronial mansion into a splendid new 'Scotch' baronial home. Inside the house, the changes were equally transformative, though the decorative elements were not especially Scottish. Colin McWilliam, who described the rooms in detail, summed up: 'The main rooms, eclectic but perfectly assured, are the most beautiful of their time in Scotland.'[17] The beauty of the rooms may or may not compensate for the impracticality of living in an old house, and Tyninghame must have been a very

impractical house in which to live prior to Burn's remodelling of the interior.

One of his skills as a designer lay in his systematic approach to organising the internal layout and modernising it. Doorways were bricked up and new corridors and bathrooms were installed. Windows were replaced, enlarged and re-aligned. Inadequate heating was addressed by installing a hot-air partial central heating system for the main public rooms, ordered from the London heating engineers Messrs. William and Mark Feetham, who had the Royal Warrant.

It was a complex operation, executed by one of their engineers who travelled from a job they had just completed in Ireland. Before work began, a local joiner spent five and a half days, 'boarding up doors to enable Mr Feethams man to judge the draught of the chim-

Tyninghame House, engraving by J. B. Allen, 1837

neys @ 3/- (per day) 16/6'.[18] The total bill came to £205 2s. 6d., which included forty-four days of a man's time for the installation, at seven shillings a day (more than twice the wage of the then mason's three shillings per day), and his travel expenses, plus lodgings and coach hire, from Ireland and then back to London.

Additional heating was provided by a charcoal burner with heated air flues installed by masons from the Edinburgh firm of James Dorward, who also installed new marble fireplaces.[19] Most of the plumbing was undertaken by George and Charles Hay, who spent two years from 1831 to 1833 on site. Carpentry and joinery work were ongoing and the payments appear to have been irregular. When John Swinton, the builder responsible for the joinery, was paid in May 1833, his invoice covered seven sides of foolscap.

The new plasterwork that William Burn designed required more skill than could be found locally; in this case the plasterer was James Anderson of Lothian Road, Edinburgh. Burn gained a reputation for handsome 'Jacobethan'-style plasterwork and James Anderson was a skilled craftsman. His elegantly written invoice included some basic work as well as decorative elements that are given their distinctive descriptions: double cut beads, large egg and tongue, laurel wreaths, enriched Grecian leaf and bead, sunk spindle bead, even a flower in the centre of the dairy ceiling.

The quantities are eye-watering: 2,073 feet of double cut bead moulding, 1,338 feet of cornices in the public rooms and staircase, together with 899 feet of 'large enrichments in underparts of cornices in these rooms'. More than 1,500 feet of the same moulded

Right Hon.ble Earl of Haddington

To James Anderson Plasterer

Measurement of Plaster Work in Tynningham House

Per Report of J.r W.m Spottiswood

feet	inch				£ s d
3	9	Sup.t 3 Coats Plaster	@6	£	230 2 8
5	"	" Deafening partition on Two Sides	4.d		5 19 10
4	6	" Composition Deafening on Floors with 1 Coat Plaster	6.d		39 17 2
2073	"	Lin.l Double Cut Beads	0½		4 6 4½
1258	"	Sup.r Cornices in Public Rooms Staircase &c.a	4.d		20 19 8
899	"	Lin.l Large Enrichment in under part of Cornices in these Rooms	8.d		29 19 4
637	"	" Enrichments in upper part of these Cornices	4.d		10 12 10
1637	9	" Moulded D.o Ceilings of Library & Soffits of Staircase	1½		10 4 8
140	"	" Large Egg & Tongue in Library	5.d		2 18 4
99	"	" D.o in Staircase	5.d		2 1 3
203	4	" Laurel Wreath on Ceiling of Library 5½ Girth	10.d		8 9 6
50	"	Sup.r Bands round Circular part of Ditto	4.d		" 16 8
129	"	Lin.l Enriched Grecian Leaf and Bead D.o	4.d		2 3 "
365	"	" D.o D.o Leaf in Pannels	4.d		6 1 8
116	"	" Sunk Spindle Bead	3.d		1 9 "
289	"	" Stiles in Library & Din.g Room 9 Inches broad	3.d		3 12 3
88	6	" D.o D.o 7½ " "	2½.d		" 18 5
87	"	" D.o D.o 6 " "	2.d		" 14 6
		11 Patras each 11 Inches Diameter	2/6		1 7 6
46	9	Lin.l Enriched Wreath round D.o	6.d		1 3 4½
		2 Patras each 7 Inches Diameter	1.d		" 2 "
5	6	Laurel Wreath round D.o	6.d		" 2 9
87	"	Sup.r Mouldings on each Side Window	4.d		1 9 "
62	"	Lin.l Enriched Grecian leaf in Pannels over Dining Room window	3½		" 18 1
56	"	" Stiles in Ceiling of Dining Room 9 Inches Broad	3.d		" 14 "
118	"	" Arrases on Beams of D.o	2.d		" 19 8
68	6	" Moulding on Ceiling of Staircase	4.d		1 2 10
		4 Cut Ornaments in Angles of D.o	20.d		" 6 8
579	"	Lin.l Rib Mouldings on Ceilings of Flats & Soffits of Stair with Spikes &c.a	5.d		32 7 "
1762	"	" Plain Cornices in Bed & Dressing Rooms &c.a and in Dairy	4.d		29 7 4
563	"	" Ovolo Moulding in Passages &c.a	3.d		7 " 9
102	"	" Moulded Beads in House and Dairy	3.d		1 6 "
		Flower in Centre of Ceiling of Dairy 2 " 8 Diameter			" 15 "
16	"	Lin.l Moulded Fillet round D.o	2		" 2 8
		2 Plasterers each 14 Days at alteration of Ceiling of Library			4 13 "
		2 Cwt of Fine Stucco			1 " "

enrichments went on the soffits on the staircase and the ceiling of the library. It took two plasterers fourteen days to alter the ceiling in the library. Anderson's total bill came to £544 5s. 1d.[20]

In the new bathroom in the west wing, a bath of the best marble, 'finished in the Best manner', and black marble covings for the ante room were supplied by David Ness, marble cutter and sculptor of 15 Leith Walk. Ironwork including grates, window bars, locks, shutter fastenings and foot scrapers, was supplied locally by John White, ironmonger in Haddington. The newel posts on the central staircase were decorated with eight carved oak urns by John Steell, the celebrated carver and gilder from Edinburgh.

Once the alterations were complete and the rooms were plastered, decoration could begin. James Deans from Haddington undertook the painting and/or papering of every room in the house. In the public rooms the preparation and execution were thorough – six coats of paint on walls and ceilings was standard. The walls and ceiling of the entrance hall and principal staircase were painted in a 'stone colour'. In all the public rooms, doors, windows and shutters were all given the same treatment to achieve an 'imitation oak' finish. It required a special skill and decorators were not always keen to share their secrets. Rags, sponges and flat brushes were used to create pattern and knots and special brushes of badger hair softened the finish. Whereas Deans charged one shilling and sixpence per square yard for painting bedroom woodwork in a plain stone colour, this skilled technique cost two shillings and sixpence per square yard. Even at double the price, it was far cheaper than using real oak.

For the drawing room the 'finishing paper' was ordered from Cowtan and Sons Ltd of Oxford Street, who specialised in fine hand-blocked wallpapers, fabrics and trimmings. Their order book, now in the

Victoria & Albert Museum, records the choices made for Tyninghame on 8 September 1832.[21] The pale green paper chosen for the drawing room is the only wallpaper still *in situ*.

All the rooms in the east and west wings were papered including the bedrooms, turrets and water closets, the only detail given by Deans was the price: one shilling and sixpence per piece. The one exception was the gallery, the room at the heart of the house that had once been part of the original tower. It had a white ceiling and cornices, and was papered with 'Crimson Flock Wallpaper', at two shillings and sixpence.[22] James Dean's total bill came to £616 12s. 6d.

By February 1833, four years and three months from the first drawings dated 19 October 1829, the house was becoming habitable again. A Brussels weave carpet for the drawing room, complementing the wallpaper, was woven by Crossley of Halifax. Payment was made to 'Baldock, Chinaman to his Majesty', for a mirror in a gilt frame, a sideboard and some china. The furniture, books and pictures which had been in storage were brought back; paintings were cleaned, varnished and re-hung by Chalmers and Son of Princes Street, who also gilded the frames. The library was arranged by Mr George Goldie. More furniture was purchased from William Kirkwood, Edinburgh, together with washstands, commodes 'of good Spanish mahogany', mahogany 'towel horses', dressing tables, beds and bedding. While a fuller picture of the furnishings might be gained from further archival research, some of the public rooms are illustrated in the Sotheby's catalogue for their sale in September 1987. The photographs show the rooms as furnished for the 12th Earl and Lady Haddington; the wallpaper in the library is not the original but the plasterwork is that of James Anderson; in the drawing room, the marble fireplaces, possibly by Lorenzo Bartolini, are those installed by James Dorwood, the paintings shown are those re-hung by Chalmers and Son and the wallpaper and carpet are original.

Opposite: Page from James Anderson's account (Courtesy of the Earl of Haddington)

The gallery with 'Crimson Flock Wallpaper', 1987 (Courtesy of Sotheby's)

While work was going on to finish the interior, Burn turned his attention to the outbuildings and finally the garden. The outbuildings named on Burn's invoice covering the years 1832 to 1834 included plans and specifications for an icehouse, dairy, stables and offices, laundry and wash house buildings, and gate lodges. His fee, as for the house, was five per cent of the estimated total of £3,000. The accounts of Mr Balsillie, the builder, and James Deans, painter, both bring the detailed workings of a grand house and its staff into relief. In the stables complex there were haylofts, an old granary, a harness room, a saddle room, a coachman's house, as well as a four-stall stable and three two-stall stables and coach houses. By the dairy there was also a piggery (pigs were often given the whey and by-products from cheese making). The

laundry buildings included a laundry room, brewhouse, wash house, mangle house, larder, potato and poultry houses, a fish house and a charcoal house. In all, the mason's work for the stables, including the 'Dundee stone', came to £1,036 13s. 9¾d. The work on building the laundry buildings came to just over £700. James Deans's bill came to roughly £1,800. This further expenditure was over and above the £10,000 in Burn's original estimate for the house.

The icehouse at Tyninghame was cut into a north-facing slope, to the north of the house and offices. It is disguised and insulated under a grassy mound, with an entrance to the north opening into a short flagstone passage which leads to a perfect egg-shaped chamber of smooth ashlar. Tim Buxbaum refers to an icehouse at Whim House in Peeblesshire, older than the one at

The drawing room in 1987 with the original wallpaper (Courtesy of Sotheby's)

Tyninghame but of the same egg-shaped design.[23] There was very probably a drain at the bottom, which allowed for meltwater to escape. In a hard winter, snow and ice could be collected locally with comparative ease. It was packed in layers with straw or sawdust, but with the advent of refrigeration in the twentieth century it became obsolete. It remains in perfect condition.

In Scottish country estates the dairy played a significant role and was often a freestanding building to be visited on the garden tour. F. Marian McNeill quotes from Dr Johnson, 'A dinner in the Western Isles differs very little from a dinner in England, except that in place of tarts there are always set different preparations of milk.'[24] 'Milk-meats' were never just butter and cheese. McNeill gives recipes for Corstorphine cream, hatted

kit, crowdie, wine whey, green whey, frothed whey, frosted milk and buttermilk, besides recipes for cheese. A simple, free-standing octagonal dairy was built in the garden by the stables and stable cottages. It was both ornamental and functional: a place where visitors could be taken for refreshment and would have been in use until the early twentieth century. It had a louvred 'lantern' at the top, for extra ventilation and to keep the internal temperature cool as did the shade from surrounding trees. The plaster ceiling had what the plasterer called a 'flower' in the centre. It was an intriguing design as the spaces between the curling petals of the flower allowed the air to flow in and out through the slats on the lantern above. It was in fact, a churning room: 'The churning room, at the heart of the dairy, would be furnished with a slate dresser round

Redrawn copy of Burn's plan of the garden at Tyninghame; proposals are in ink, existing flower beds and trees are outlined in pencil

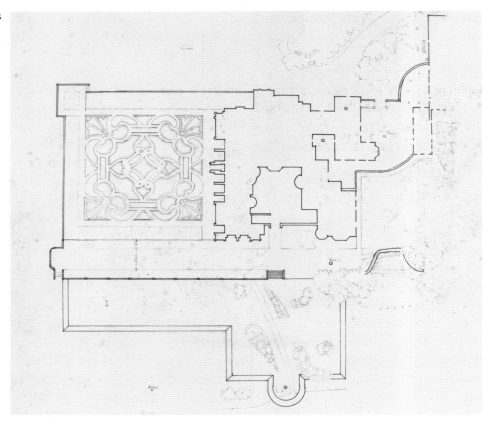

the walls, and a marble topped table in the middle. There would be pats to stamp the family crest on the butter, heavy stone presses to produce cheese . . . and other wooden utensils.'[25] Instead of slate dressers, slate shelves were fixed in the window recesses, where cheese, butter and milk could be kept cool. additional ventilation panels were set into the walls below the windows. Instead of a stone floor, it was boarded with oak and the stone flags kept to the outer edge where their cooling effect was most needed.

Sadly, the only plan of the garden around the house to survive is very discoloured and barely legible. Redrawn, the plan shows an extravagant design for the parterre to the west, a long terrace across the south front of the house with two flights of steps leading down to a rather narrow L-shaped lawn edged with a

wall. The drawing shows a pre-exisiting path and that flower beds, cut into the lawn, had already made an appearance.

What Burn was proposing as landscape and garden design was in line with ideas that Humphry Repton had developed by the end of the eighteenth century and which were eventually endorsed by John Claudius Loudon, the most eminent horticulturalist of the day. Terraces, balustrades and flower gardens in the vicinity of the house began to make their return. Repton acknowledged that a garden was an 'artifice' and that attempts to replicate nature within its precincts were futile: 'a garden . . . is a piece of ground fenced off from cattle, and appropriated to the use and pleasure of man: it is or ought to be, cultivated and enriched by art, with such products that are not natural to this country, and, consequently, it must be artificial in its treatment . . . yet there is so much littleness in art, when compared with nature, that they cannot be well blended . . .'[26] Repton goes on to recommend the separation of the exterior of a garden, further from the house and which should blend with park scenery, while 'the interior may then be laid out with all the variety, contrast, even whim, that can produce pleasurable objects to the eye'.[27]

Although Repton himself never visited Scotland, he was responsible for redesigning Valleyfield, in Fife, which his sons visited and surveyed. However, the 9th Earl spent at least as much time in England as he did in Scotland. When in London, he and his wife lived in Berkeley Square with a wide circle of friends, including many of Repton's clients who were also peers and MPs. As the leading garden designer in England at the turn of the century, Repton's ideas would have been familiar both to architect and client who would have approved of the separation of the artificial (the garden) from the natural (the park). Repton advised a deliberate partition – fence or balustrade for example – between the lawn of a garden and the landscape beyond. Burn's plan drawing indicates a wide wall dividing the lawn from the pasture but, as no elevations of the garden survive, there is no indication of its intended height. When it was built, it had become a low parapet, finishing a retaining wall with a ditch in the manner of a ha-ha, separating the garden from the parkland with its cows beyond. The lawn area was enlarged to make a longer, wider rectangle. Within this 'frame', gravel paths, flower borders and a variety of island beds were cut into the lawn and the path to the old St Baldred's kirk was re-aligned (p. 151).

Two features not shown on the drawing are the large, raised sandstone beds, supported by inverted, spiral scrolls in the lawn below the parterre. Their date is uncertain. They may predate Burn's work at Tyninghame, and were possibly moved as part of his re-organisation of the garden. On the other side of the lawn

was a sixteenth-century Venetian well-head, accompanied by a further scattering of flowerbeds, the 'pleasurable objects to the eye' that Repton recommended.

Burn's swirling and interlocking pattern for the parterre shown in the drawing (p. 132) resembles in spirit the 'Parterres of Embroidery . . . so called, because the Box wherewith they are planted, imitates Embroidery upon the Ground. They are the finest and most magnificent of all and are sometimes accompanied with Knots and Scrolls of Grass-work.'[28] They occupied pride of place nearest the house. Burn's interlaced pattern was not implemented. Instead, the present design consists of a square lawn divided into four sections by two cross-paths. Two opposite quarters have four triangular-shaped beds, the other two have elongated diamond-shaped beds, set on the diagonal. It could be a relic of a much earlier date or may have been designed at the turn of the century when the sundial was erected.

The beds would have been filled with hardy and half-hardy flowering annuals grown in the Walled Garden greenhouses. Each quarter has a central squat vase of imitation stone on a square plinth. The vases, decorated with rams' masks and festoons of vines with grapes, were supplied by Felix Austin, artificial stone manufacturer.

The firm was rated highly. When their 'Specimen Book' was published in 1841 it was reviewed in the *Gardeners' Magazine*: 'Everyone who has passed along the New Road, . . . near Fitzroy Square, has seen Mr Austin's splendid assemblage of sculptural works in artificial stone; and there is scarcely a flower-garden in any part of England which does not boast of a vase, a fountain, a sun-dial, or a statue, from his manufactory.'[29] The manufacturers claimed that their artificial stone was remarkably durable, impervious to water and 'will not sustain any injury from the severest winter'. It was made from Portland cement, broken stone, pounded marble and coarse sand and was much cheaper than real stone.

Above: Parterre with geometric flower beds
(Courtesy of Andy Semple)

Left: Artificial stone vase by Austin & Co.

The 9th Earl was probably running short of money as his building project came to an end, and he joined the increasing number of architects, gardeners and landed gentry who patronised the firm. In December 1833, his factor paid £64 12s. for garden ornaments. Although no details were given, in July the following year, a further order was placed for 'a large French Foliage Vase', Grecian tazzas, one with a circular plinth and a pair of shells.[30] Besides free-standing urns, others were destined for positions on pillars by flights of steps and at intervals along the length of the terrace wall. A watercolour, painted in October 1837, a few years after the terrace was completed, clearly shows the triangular flower beds, the sundial and the urns on pedestals along the parapet wall to the north. The yew trees have

Watercolour of north section of the parterre, 1837

since grown and they now enclose the garden on this side. The urns have been removed.

A local builder, Thomas Hannan, was responsible for building the enclosure walls and the terrace which had a curved wall at each end with curved wooden bench. It was probably he who was responsible for the extensive ha-ha which must have been constructed around 1856 when the 9th Earl again approached William Burn, this time to design an obelisk to commemorate his namesake, Thomas, the 6th Earl, and his wife Helen. It was to be situated as a focal point at the end of the Sea Avenue, the mile-long avenue that runs east–west to the estuary of the Tyne at Hedderwick Bay.

The tradition of using an Egyptian obelisk as an 'eye-catcher' had begun in Roman times. They appeared in eighteenth-century gardens, both on a small scale, as in the commemorative obelisk to his mother in Pope's Twickenham garden, and on a larger scale as in the Ilex Grove at Holkham Hall, the work of William Kent. In Scotland, they appeared in the policies of Blair Castle, at Penicuik House and on bridges – Aberfeldy (William Adam) and Dumfries House (John Adam). In the nineteenth century, their appearances became more frequent. Napoleon's Egyptian campaign and the involvement of Scottish regiments, as well as the official illustrated accounts of the campaign that ensued, stimulated an increased interest in Egypt. However, when obelisks were used in Scotland, they were not 'the dominant feature in some

Aerial view of the obelisk and the Sea Avenue (Courtesy of Andy Semple)

central square'. In Glasgow, the tallest obelisk in Scotland, at 148 feet, commemorating Nelson, was placed on Glasgow Green. Edinburgh's commemorative obelisk to the political martyrs of 1793, was erected in the Old Calton Burial Ground where it rises from the cliff face on Calton Hill. Other obelisks appeared, like the one at Tyninghame, 'enhancing the landscape and crowning hills to add there a Picturesque and Romantic focal point'.[31] Besides their exotic attraction, the symbolism of obelisks appealed to aristocratic Scottish families, many of whom, including the 9th Earl of Haddington, were Freemasons and held prominent positions in the Brotherhood.

In 1856, William Burn had just finished working for the 2nd Earl of Leicester at Holkham Hall in Norfolk so it is perhaps not surprising that the obelisk at Tyning-hame bears some resemblance to that of William Kent.

It occupies a position on a slight rise, facing east down the long avenue of beech trees to the estuary; to the west, it looks across the park and fields to the Binning Wood. The ha-ha surrounding the obelisk on three sides and continuing to the north and south is in an unusual place. Traditionally these sunken ditches with a stone retaining wall were constructed at the end of a lawn, where they could unobtrusively separate the well-tended garden from the park, with its animals, and afford an unimpeded and extensive view for their owners. Perhaps it was built before the belts of rhododendrons were planted and there were still open views across the 'Big Park'. A long straight wall is shown on the OS map of 1854, already possibly the ha-ha, in which case, when the obelisk was erected the sunken ditch and wall were extended around it to provide an unimpeded view from any point on the avenue.

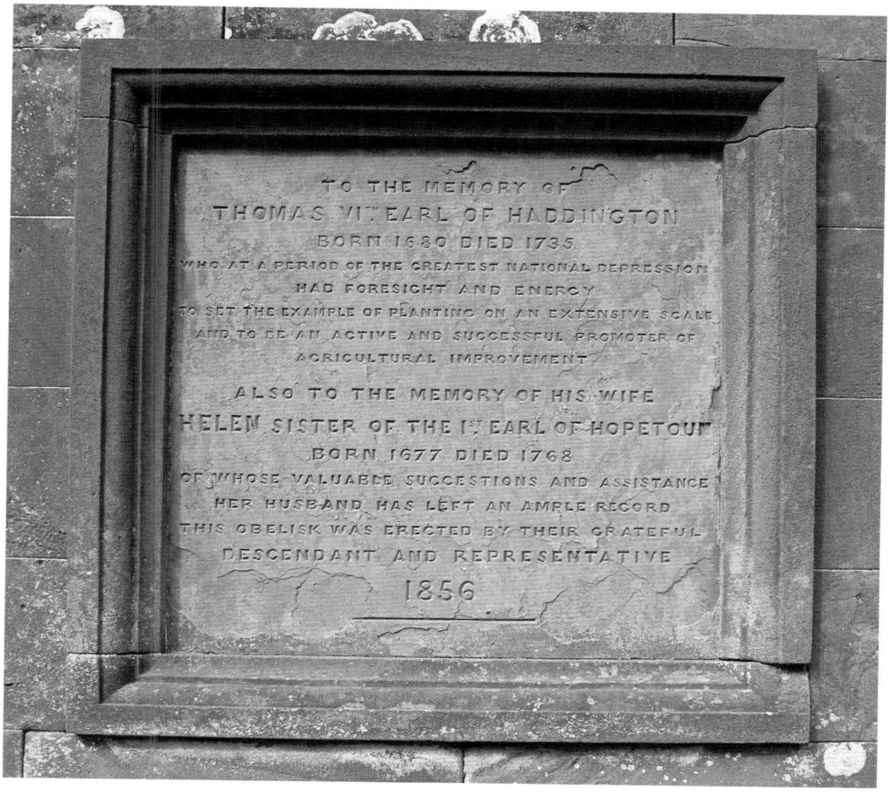

When Thomas, the 9th Earl, died on 1 December 1858, he was buried at Tyninghame. As he and his wife had no children, the estate passed to George Baillie of Jerviswoode and Mellerstain, the great-grandson of Helen Hope and Thomas, the 6th Earl. The 9th Earl's improvements to the house and its gardens were more extensive than those of any of his forebears, apart from Thomas and Helen, who had designed the basic layout of the estate that he had not changed. Of all his predecessors they were the ones who had contributed most to shaping the landscape and Thomas may have felt that, with the help of William Burn, he was finishing their work. The obelisk has a memorial, fittingly dedicated to their memory:

TO THE MEMORY OF

THOMAS VIth EARL OF HADDINGTON

BORN 1680 DIED 1735

WHO AT A PERIOD OF THE GREATEST NATIONAL DEPRESSION

HAD FORESIGHT AND ENERGY

TO SET THE EXAMPLE OF PLANTING ON AN EXTENSIVE SCALE

AND TO BE AN ACTIVE AND SUCCESSFUL PROMOTER OF

AGRICULTURAL IMPROVEMENT

ALSO TO THE MEMORY OF HIS WIFE

HELEN SISTER OF THE 1ST EARL OF HOPETOUN

BORN 1677 DIED 1768

OF WHOSE VALUABLE SUGGESTIONS AND ASSISTANCE

HER HUSBAND HAS LEFT AN AMPLE RECORD

THIS OBELISK WAS ERECTED BY THEIR GRATEFUL

DESCENDANT AND REPRESENTATIVE

1856

No of House holders Schedule	Name of Street, Place, or Road, and Name or No. of House	Name and Surname of each Person who abode in the house, on the Night of the 30th March, 1851	Relation to Head of Family	Condition	Age of Males	Age of Females	Rank, Profession, or Occupation	Where Born	Whether Blind, Deaf-and-Dumb
67	Tynninghame Garden	Thomas Lees	Head	Mar	33		Gardener & Laborers under his charge	Roxburghshire Melrose	
		Ann H. Do	Wife	Do		28		Ayrshire, Girvan	
		Thomas Do	Son		6		Scholar	England	
		William Do	Do		5		Do	Haddingtonshire Whitekirk	
		Andrew Do	Do		4			Do Do	
		Mary Jella Do	Daur			2		Do Do	
		John Do	Son		1			Do Do	
		Catherine Scott	Serv	U		23	House Servant	Do Athelstaneford	
68	Tynm. Garden, Bothy	Christopher Ryan		U	29		Gardener Journeyman	Ireland	
		James Weir		U	23		Do Do	Stirlingshire Polmont	
69	Tynninghame House	Thomas, Earl of Haddington	Head	Mar	70		Earl of Haddington occupying 750 ac employing 9 Lab	Midlothian, Edin	
		Maria, Countess of Do	Wife	Do		70	Countess of Haddington	England	
		Jane Hope	Visitor	U		44		Midlothian Cramond	
		Mary Porteous	Serv	U		58	Housekeeper	Lanarkshire Lesmahagow	
		Esther Frost	Serv	Mar		46	Cook	England	
		Dorothea Ranzen	Serv	U		56	Lady's Maid	Hanover	
		Mary Edington	Serv	Widow		52	Laundress	Midlothian Cranstown	
		Jane Dixon	Serv	U		39	Housemaid	D1 Dalmeny	
		Elizabeth Gunn	Serv	U		35	Do	Do Edinburgh	
		Marion Alison	Serv	U		28	Dairymaid	Haddingtonshire Whitekirk	
Total of Houses 1 3 0 — B —				Total of Persons	8	12			

CHAPTER 11

People and Plants

The garden and policies had probably never had so much attention lavished on them as they did during the lifetime of Thomas, the 9th Earl. The more time he spent at Tyninghame, the more his father had become committed to planting, and enormous advances in horticulture coincided with their tenure. Horticultural societies were established in England (1804) and Scotland (1809), and their transactions were published; gardening magazines for the general public appeared together with a steady stream of new plants introduced by (mainly Scottish) 'plant hunters', all contributing to an expansion of the market. Nursery businesses became more and more profitable: 'Four leading nurserymen died in the 1860s, each leaving over £4 million in modern terms, though none could approach their contemporary, Joseph Paxton, who died in 1865 worth £112 million (£180,000).'[1] Technical innovations followed and, as more and more half-hardy and tender plants were cultivated, designs and systems for heating greenhouses were refined and improved. Labour though was relatively cheap and plentiful. At Tyninghame, there was no mention of any difficulty in finding or paying men – and women – to work in the garden and on the land.

Opposite: 1841 census, Tyninghame House (Courtesy of the National Records of Scotland)

With the introduction of the first official census of the population in 1841, the names and ages of all the members of households were recorded county by county. In Tyninghame (Haddingtonshire), it gave a snapshot of everyone living on the estate and in the village at midnight on 6 June 1841. Apart from 1941, a census has been taken every ten years since, and the 1851 census required more details and thus gave a fuller social picture. None of the Haddington family were in residence when the first census took place, though there were five female servants and four male servants in the house, all unmarried and only three born in Haddingtonshire. There were approximately nine other married servants who lived in the surrounding cottages and offices. Their specific roles were not described; their names were followed by initials: FS for 'female servant' and MS for 'male servant'. In the case of David Ford, 'Gardner' was crossed out and replaced with MS. Neither he nor three of the other servants were born in the county (their actual birth places were not requested).

In the lodges and in the village, the occupations of the householders and those residing with them were more explicit. The majority were agricultural labourers, 'Ag. Lab.'. In the village itself there were forty-nine men, aged between fourteen and eighty-eight and twenty-three women, aged between twelve and thirty-five so described. In Tyninghame Links there were another eight men, the youngest a boy of ten years old and another three women and a girl of ten, all described as 'Ag. Lab.'. In Brownrigg, Old and New Lochhouses there were another thirty male labourers, from boys of ten to a ninety-year-old! The twelve women agricultural workers were younger, from age fourteen to thirty-five.

Other occupations listed in the 1841 census for Tyninghame were a forester and foresting labourer, one builder, three masons, three journeymen masons (who had finished their apprenticeships and were employees) and one mason's apprentice. The builder and masons were all members of the Hannan family, involved in the remodelling of Tyninghame House and responsible for many of the buildings in the village. There were also three joiners and three joiner's apprentices, two bakers and one baker's journeyman, one 'sawyer', two shoemakers and two shoemaker's apprentices, one cooper, a teacher and the parochial schoolmaster, a grocer and spirit dealer, a public coachman, a tailor, two journeymen tailors and one apprentice, a blacksmith with one journeyman and two apprentices, and the factor, Matthew Buist. There were also nine women described as paupers. Only seven of the village inhabitants had been born outside the county.

In the census of 1851, the householder had to fill in the birthplace of everyone staying under his or her roof (and whether blind, deaf or dumb). In addition, he or she noted how many they employed, if any. By then, there were seventeen members of staff living in Tyninghame House, almost double the previous number. This might be explained by the earl and countess being in residence this time; the earl, who had been First Lord of the Admiralty from 1841 to 1846, was now Lord Privy Seal, and had a substantial career behind him. With a London house in Berkeley Square, he and his wife, who had her own inheritance, lived well. Their household was still headed by Mary Porteous, their unmarried housekeeper from Lesma-

hagow in Lanarkshire. There was a cook, a lady's maid, a laundress, three housemaids, a dairymaid, a still-room maid, a kitchen maid and a scullery maid. Most of the manservants came from England: the butler, the coachman, the footman and the groom, who lived in the Stables. Several members of the extended staff lived in the village: the gamekeeper and his assistant, a house porter, two gardeners and a gatekeeper, for example. As the gardener had nine labourers 'under his charge', this census suggests that, besides the factor, there were over thirty men and women working in the house and grounds.

These census details give a tantalising outline of life in the big house and its gardens. Who were they, the head gardeners, journeymen and labourers who tended the hothouses and the garden? Their names appear in parish records but there is no surviving correspondence between head gardeners and owners. Nevertheless, with the establishment of the Caledonian Horticultural Society (CHS) in 1809, following the establishment of the Royal Horticultural Society in London in 1804, and the reports of its meetings in the Scottish press, a picture emerges of the expertise of Tyninghame's three nineteenth-century head gardeners. They all joined the CHS, 'the Caley' as it became known, as corresponding members and exhibited regularly.

The first was David Ford (b.1787?), possibly from Chirnside.[2] He came to Tyninghame some time before 6 March 1810, when he was listed as a corresponding member of the Caledonian Horticultural Society.[3] His first prize at the Caley was on 12 May, for early grapes.[4] Other prizes for vegetables followed, and in October that year he delivered one of the communications that formed part of the general meetings. His paper 'On diseases in the bark of fruit trees', suggests that David Ford was an educated gardener who was keen to establish his reputation.[5] After the meeting, about fifty members sat down to dinner. Dessert was provided by the specimens of fruit submitted in the competitions together with other fruit presented by members. On this occasion, at the head of the table, a very large flowerpot was placed in which was growing a vine bearing fourteen bunches of Black Hamburg grapes. It came from the Duke of Buccleuch's garden at Dalkeith.

From this date *The Caledonian Mercury*, *The Scotsman* and the *Edinburgh News* all reported the prizes Ford won regularly in Edinburgh at the Caley and at the East Lothian show in Haddington. He won the prize for grapes in 'the best state of preservation' in March 1814 with late white muscadines, which had been kept six months in good condition. Exactly how he managed this might have been his 'trade secret' as there were many elaborate ways devised to keep grapes fresh for several months.

Besides preserving grapes, Ford also won a medal for the largest and heaviest bunch of white muscat grapes in September 1821. His many prizes indicate that peaches were being grown at Tyninghame on heated and unheated walls. On 18 September 1823, *The Caledonian Mercury* reported that besides a silver medal for peaches, he won another: 'For the greatest variety of Fruits of good quality, produced by any one competitor, to Mr David Ford gardener to the Rt. Hon Earl of Haddington.'[6]

Given the interest in raising pineapples, or pines, and the expertise of the gardeners, it would be surprising if these were not also grown. In his *Encyclopoedia on Gardening*, the Scottish horticulturalist, J. C. Loudon, born in Cambuslang, Lanarkshire in 1783, describes Tyninghame as having 'a good kitchengarden. In 1805, pineapples were grown here in a pit, with a brick vault below, into which steam was introduced. Some of the plants were in pots, and the rest planted in the soil.' The Earl of Derby's gardener had been the one of the first to successfully introduce steam to heat a vault in the cucumber house in 1788, and steam-heated pits for melons and pineapples followed. By the beginning of the nineteenth century all the most advanced houses were heated by steam.[7] In Scotland,

John Hay, who was working at Archerfield home farm, Collegehead, from 1799, was an early designer of greenhouses and a pioneer of steam heating who undertook commissions outwith the estate.[8] As he was nearby, it is tempting to link him with the design and construction of hothouses and steam heating at Tyninghame but there is, to date, no evidence of this connection. Steam heating was an expensive initial outlay; J. C. Loudon was not entirely convinced of its practicality for the non-commercial grower, preferring the tried and tested 'fire, dung and tan heat' method.[9] Tyninghame was evidently in the vanguard by 1805. In spite of this early adoption of steam heat, David Ford did not win prizes for pineapples until 1837 when even his fellow horticulturalists at the Caley were surprised at 'a splendid specimen of the Otaheita Pine Apple in a flower pot' that Ford produced for their September meeting, and they awarded him a special premium.[10]

The only other gardener mentioned in the 1841 census was David Gibson, aged thirty. Other help in the garden would have been provided by men, women and children listed in the census as 'Agricultural Labourers'. Based on the number of labourers working in the garden in the 1851 census, the head gardener and David Gibson would probably have had another ten helpers giving regular assistance.

David Ford's final claim to fame appeared in *The Caledonian Mercury* in October 1843 with the headline 'The Egyptian Mummy Wheat at Tyningham.' From four special grains of wheat that had been presented to Lady Haddington, he produced 189 ears of wheat, 'which at a modest calculation would not yield less than 20 grains to the ear, or in all 3,380 distinct grains, showing an increase of 845-fold – an increase far beyond anything of the kind ever before heard of'.[11]

The grains had not been taken directly from the casement of a mummy but had been taken from a 'parent wheat . . . planted in Egypt when taken from a tomb in Phebead'. Wheat or other grains were frequently found in excavations of Egyptian tombs in the nineteenth century, and stories of their germination captured popular imagination. They regularly made entries into the newspapers, particularly in the 1840s but even into the twentieth century.[12] Serious botanists were never taken in by the claims that wheat from these ancient tombs could germinate. Lady Haddington and her gardener were not the only ones to have been duped but the story made a fitting highlight at the end of David Ford's career.

He was succeeded in his post by Thomas Lees, who was born in Melrose in 1818. He was the nephew of the distinguished gardener for Lord Douglas at Bothwell Castle (Lanarkshire), Andrew Turnbull, and was trained by him. Turnbull made a name for himself raising new varieties of *Ericas* (heaths), *Calceolarias*, camellias and orchids.[13]

Lees' name is reported for the first time in 1846, when he followed in his predecessor's footsteps by winning first prize for White Muscat of Alexandria grapes and in the same year was elected as a corresponding member of the Caley. As Head Gardener at Tyninghame in 1851, he had four experienced gardeners, nine labourers and an apprentice under his supervision. Lady Haddington, in an article for the Journal of the RHS in 1971 wrote, ' . . . there was a head gardener for some years by the name of Lees. Records do not mention his fame in the horticultural world but he is remembered as having fifteen children which included three sets of twins!'[14] While it is true that Thomas Lees did not acquire the fame of his successor, Robert Pace Brotherston, nevertheless his name frequently appeared in the reports of prizes at the Caley shows.

In the course of his career at Tyninghame (1846–74?) he regularly won prizes at East Lothian and Edinburgh horticultural shows as well as those at the Caley. For the East Lothian shows he often entered flowers – perhaps the result of the training he received from his uncle – as well as fruit and vegetables. He won prizes

for grapes, both muscat and Black Hamburg, as had his predecessor, David Ford, and for peaches and nectarines.

When the Caley held an 'International Fruit and Flower Show' in September 1869, *The Scotsman* reported that, 'Mr Thomas Lees, gardener to the Earl of Haddington, Tynninghame, has taken second prize with a very good collection (of sixteen sorts of fruit). The lot includes grapes, melons, peaches, nectarines, apricots, figs, pears, plums &c. Among the grapes are two fine bunches of the Tynninghame muscat.'[15] The Tynninghame muscat, was eventually found, like the Bowood and Tottenham Park muscat, to have arisen 'from seedlings having been raised at these places, which have eventually proved to be merely seminal reproductions of the old variety'.[16]

It was probably during Lees' tenure as head gardener that rhododendrons were introduced to the estate on a large scale. One piece of evidence is the rhododendron 'Countess of Haddington'. It is a cross between *R. ciliatum* and *R. dalhousiae* which was raised by William Evans and 'passed to Lees, gardener to Earl of Haddington at Tynninghame, where it was probably named'.[17] The flowers are trumpet shaped, white flushed pale rose and born in a truss; the leaves are dull olive green with golden brown scales below. It is a small plant, extremely floriferous and perfumed but rather tender. Its parents were both collected in north-east India by Joseph Hooker, who started sending seeds and plant material back to Britain in 1849. Joseph's father, William, was Regius Professor of Botany at Glasgow from 1820 until 1841 when he became director of the Royal Botanic Garden at Kew until his death in 1865.

William Wilson Evans, a gardener from Fife, was assistant then curator of the Caley's 'Experimental Garden' at Inverleith from 1848. When the garden became part of the adjacent Botanic Garden of Edinburgh in 1857, Evans' job as curator became redundant and he moved out with his young family to Tynefield, a small farm on the Tyninghame estate, close to the village.[18]

The rhododendron 'Countess of Haddington' must have been raised by Evans sometime before 1857 as its origin was described as 'Experimental Gardens Edinburgh'. It was one of, if not the first, highly scented rhododendron to be hybridised. It was awarded an RHS First Class Certificate (FCC) in 1862. Slightly tender and needing a cool greenhouse in winter, it proved popular for its beautiful scent and prolific flowering. In 1888, an illustration of one of a pair of rhododendron 'Countess of Haddington' appeared in *The Gardeners' Chronicle*, shown by the nurseryman James Cypher of Cheltenham. He said: 'the plant here illustrated, and its fellow, are 6 feet high and 6 feet across

Rhododendron 'Countess of Haddington', 1888

Rhododendron 'Countess of Haddington' at Caerhays (Courtesy of Caerhays Estate)

Paradise Wood and the Garleton Walk

and at Easter last year they bore over 1,000 flowers each'.[19] It is still in cultivation and at Caerhays, Cornwall, it grows well in groups in sheltered, open ground.

At the beginning of the nineteenth century, rhododendrons and azaleas were introduced tentatively, grown in glasshouses and pots, rather than in the pleasure garden. As their hardiness became established and more species were introduced (mainly from America), they advanced outside into shrub borders and collections often called 'American Gardens'. By the middle of the century, plant collectors in Asia were sending back seeds and plant material to individuals, botanic gardens and nurserymen; by the end of the century their place in gardens and woodlands was established.

The 9th Earl 'greatly improved the place by plant-ing Rhododendrons by the woodland paths'.[20] It was probably during his tenure that rhododendrons also made their way into the Binning Wood. A special Rhododendron Walk, or *allée* as it was also known, was planted along the Garleton Walk, the most northerly of the three long avenues that run west–east to the shore. At its western end, by the Binning Wood, the path splits into two parallel paths which continue for a short length and then come together. The name for the woodland at this point on the 1859 estate plan is 'Paradise'.

Evans lived nearby at Tynefield for seven years, so he might even have advised the 9th Earl on the choice of rhododendrons and azaleas to be planted there, although this can only be a matter of conjecture. He would have known Thomas Lees from the Caley and it would be surprising if he did not make frequent visits to his colleague and the gardens and greenhouses under his neighbour's care. As the curator of the Experimental Garden at the time when rhododendron seed was being sent to Edinburgh by Hooker, he was very familiar with the species grown and hybridised in Scotland. Some of them may have found their way to the Rhododendron Walk. A long serving estate worker, Rick Clark and former head gardener Albert Johnston recall the variety of tall rhododendrons that formerly grew along this walk. They survived until the 1960s by which time many were damaged or in poor health and they were grubbed up when new drains were laid; now only *Rhodendron ponticum* remain.

Today, this is considered a pest, an undesirable foreign invasive species which reduces bio-diversity: its leaves are unpalatable to native fauna and it outcompetes native groundcover so its removal is encouraged. It is native to southern Europe and was introduced in the eighteenth century but it was not until the 1840s that it became widely used as cover for game. Not only could it be useful, but it was also beautiful, easy to grow and it was new. It was sown and planted by the million in estates across the British Isles. In an article on the history of rhododendrons in British gardens, Brent Elliott quotes from the first volume of *The Gardeners' Chronicle* (1841), in which Philip Frost, head gardener at Dropmore wrote, 'In woods here we have, by a little attention, thousands of self-sown seedling *Rhododendron ponticum*, growing on any kind of soil excepting stiff clay . . . When in bloom, nothing can surpass the beauty of Rhododendrons in woods'.[21] The temptation to introduce them to the Binning Wood was too strong to resist – and the consequences unforeseen.

William Evans moved away to the Penicuik estate of Sir George Clerk in 1864 to become his estate manager. Lees stayed on at Tyninghame a few more years; the 1871 census showed he and his wife were still living at Tyninghame Garden, in the Head Gardener's House designed by William Burn. Six of his children

were still living at home, but two of his sons, Thomas aged twenty-six and James aged nineteen, had moved into the gardeners' bothy where they were living with three other young gardeners. It was a credit to Thomas that five young men, including two of his sons, chose to train with him.

The fame of the gardens at Tyninghame and the Binning Wood was spreading and beginning to attract visitors as well as apprentices. The 10th Earl and his gardeners were undoubtedly proud of the appearance of the gardens and the Binning Wood, and as tourism developed both were opened to the public towards the end of the summer. A notice of opening times, dated 8 August 1867, stated that they 'will be shown on saturdays from the 17th August to the 26th October, between Twelve and Five p.m. . . . except in wet weather. It is requested no fires may be lit in the woods'.[22]

Thomas Lees was living at the home farm at Archerfield when he died of pleurisy, aged sixty-one, on 7 November 1878.[23] He had been Head Gardener at Tyninghame for over thirty years during which time he worked for the 9th, 10th and the 11th Earls of Haddington. When the 9th Earl died in 1858, he left Thomas an annuity of £200, with a statement 'to mark the Earl's respect for his character and conduct, and his entire satisfaction with his service as "a first rate gardener"'.[24]

George Baillie of Jerviswoode and Mellerstain was fifty-seven when he inherited Tyninghame in 1858 and succeeded to the title of Earl of Haddington. His grandfather had changed his name to Baillie when he inherited Mellerstain in 1730, and George obtained a royal licence to add the family's original name, Hamilton, to that of Baillie. Baillie-Hamilton thus became, and continues to be, the family name of the Earls of

Overleaf: Part of the plantations of Tyninghame, showing the holly hedges, Garleton Walk, Limetree Walk and field names, surveyed by John Mason, 1859 (Courtesy of the Earl of Haddington)

Haddington. From 1858 they had two country seats: Mellerstain and Tyninghame.

One of the first things George undertook on his accession was to commission a survey of his Tyninghame estate. The sketch plan of the plantations of Tyninghame by John Mason in 1859 is the oldest surviving plan of the estate (although an earlier plan of the Knowes and the village surveyed by William Dickinson in 1814 and drawn in 1825 by John Mason also exists).

It provides names and estate details that are absent from the six inch to the mile Ordnance Survey map of the area of 1854. Besides field names, walks, avenues and the famous holly hedges, it also indicates the melon ground by the Walled Garden and tree nurseries in the Binning Wood.

A feature appearing on both maps for the first time was Buist's Embankment on the salt greens south of the Tyne. Buist's Embankment was possibly named for David Buist, whose name first appears as factor from 1810, though the factor at this time was his son Matthew.

The lake that formed at high tide on the salt greens in front of the house was described as 'one of the enlivening and admired features of that magnificent residence. The gentle ebbing of the tide leaves no sediment to spoil the beauty of the greens, which in a short time are seen covered with sheep, and in summer with a profusion of sea-pink.'[25] However, at high spring tides and in bad weather, adjacent arable fields and the turnpike road could be flooded. The writer, the Rev. James Wallace, minister at Whitekirk, also noted that 'there was a waste and sandy marsh of about 300 acres, formed at the estuary of the Tyne which the Earl of Haddington has it in contemplation to embank, and which it is supposed will amply repay the expense'.[26]

The construction of the long embankment probably took place shortly after May 1835. Locally, the story is that it was built by French prisoners-of-war but this was unlikely. The embankment was most likely built by returning Scottish soldiers, looking for work and with experience in building field fortifications.

David Buist died some time before 1841 as his wife Helen was then living as a widow with their son Matthew in the factor's house in Tyninghame. David was succeeded as factor by Matthew, whose name appears on the census as factor in 1841, 1851 and 1861. Matthew died in 1873 and so would have spent much of his working life alongside the head gardener, Thomas Lees.

The holly hedges, which had so impressed William Boutcher in 1775, also shown on Mason's plan, were no longer as extensive as they had once been, but they were still the glory of Tyninghame. They became famous, not just in Scotland through the *New Statistical Account* of 1835, but across the whole of Great Britain. Joseph Sabine gave a paper to the London Horticultural Society in 1827: 'An Account of some Remarkable Holly Hedges and Trees in Scotland' which was published in their *Transactions* in 1830.

He admired the beauty and size of the hedges at Tyninghame as well as their extent – 2,952 yards, in other words over a mile-and-a-half (2.7 kilometres). They were regularly clipped in April and took five labourers about three weeks. The most remarkable were those along the former Hard Gait: ' . . . the walk is 743 yards long. These hedges are eleven feet broad at the base, and fifteen feet high.'[27] J. C. Loudon relied heavily on this paper when he included a description of the hedges in his *Arboretum et Fruticetum Britannicum*, concluding that they were the finest in Britain.

By the time R. P. Brotherston became head gardener in 1874, the hedges had been reduced and, although still impressive, they were beginning to exhibit signs of decay. David Croal visited and described them in 1873: 'here and there large gaps are visible in the rows, those who are still alive recollect when they presented such a solidity of vegetation that it was quite a common feat for the boys in the village to walk on the top of them!'[28]

CHAPTER 12

The Head Gardener and the Painter

At the Drill Hall in Westminster on 23 July 1895, members of the Royal Horticultural Society enjoyed an afternoon lecture on 'The History of the Carnation in Scotland', given by Mr R. P. Brotherston. Robert Pace Brotherston was the Head Gardener at Tyninghame from 1874 to 1923.

R. P. Brotherston

His choice of subject revealed his long-lasting love affair with flowers, especially 'old-fashioned flowers', their history and his native country, Scotland. His interest in the history of horticulture in all its aspects became something of a passion; during his lifetime he assembled a remarkable collection of antiquarian books which was auctioned by Sotheby's in London after his death. It was an unusual legacy for a gardener.

Brotherston, like his predecessors, was from the Borders. Born in Ednam, Berwickshire, he not only enjoyed the practical side of horticulture but he also enjoyed writing about it, its history and its literature. He wrote well over 300 articles in gardening journals as well as three books, *The Book of the Carnation* (1904), *The Book of Cut Flowers* (1906) and *Gardening in the North* (1909), written with S. Arnott. His writing painted a detailed picture of the practical horticulture of his day, when labour was plentiful at Tyninghame.

He won prizes at national and local horticultural shows as his predecessors had done – not usually for grapes but on several occasions for apples, gladioli and occasionally for vegetables. When the RHS decided to hold a 'National Apple Congress' at their garden in Chiswick in October 1883, Brotherston was on the Scottish committee and exhibited ninety-three varieties grown at Tyninghame. (The gardener to the Duke of Buccleuch exhibited 220.) He was awarded the Patrick

Neill Memorial Medal by the Caley in 1904. It is one of the highest accolades for horticulture in Scotland and is still awarded biannually.

Even before Brotherston came to Tyninghame as head gardener, he had begun writing for horticultural journals. His earliest articles appeared in 1871 in *The Gardener – A magazine of Horticulture and Floriculture*, edited by fellow Scot, David Thomson, gardener to the Duke of Buccleuch at Drumlanrig. He signed his articles for *The Gardener* either R. P. Brotherston or R.P.B., and continued with them until 1881, just before the magazine ceased publication in 1882. His favourite theme was the flower garden and its contents, although his contributions covered all aspects of the culture of fruit and vegetables, the maintenance of the garden and hothouses, and the cultivation of flowers for the house.

Cut flowers became the subject of his second book – it was the head gardener's responsibility to provide decorations already prepared for the table and for the rooms of the house at all seasons of the year. His writing was always informed, full of examples and invariably accompanied with his personal observations – and his opinions. Writing on 'The Tomato', which was still a novelty in 1876, he noted that in America it was appreciated in its raw state and that some hotels in England even included it for breakfast. He prophesied 'it will only be a matter of time when it is a necessity for private families to eat it raw, rather than as cooked at present'.[1]

Another, more significant early observation on fashion in flower gardens, written just at the time he came to Tyninghame in 1874, was prophetic: 'The taste for hardy flowers appears to be on the increase, so much so, that the hardy herbaceous border will, before long, be in all probability a recognised institution in a well-appointed garden.' He then went on to list those hardy perennials and biennials he thought suitable – a long list including varieties of *Campanula*, *Dianthus*, *Delphinium*, *Gladiolus*, *Penstemon*, *Phlox*, *Aquilegia*, *Anemone japonica*, *Linum perenne*, *Crinum*, *Agapanthus*, *Lithospermum*, *Papaver alpinum*, *Nepeta*, *Gentiana*, *Geranium*, *Lilium*, *Antirrhinum*, *Alstroemeria*, *Lychnis*, *Lupinus*, *Sedum*, and many native plants such as 'the sweet blue-bell' of Scotland (*Campanula rotundifolia*), sea pinks (*Armeria maritima*), thyme (*Thymus*), Dame's violet (*Hesperis matronalis*) and Jacob's Ladder (*Polemonium var.*). If the border was wide enough, he recommended hollyhocks, dahlias, sweet peas 'and taller growing sorts of herbaceous flowers' as a fine background.[2]

Throughout his career Brotherston showed an interest in 'old fashioned flowers' by which he meant the flowers traditionally grown in Scottish gardens in earlier centuries rather than the tender new arrivals flooding in from abroad. He was was not only interested in native plants but in their old Scottish names too.

The Irishman William Robinson is generally credited with giving hardy perennials a predominant place in the garden. His book *The Wild Garden* was published in 1870, and the seminal *The English Flower Garden* appeared in 1883 before going into fifteen editions during his lifetime. Many of these editions had a quotation from William Morris as a frontispiece: 'Another thing, also much too commonly seen, is an aberration of the human mind, which otherwise I would have been ashamed to warn you of. It is technically called carpet gardening. Need I explain it further? I had rather not, for when I think of it, even when I am quite alone, I blush with shame at the thought.'[3]

'Carpet' bedding was one of the main features of the Victorian garden. At Tyninghame the original parterre to the west of the house and the beds cut into the south lawn that Burn had created in 1830 were the obvious sites for these 'carpets'. Typically, they could be displays in which single rows of the same plant were set out like ribbons, with space between the rows and sometimes with a measured gradation in height. These were particularly suitable for long beds and the

A Valentine's postcard of Tyninghame House from the south, with regimented 'carpet bedding', 1888

patterns could be sinuous scrolls or more geometric, as in a Greek key design. An alternative was the 'panel' in which a pattern was created with different coloured plants in an island bed. These often had a taller standard plant or even mounds at the centre, raised above the groundwork, all carefully graded.

A Valentine's postcard of the garden at Tyninghame in 1888 shows the island beds cut into the lawn in a variety of shapes including an H for Hamilton (or Haddington) and some are mounded.

Two old raised stone beds in the lawn were also filled with annual plants. The ivy and other climbing plants, including roses, against the house were popular at the time (although William Robinson banned ivy from house walls). The clipped evergreens in Versailles tubs under the balcony were probably bay, *Laurus nobilis*, rather than citrus fruit trees. They masked the rooms on the ground floor where the staff were working.

No doubt Morris would have blushed at the sight of this postcard from Valentine, and Robinson would have remonstrated fiercely, but Brotherston may have felt duty-bound to include the half-hardy bedding plants and tender plants he had been trained to produce. All over the country there was still a strong demand for such long-lasting brightly coloured displays which justified the considerable investments

Overleaf: The double herbaceous border in the Walled Garden (Courtesy of *Country Life*)

made in the latest greenhouse technology by the owners of large gardens like Tyninghame. Even Robinson included a chapter on bedding plants in the first twelve editions of *The English Flower Garden*, perhaps in acknowledgement of their on-going popularity.[4]

For Robinson, the ideal was for the flower garden to be within easy access of the sitting rooms. 'In olden times . . . the place for the flower garden was quite near the house; and that is the place for it now. The Scottish way of going half a mile to the kitchen garden to find the flower garden there is not the best.'[5] But that is exactly where Brotherston introduced double herbaceous borders and his garden of old-fashioned flowers. Writing about Victorian gardens in his *History of Gardening in Scotland*, E. H. M. Cox noted that 'The mixed border at Tyninghame must have been very fine, for it was one of the few that was regularly mentioned. But as a rule herbaceous plants were ignored; the relics of the old borders so loved by previous generations were relegated to the edges of the shrubberies where they gradually succumbed.'[6]

The earliest photograph of the borders appeared in an article in *Country Life* in August 1902. It showed them stretching the whole length of the garden, a distance of roughly 150 metres, backed by a low yew hedge which marked the division with the vegetable garden. There were good reasons why the splendid borders should look their best as this was an important year for Tyninghame. The 11th Earl was appointed a Knight of the Thistle in the Coronation Honours, and King Edward VII visited the garden later that year.

Brotherston established the double border at Tyninghame well before Gertrude Jekyll's books appeared at the beginning of the twentieth century, but evidence for an exact date is lacking. However, he never gave up his use of 'carpet bedding' around the house; the two approaches existed alongside each other and planting on the south lawns and parterre continued in this style until the mid twentieth century.

The Walled Garden featured both half-hardy and hardy annuals in a different way: as 'fillers' among the hardy herbaceous plants. Here, besides the double herbaceous borders, Brotherston took pride in a formal knot garden of low box hedges, described in *Country Life* as 'a little old-world garden, presided over by the cut yew peacock, which is dedicated to old-fashioned English flowers, herbs and the rarer bulbs'.[7]

Roses featured all over the garden – some growing against the perimeter walls alongside the fruit trees – the pale yellow *Banksiae* climbing rose was mentioned; the old favourite 'Gloire de Dijon', together with 'Cheshunt' hybrid and Ayrshire roses, were some of those growing against the trellises that bordered a wide grass path. This was a cross-path known as the Green Walk, which had arches covered with honeysuckle intersecting the trellises. The rose garden itself, was 'of dainty formal design and high box edgings, planted out lately with teas and hybrid teas, each bed containing a different variety'.[8] The design of this section of the garden, on either side of the steps to the Camellia House at the north end, has not been changed: the 'high box edgings' are still there, although the roses have been replaced with lavender.

Another of Brotherston's innovations was the Apple Walk, over 100 metres long, to the south of the Walled Garden and accessed from the central path through the old stone doorway at the southern end.

In the photograph (p. 156) a small fountain of a cherub as a water carrier can be glimpsed. Neither the fountain nor the lead figures remain; the fountain has been replaced with a small statue of a monk, recalling Tyninghame as the home of St Baldred. The main apple variety in the photograph was 'Keswick Codlin', chosen for the beauty of its flowers rather than for its fruit, but many of these have been replaced over the years. All around the kitchen garden apples had been grown as free-standing espaliers along paths, against walls as well as in a small, grassed orchard area so there was plenty of choice when it came to exhibitions. At the National Apple Congress in 1883, Brotherston was

The Apple Walk

complemented in particular for 'Ecklinvale Seedling', 'Mère de Ménage' and 'East Lothian Seedling'.

Brotherston won several prizes for apples from Tyninghame exhibited at the Caley autumn shows in the mid 1880s. His articles for *The Garden* included pieces on apple culture as well as others on the cultivation of apricots, cherries, pears, plums and, of course, grapes. In *Gardening in the North*, the authors state: 'Fruit is the highest type of garden produce; success in its production is the greatest attainment of the culti-

vator.'[9] It was invariably the domain of the head gardener, and Brotherston was confident in his expertise. He wrote several articles on pruning, even giving another lecture to the members of the RHS in London on 15 August 1899, but he was always keen to point out that pruning could only be learned by experience and observation. Needless to say, he was familiar with fruit varieties which did well in Scotland, often providing the Scots' equivalent alongside their Latin names: peres, plumes, brambles (blackberries), blackberries

Old stone doorway in the south wall with eighteenth-century painted lead figures, from *Country Life* (Courtesy of *Country Life*)

(blackcurrants), rizzers (red and white currants) and grosars (gooseberries).

Lying between the Walled Garden and the house is the area still known by its original name, the Wilderness, though by the end of the nineteenth century more flowering shrubs, exotic trees and bulbs had been introduced. Any formality of design had disappeared, but many of the original trees survived: beeches, sycamores, limes, sweet chestnuts, deciduous and ever-

green oaks and cedars. If remnants of holly, yew and box hedges remained (and remain) it was as single specimens here and there.

Besides replacements of native trees, the new 'exotics' from abroad were usually from the west coast of America. Seeds of Wellingtonias, *Sequoiadendrum giganteum*, for example, eventually found their way into parks and estates across the country. The exact date of their entry into Tyninghame is uncertain; one was planted to the south-east of the bowling green where it thrived and has become the tallest tree in the Wilderness. Others have been planted along the Sea Avenue, almost marking the site of the old farm that once stood there. Further nineteenth-century American introductions included coast redwoods (*Sequoia sempervirens*), Monterey (*Pinus radiata*) and Ponderosa pines (*Pinus ponderosa*), and Douglas fir (*Pseudotsuga menziesii*). Other trees introduced into the Wilderness about this time were a deodar cedar (*Cedrus deodara*) from the Himalayas, the Atlantic cedar (*Cedrus atlantica*) from the Atlas Mountains in Morocco, and the Oriental, or Caucasian, spruce (*Picea orientalis*) from the eastern end of the Black Sea. Although its name had not changed and it was still considered a place for pleasure rather than for scientific study, the Wilderness had become, in effect, an arboretum, reflecting the taste which developed as the nineteenth century progressed and as exotic trees became available.

Sadly, the great gale of 1881 destroyed thousands of trees and uprooted some of the best specimens.[10] It struck the Borders and the south-east coast of Scotland with particular force, causing 189 fishermen, mostly from Eyemouth, to lose their lives. Given their coastal position, the woods at Tyninghame were among the worst affected.

An account of the havoc was published in the *Transactions of the Highland and Agricultural Society of Scotland* in 1885. 'Binning Wood has been completely and irreplaceably disfigured . . . the havoc created by the storm is something quite indescribable. The stately beeches of magnificent size, which surrounded the bowling green, styled The Wilderness, have all gone and other well-known specimen trees of noble size have shared the same fate. Nowhere amongst the numerous records of destruction by this gale is there any instance to be compared with the desolation and utter blank disorder spread around fair Tyninghame . . .' Well over 6,000 Scots fir (*Pinus sylvestris*), 1,000 oaks and about 2,800 beech came down that day. The writer estimated

that it would take three years to clear the debris. In fact, during the first year 'fully 100 men have been employed in the woods, by the various purchasing firms, and four steam engines, two traction engines, and three saw mills have been erected, presenting quite a novel view of backwoodsman life in this district'.[11]

There are no images of the Wilderness at Tyninghame during Brotherston's tenure to illustrate his planting there but, after a visit in 1905, Samuel Arnott FRHS, who collaborated with Brotherston to produce *Gardening in the North*, wrote: 'The garden overflows into the woods . . . and we see what is called wild gardening of the best kind carried out on a broad and well considered style. In the "Wilderness" and elsewhere there are myriads of coloured primroses, Snowdrops, Narcissi, wild Tulips and other plants covering the ground everywhere, and making a walk among them delightful.'[12] Of all the 'wild planting' effects advocated by Robinson, extensive drifts of naturalised bulbs in grass was one of the most easily achieved and had long been a feature of the gardens. When writing one of his articles on the flower garden in 1881, Brotherston commented: 'Whilst writing this there is a "garden on the grass" close by, of some 15 to 20 acres in extent, the greater portion of which is covered with Primroses in every possible shade of colour, from white to maroon. They are absolutely countless in number. When they were first planted, no-one seems to know . . .'[13]

At the beginning of 1914, Brotherston wrote a series of six articles on making and maintaining an herbaceous border for *The Garden*, the magazine that Robinson had founded in 1872. The 'thoroughness' which had been noted by Arnott on his visit, perhaps the hallmark of a good gardener, was evident in his account. Brotherston recommended lifting every plant every year: cultivate, rearrange and replant.[14] As to whether the herbaceous border saved labour and money, as Robinson maintained, Brotherston was dubious: if 'the plants and their environs [are] kept equally well, the

Primroses in the Wilderness

hardy flower man has nothing in his favour in the above respects'.

When it came to the arrangement of plants in the border, he cautioned that perfection was elusive. Nevertheless, he offered the readers three examples of his planting designs from Tyninghame borders that had met with success the previous year. He was trying to achieve a more natural way of planting avoiding the regularity found in carpet bedding schemes.

As for the colours, much had been written on this topic and Gertrude Jekyll's book, *Colour Schemes for the Flower Garden* had appeared in 1908, although Brotherston did not refer to it in his articles. He gave no underlying theories as guidelines and instead presented his own observations on certain colours and combinations which worked and some that did not. These were combinations of strong, clear colours rather than the subtle gradations that Jekyll proposed.

Many of his observations were astute: he wisely noted white was a colour that should be used with care and for its intrinsic value rather than as a buffer between jarring colours. It went well with blues but

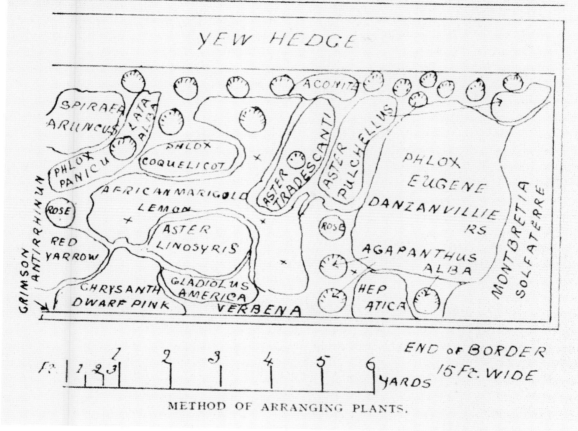

Section of a Tyninghame border including sulphur montbretia, lilac phlox, dwarf pink chrysanthemum, lemon African marigold, verbena and white and blue agapanthus

not with reds, where cream was usually preferable. As for those who criticised the repetition of colours or plants in a border, they 'have never discovered how an extensive border is to be furnished by any other means . . . some plants may be used in every little gap without giving the least feeling of sameness'. His final piece of advice showed him always willing to learn: he urged his readers not to be ashamed to ask for advice from those who had a more educated colour sense.

He had done precisely that when he consulted his friend, the painter Robert Noble, for advice on a

chapter on colour for *The Book of Cut Flowers*, published in 1906. Brotherston had been invited to write the book by the Caley after winning an essay competition on the subject of cut flowers. Many of the horticultural societies, including the RHS in London and the Caley, offered prizes for floral decoration, traditionally the domain of the head gardener. By the beginning of the twentieth century, they were all becoming increasingly concerned that the burgeoning trade in flowers was leading to vulgar excesses and that they needed to set higher standards. One of the conditions

Dinner-table decorated with Palms. (The pots are hidden under the table, as in cut below.) Reproduced, by permission of Messrs W. Blackwood & Sons, from *Domestic Floriculture*, 1874.

Dinner table decoration with palms – an illustration from *Domestic Floriculture*, 1874

of publication was that Brotherston should read the essays of his fellow competitors and take them into consideration in his text. All essayists agreed that simple ways of arranging flowers were best and none had time for any of the 'accessories used at dinner tables, nor of the devices for drawing rooms'. These had developed into 'jungles of tropical vegetation' and veritable gardens on the dining tables of those years.

A bibliography included as an appendix showed that his was one of the earliest books in English on floral arrangements – Gertrude Jekyll's book, *Flower Decoration in the House*, came out the following year. In Scotland, Miss Frances Hope of Wardie Lodge, Edinburgh, had written various articles on gardening during her lifetime, including on floral decoration and these were collected and published in 1881, after her death.

Brotherston valued her words, written in the 1870s, because 'there were no false theories of arrangement, no abnormal shapes in glasses . . .'[15] He included in his bibliography eleven books published in German or French between 1886 and 1904.

One theme came out very strongly from the pages of Brotherston's book – simplicity. He urged his readers not to despise common or native plants, 'a snowdrop . . . is not less pure and lovely because it never saw the inside of a greenhouse'.[16] Quantity was not essential, the charm of the individual flowers was important and, unless for a drawing room, the material for the vase could be quite humble – a jam jar for example.

It was not surprising therefore that he was attracted to the art of ikebana, the Japanese style of floral arrangement. Josiah Conder, an English architect working in Japan, was responsible for opening a window onto this aspect of Japanese culture for a Western audience. His illustrated book, *The Flowers of Japan and the Art of Floral Arrangement*, was published in English in Tokyo in 1891 and, with the author's permission, Brotherston reproduced some of the illustrations. While he was personally very attracted to this Japanese art form, whose 'principles bestow a due regard on every part of the plant – on flower, stem, leaf and branch . . .'[17] he conceded that many would find their methods too constrained.

Whether the copy of Josiah Conder's classic, now a rare collector's item, belonged to Brotherston or to the 11th Earl, George Baillie-Hamilton-Arden, is not known. The collection of books in the library at Tyninghame, begun by the 1st Earl, contained several volumes on gardening and forestry, going back to John Evelyn and John Reid in the seventeenth century; successive generations had added items of horticultural significance. Brotherston had an extensive knowledge and collection of horticultural books but he was indebted to the Earl and Countess of Haddington, whose library was always at his disposal.[18]

Brotherston's earliest writing was on practical horti-

Giant Christmas Rose, own leaf, leaf of Megasea, and spray of Quaking Grass in earthenware jar. The beauty of the stems should not be overlooked.

Christmas roses in a jar

cultural matters, but after 1897 he began to write on garden and gardening history for *The Gardeners' Chronicle*. Beginning with the first book published in Scotland on gardening, his first article was on *The Scots Gard'ner* by John Reid, though he was unaware of the Haddington family's connections with Niddry Castle. Later, he wrote articles on garden history for the *Journal of Horticulture*.

Above: *Whitekirk and Binning Wood* by Robert Noble (Courtesy of the Victor Murphy Trust)

Opposite: *Rhododendrons* by Robert Noble

His fascination with plant names, especially vernacular ones, and his botanist's urge for accuracy had been practiced since he was a young man. The interest he developed in the history of gardening and its literature may have come from his early education and during his apprenticeship as a gardener under Mr Thom at Newton Don, Kelso, the home of Lady Eleanor Balfour. His obituary in *The Journal of Botany* recorded that 'Chiefly self-educated, Brotherston had a good acquaintance with Latin and French and some knowledge of Greek.'[19]

Sadly, he did not live long enough to enjoy life in retirement with a garden in the village. He died three months after retiring, on 21 December 1923, and was buried at Whitekirk on Christmas Day. Several obituaries appeared in the horticultural journals for which he had written throughout his life.

The gardens at Tyninghame reached their zenith

during the years when Robert Brotherston was still Head Gardener, as the pages of *Country Life* testified. When King Edward VII visited the earl and countess in 1902, he planted an oak tree on the edge of the Wilderness. The gardens around the house, the walled kitchen garden and the holly hedges were not the only attractions: the Binning Wood, 200 years old, was fully mature with grand avenues of broadleaf trees and Scots pine; there was also 'the Garleton Walk of rhododendrons of all shades and sorts, including the Himalayan and Sikkim varieties, which run for a mile or more to the sea'.[20] It was this planting that attracted Brotherston's friend, the East Linton painter Robert Noble.

Noble (1857–1917) made his home in East Linton in 1887. He had trained first with his cousin, the landscape painter James Campbell Noble, and later spent time in France for further study in Paris, but little is known about his early life and his travels there.[21] His

paintings were mainly landscapes and scenes in France and, after 1887, mostly of East Lothian. He was part of a sociable group of painters, some of whom had studied together in Edinburgh in the 1870s, who enjoyed the landscape and working village life in East Lothian and along the Berwickshire coast. Moreover, they felt landscapes should be painted in the open air, *en plein air*, rather than in the studio. They followed a path similar to that of their more famous contemporaries – the Glasgow Boys and Girls.

Noble was drawn to the expansive landscapes of East Lothian, which he often painted in fading light, as in *Whitekirk and Binning Wood*. He returned often to paint scenes along the banks of the Tyne in East Linton and the surrounding farmland; on at least one occasion he painted rhododendrons at Tyninghame. His painting *Rhododendrons* does not mention Tyninghame by name but it can be placed there, and possibly dated, through another painting of the same scene by his friend, Robert Payton Reid (1859–1945). This is titled *In the Rhododendron Alley at Tyninghame, Haddington, Scotland, 1889*, and bears a striking likeness to the painting by Noble. In both paintings towering white (possibly *Rh. Griffithianum*), and pink and mauve (*Rh. Ponticum?*) rhododendrons border the grass path. Noble included golden yellow azaleas, absent in Payton Reid's painting, and in the middle distance, a seated figure of a painter at his easel, possibly Payton Reid, executed with a few suggestive brush strokes. Noble's painting was probably also painted in 1889 and was sold at Christie's in 1917, the year of his death.

The size of the rhododendrons indicate they were at least thirty or forty years old when they were painted, which coincides with the evidence given orally by the 11th Earl in the article in *Country Life* (August 1902). Some of these Asian introductions, although hardy, were (and are) fairly short lived, whereas *Rhododendron ponticum*, on the other hand, which had been introduced earlier, readily increased.

During and after the First World War, country estates all over the British Isles had to economise and their priorities had to change. Around the house and in the Walled Garden at Tyninghame, Robert Brotherston took it all in his stride, cleverly combining efficiency with economy, showing that he could 'carry on' when circumstances were not propitious. But maintaining the rhododendrons in the Garleton Walk was not one of his priorities.

Throughout his forty-nine years as Head Gardener, the gardens at Tyninghame had never been so well cared for. The 11th Earl and Countess gave him every encouragement and were reluctant to see him retire. The friend who wrote his obituary for *The Gardeners' Chronicle*, remembered him as a valued contributor who always had his own opinions on horticultural matters but who never maintained his was the only view:

> He never spoke roughly or dipped his pen in acid . . . A gardener by nature, by training and by choice, he did all he possibly could to ennoble the profession he so greatly loved. To have the care of a garden, to discuss plants and flowers with plant and garden lovers, and to study old gardening literature were his chief interests, and he could no more help writing of the matters he discovered or discussed than he could do an unkind or mean thing.[22]

Much of his legacy survives – the Apple Walk, the yew hedges and design of the cross-walks in the Walled Garden, for example, not to mention the succeeding generations of plants he loved, from honeysuckle to the hardy anemone 'Honorine Jobert' which still thrive in the garden. But in the 1960s, the rhododendrons in the Garleton Walk and the double herbaceous border he had designed and which had been the pride of Tyninghame, were both taken out. Change was on the way.

CHAPTER 13

Destruction and Renewal

Robert Brotherston, Robert Noble and the 11th Earl of Haddington all lost sons in the First World War. All were deeply affected, but the war itself left barely a mark on the landscape at Tyninghame. The regiment that had been formed as the Lothians and Border Yeomanry in 1797 in the face of the threat of a Napoleonic invasion, after several name changes, had become the Lothian and Border Horse Yeomanry, sometimes known as the 'Princes Street Lancers' or 'Loathsome and Bloody'. Their annual summer camps

Off duty on Race Day, Belhaven Sands, 1891, by Robert Payton Reid (Courtesy of the Scottish and North Irish Yeomanry)

took place across the county often with exercises in the Lammermuir Hills but always finishing at Belhaven Bay, which then formed part of the Tyninghame estate. There was a concert party, a parade and horse races along the sands – quite a social event. Robert Payton Reid's painting of officers relaxing on the beach at the end of the century captured part of the ambience.

It was a scene that would have been familiar to Brigadier General George Baillie-Hamilton, Lord Binning (1856–1917). At the time, his father was living at the Tyninghame estate while he and his family lived at Mellerstain. Although he had retired from the army in 1907, he presided over the military and social events of the 'Lothians' as he remained their Lieutenant Colonel.

However, social events at Belhaven Sands became a thing of the past once war broke out in 1914. The 'Lothians' were deployed abroad when more men were needed in France to support the British Expeditionary Force. The *Hawick Express* reported on Friday 15 October 1915: 'Although in his 59th year, Colonel Lord Geo. Baillie Hamilton, CB, MVO., (Lord Binning,) has left for the front in command of the Lothian and Border Horse.' Lord Binning's eldest son, also George, was an officer in the 2nd Dragoons (Royal Scots Greys) and served with them in France.

In December 1915, Lord Binning was made a temporary brigadier general, put in command of the 41st Brigade and assigned to the 14th Light Division. He saw no significant military action during these months but his health was badly affected by the winter conditions. In April he returned to Britain to take charge of the 11th Mounted Division.[1] He was on furlough at home at Tyninghame with his ailing father when his health deteriorated further and 'flu turned into pneumonia. He died aged sixty on 12 January 1917, a few months before his father, the 11th Earl, who died on 11 June 1917 aged ninety.

The estate then passed to the earl's grandson, George (1894–1986), who was awarded the Military

Cross in the same year. He was twenty-three and was to fight in two world wars. Having served in the intervening years with the 'L and B', which from 1921 to 1938 was called the 19th Armoured Car Company (Lothians and Border Yeomanry) as tanks replaced horses (and bicycles), he became a major in 1938.[2] George, or Geordie as he was known, was second in command to his friend, CO Lieutenant Colonel Harry Younger. It was one of the coldest winters on record, and in February 1940 he caught pneumonia and was evacuated home from France. From then on, he could only follow the news from afar as the regiment joined the famous 51st Highland Division and took up positions in front of the Maginot Line.[3] Its defence eventually proved impossible, and they were ordered to retreat but were then cut off from evacuation at Dunkirk and from Le Havre. 'Of the 500 officers and men of the 1st Lothians and Border Yeomanry, only 20 returned to the UK. The rest were either killed, wounded or captured . . .'[4] In 1941 George joined the Royal Air Force Volunteer Reserve (RAFVR) and became Wing Commander.

The Second World War left deep scars, not only on the people, but on the fields, woodland and beaches of the Tyninghame estate. The evacuation of Dunkirk at the end of May had been a much-needed boost to civilian morale which helped to alleviate the defeat. But defeat it was. In Scotland there was anticipation of an invasion by German troops from occupied Norway. In the same month General Ironside was hastily made commander-in-chief of the Home Forces. His plan for Home Defence included providing a defensive 'coastal crust' to fight off small raids and delay enemy landings.

The naval dockyards at Rosyth and the Forth Railway Bridge were seen as possible targets in need of special defensive measures and, in June 1940, the Tyne estuary was identified by Scottish Command as one of two areas vulnerable to attack and of concern.[5] Many of the coastal defences – tank traps, pillboxes,

Anti-tank blocks at Mosshouse Point

trenches and anti-glider poles – erected on the Tyningham estate in 1940 still remain in place to this day.[6]

The most noticeable reminders are the large concrete blocks, one and a half metres high and just over a metre square, in single, double or even triple lines marching along the dunes, through the trees and occasionally onto the beaches where they are now sinking into the sand. They extended along the low shoreline from Mosshouse Point, for almost two kilometres, through the Tyninghame Links and Fir Links Wood, ending at Scoughall, where the cliffs and rocks made tank invasion impossible.

Concrete pillboxes were sited where there was a wide field of view. The best preserved is on the edge of Fir Links Wood, with views across Hedderwick Bay towards Dunbar. It is partly sunk into the ground, now covered in grass with large bushes of sea buckthorn growing round about which hang low and camouflage it from the seaward side. Two other structures that were built into the cliff face on the north-western side of Whitberry Point have almost fallen into the sea. Some forty or fifty metres inland are the remains of a small trench system.

Two of the main tracks leading down to the beach have wartime gate 'buttresses', massive blocks with slots on one side and holes on the other for horizontal

Second World War pillbox at the edge of Fir Links Wood

railway lines or steel joists which could be slotted into position. Together with large corrugated concrete cylinders that could be man-handled into position, they made roadblocks which could be quickly opened or closed.

The final vestiges of wartime defences are the remains of anti-glider posts on both sides of Hedderwick Bay. The salt flats that make up the estuary of the Tyne were identified as a possible landing area for enemy planes. At low tide two or three lines of wooden stumps, roughly twenty-two metres apart, extend for several hundred yards. They indicate the positions of

'Rommel's Asparagus', as they were known by both sides. Originally two or three metres tall, they have either been cut or have worn down and are now rotting in the mud in their concrete bases. Taken together, the reminders of the Second World War scattered along the coastal fringe of the Tyninghame estate form one of the best preserved sea defence complexes, now recognised as part of Scotland's heritage.

The war had a much greater impact on the Tyninghame woodland however. Under the Control of Timber Order (1941) the Ministry of Supply requisitioned timber to maintain 'supplies, and services, essential to the life of the Community'. Both Binning Wood and Brownrigg were clear felled, along with others in East Lothian. The 6th Earl and his wife had always understood that planting trees on a large scale could be a commercial enterprise for the estate, and their descendants had upheld the estate forestry for over 300 years. As the 12th Earl made clear in a paper he wrote for the *Journal of the Royal Scottish Forestry Society* in 1967,[7] the estate would never have countenanced the clear felling of the entire Binning and Brownrigg woods, but there was no choice. In total, just over 10,000 trees of good quality were felled between 1942 and 1945. 'Some of the Beech was of a very fine quality and this was used to make the fuselages for Mosquito Aircraft, the famous reconnaissance bomber of the period.'[8] Huge as these losses were in the Binning Wood, they had been surpassed by the losses across the estate sixty years before in the gales of 1881. In neither case could the estate realise the full value of the timber as merchants were over-supplied after the gale and prices were strictly controlled during the war.

In the story told by the earl, he concentrated on his own personal recollections, and he included the statistics in appendices. As a boy he recalled that the avenues of the Binning Wood were easy to maintain as there was more moss than grass because of the shade. 'I can remember my grandfather on his old chestnut hackney "Cockatoo". When his horse was 40, and my grandfather 80, he still rode him about the wood.'[9] Although there was a strong iron fence along the North Berwick road, the gates were not locked and there was free public access.

Felling the Binning Wood took barely two years, but its replanting after the war began in 1947 and took more than ten years to complete. There were six foresters on the estate at this time. The main problem preventing the establishment of young trees was the *Rhododendron ponticum* which was a constant menace. After the clear felling 'many acres of rhododendrons

Plaque commemorating the replanting of the Binning Wood, 1960

remained, drawn up by the high trees, in some instances to 50 ft. or more, and with trunks of 6 ft. circumference'.[10] It proved impossible to remove all the roots, which resulted in a higher proportion of Scots pine planted than previously; they grew faster than hardwood transplants and could, in theory, suppress the weeds. A further complication was that beech and oak were in short supply after the war, and expensive. As a result, most of the beech was raised in the Tyninghame nursery (some from Tyninghame beech masts). As for the pine, much of these were also raised in the nursery from seed from Darnaway, Cawdor and Mellerstain.

The Earl of Haddington himself visited the wood regularly to make sure the original rides, which could still be traced on the ground, were accurately replanted and from time to time he even helped with the work.[11] It was eventually completed in 1960 and commemorated with a plaque on a stone cairn in the middle of Helen's Circle.

With its long rides and majestic avenues of trees, the Binning Wood had been open to the public at regular intervals from at least 1867, and possibly earlier. When Queen Victoria was driven past on the way back to Broxmouth from North Berwick in August 1878, she said it had reminded her of Windsor Forest.[12] It was many years before the trees formed the kind of stands and woodland canopy that attracted visitors again and during this time the gates remained locked. On the other hand, the gardens around the house at Tyninghame were among the first to open to summer visitors under Scotland's Gardens Scheme. Garden open days began to raise money in 1931 for the Queen's Nursing Institute in Scotland, as the Queen's Nurses, or District Nurses, were known. At the time, the Queen's Nurses had neither pensions nor adequate funds for training. Entry was one shilling.

The 12th Earl and his Countess came to live at Tyninghame in 1953. While George was serving as aide-de-camp to the governor-general of Canada in Montreal, he had met Sarah Cook. They married there in 1923 and then returned to Scotland, living at Mellerstain until the death of his mother, Lady Binning, in 1954. She had been widowed in 1917 but had stayed on, looking after the estate. Once at Tyninghame, both became actively involved in improvements: he in the Binning Wood and she in the gardens.

These were not the only interests of the 12th Earl and the Countess of Haddington. She was a concert pianist and was involved in setting up the first Edinburgh International Festival in 1947 and remained a member of the Festival Committee for fourteen years. The earl was the first president of the Edinburgh Georgian Group, which became the Architectural Heritage Society of Scotland. He was also a trustee of the National Library of Scotland (1963–86), president of the Society of Antiquaries of Scotland (1945–50) as well as chairman of the trustees of the National Museum of Antiquities of Scotland. (He donated over 150 items of costume and textiles to this museum in 1977. Three are still on display.) There were also public duties associated with his aristocratic title – he was a representative Scottish peer in the House of Lords from 1922 to 1958, Lord Lieutenant of East Lothian from 1952 to 1970 and was made a Knight of the Thistle in 1951.

While her husband concentrated on the forestry, the Countess of Haddington was drawn to garden making. The land on the clifftops and above the beaches was still part of the estate. The first of the many garden design projects that Lady Sarah began when they came to live at Tyninghame was a surprising choice: to replant the clifftops above Bathan's Strand and Ravensheugh beach. She was particularly attracted to this spot and wanted to enhance the planting to make a wild, seaside garden on what was then a fairly barren site. She turned for advice to James Russell, an Old Etonian whose family owned Sunningdale Nurseries in Windlesham, Surrey, and who was to advise her for the next eleven years.

As the nursery trade began to recover gradually after the war and Jim Russell's reputation as a plantsman established itself throughout Britain and Ireland, many of his Old Etonian friends asked him for help with their estates. His passion for plants took him all over the country, from Gosford House, East Lothian, for the Earl of Wemyss and March from 1951 to 1953, to Culzean Castle, Ayrshire, for the National Trust for Scotland between 1952 and 1956.[13] In all, he was involved in the design and planting of fifty-five gardens in Scotland between 1951 and 1991, and yet his name is not well known by the general public.

His first letter to Lady Haddington, dated 15 October 1955, consisted of seven folio sheets of single-spaced typing with ideas for planting the clifftop garden and the promise of a plan to follow, together with suggestions for other parts of the garden, plant lists and prices.[14]

For the approach to the clifftop he suggested wild

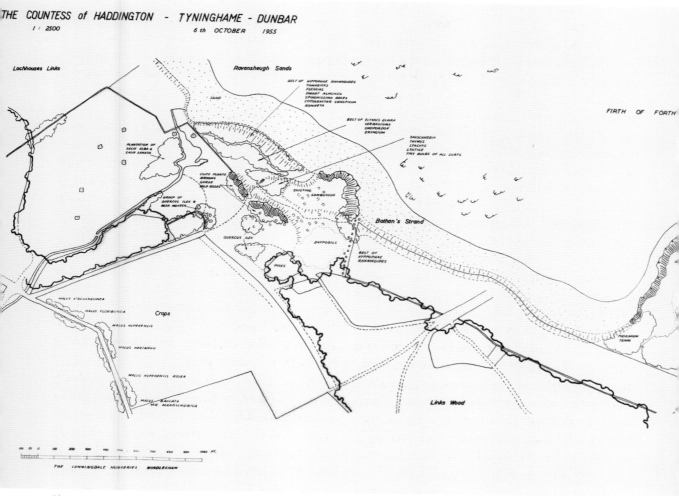

Planting plan for a clifftop garden (Courtesy of the Borthwick Institute, University of York)

crab apples: 'they are a wonderful sight in full flower and usually bear a heavy crop of small scarlet or yellow fruits as well. Their season is May but if planted in long, rather narrow banks, as shown, they will be shaped by the wind and form a very dramatic tunnel effect.' For the top of the dunes he suggested framing the view to Whitberry Point (which he calls the headland) with groups of evergreen oak (*Quercus ilex*), with sea buckthorn (*Hippophae rhamnoides*) as a 'nurse' to help them establish, and the single, scarlet *Rosa moyesii* and

the darker red *Rosa m. Hillierii*, with orange flagon-shaped hips, grouped with an existing clump of sea buckthorn. It would have made a dramatic grouping of blazing reds when in flower followed by the bright orange berries and hips. On the headland itself he suggested groups of the 'tough grey *Cypress Arizonica*',[15] and included a small pencil sketch of this equally dramatic transformation.

On the top of the small cliff, he suggested fuchsias, Romneyas and tamarisks: 'I have seen a very beautiful

Sketch of Whitberry Point with *Cupressus arizonica* (Courtesy of the Borthwick Institute, University of York)

effects near The Blaskets in Co. Kerry where the fuchsias and *hippophae* have been blown by the wind into a tapestry of silver and scarlet.' More silver was to be introduced on the landward side with the silver willow, *Salix alba argentea*, where the ground becomes marshy.

Plant names in Latin and English, their colours and effects, tumbled from his pen and his beguiling prose persuaded his clients to follow his vision for their estates. Russell was not in the busines of instant 'makeovers'. His plans, often extensive, would take many years to establish and he was well aware of the pitfalls along the way. Later, he wrote to Lady Haddington: 'I think that from the point of view of the sand dunes, it would be very interesting to try two or three each of the plants suggested and see how they flourish before embarking on any large planting. Sea shore planting is always tricky.'[16]

As well as his proposals for new planting above Bathan's Strand, he made suggestions for introducing buddleias, and grey and silver foliage plants in the herbaceous border on the south lawn as well as roses with glaucous foliage: *Rosa* 'Queen of Denmark' and *R.* 'Celeste' for example. In her reply a month later, Lady Haddington thanked him for his plans but added that she thought she must concentrate on a very few of the suggested plants – she underlined very! Clearly the clifftop garden was going to have to wait; an order was sent for a few shrubs and four Angel's Trumpets (*Datura*) for the conservatory. If Russell was disappointed, his enthusiasm for the garden was not diminished and their correspondence continued over the next eleven years. He made several visits to the garden, usually followed by long letters and plant lists, and occasionally by plans. While many of his planting suggestions were adopted, neither the design for the clifftop garden nor a later design for an Italian garden to the east of the house ever materialised.

Instead, the clifftop garden became the site for a Canadian style log cabin, built in the mid-sixties by the

View from the cliff by the log cabin to Ravensheugh beach

12th Earl for his wife, to remind her of home. Some planting of sea buckthorn had taken place but none of the decorative planting envisaged by Russell, nor the placing of Arizona cypresses on Whitberry Point, was ever implemented. Rather than a private seaside garden, this part of the coast was to become a public garden, a country park, which was eventually secured when the Tyninghame estate signed an access agreement with East Lothian Council on 18 December 1974.

'Amendment No. 21 to the County Development Plan zoned this stretch from Seacliff to Tynemouth and its agricultural hinterland up to the A198 as an Area of Great Landscape Value in which there would be no more commercialisation of the coast.'[17] Lady Haddington had not been alone in falling in love with this spot. Frank Tindall, East Lothian County Planning Officer from 1950 to 1975, wrote in his memoirs, 'it is one of the glories of East Lothian and its conservation and opening up to the public of Central Scotland was one of my proudest achievements. Never was I more

pleased with myself than when I reached an agreement that gave the public rights over Belhaven Sands, Tynemouth and Ravensheugh Sands, all now embodied in the John Muir Country Park.'[18]

East Lothian was late to recognise the enormous contribution that John Muir (1838–1914), the environmental campaigner who had been born in Dunbar, had made to the preservation and conservation of wilderness areas in the United States – Yosemite National Park and Sequoia National Park, for example. The Sierra Club, the American environmental organisation founded by Muir, was keen to raise awareness of East Lothian's famous son and donated photographs by Ansel Adams of Yosemite for an exhibition organised in Dunbar in 1970. Although not 'wild' by Yosemite standards, the windswept shores and salt flats of the Tyne estuary became part of the country park named after this great environmentalist.

From this point it made no sense to pursue the original idea of a seaside garden, and it was never mentioned in the pieces Lady Haddington wrote about Tyninghame. She contributed an article for the *Journal of the Royal Horticultural Society* in 1971[19] and a chapter to *The Englishwoman's Garden*, edited by Alvilde Lees-Milne and Rosemary Verey in 1980,[20] even though she was Canadian and the garden was in Scotland. 'When we came to live at Tyninghame in 1953, it was not long before the urge to continue the work of previous generations in the garden was put into practice, using our own interpretation and with a view to as much labour saving as possible.'[21] One of the first results was to redesign the planting around the house and to abandon the bedding-out schemes on the parterre that been the tradition for over a hundred years. A scheme of white and yellow roses was chosen to contrast with the pink sandstone of the house. The white floribunda rose 'Iceberg' thrived but the yellow ones took longer to establish: 'King's Ransome', 'Kerry Gold' and 'Golden Jewel' were all tried. Today the yellow roses are 'Graham Thomas' and 'China Town'. Originally the white climbing rose 'Leverkusen' was grown as a standard in the centres of the triangular beds but by 1979 these had been replaced with standard 'Iceberg' and 'Golden Showers', grown on a wooden support.[22] The beds were edged with silver-grey leaved *Artemisia arborescens* and *Cerastium tomentosum*.

The terrace with its long gravel path was also replanted with roses: yellow and white beside the parterre and pink roses, including the hybrid musk 'Felicia', along the edge by the balustrade, both sides edged with lavender. Plants with grey foliage became particular favourites, appreciated as a foil to the pink sandstone of the house. *Cineraria maritima* and *Senecio* 'Sunshine', tree peonies and lavender were introduced into the herbaceous border below the terrace. It was James Russell who, on his first visit, had originally suggested these introductions together with white buddleias at the back of the border. The plant with silver leaves that made, and still makes, most of

an impact at Tyninghame is the silver leaved pear, *Pyrus salicifolia* 'Pendula', a small tree with a weeping habit that proved a sympathetic companion to the many old-fashioned roses along the terrace and elsewhere in the garden.

'[In] the woodlands beyond, one finds some magnificent widely spaced trees, oaks, beech, sycamore and Ilex. A path leads to the [Walled] garden but as no under-planting had been done, we decided to make large beds for woodland plants.'[23] The choice of shrubs and ground cover plants – varieties of *Williamsii* camellias, azaleas, hydrangeas, Philadelphus and shrub roses, for example, together with bergenias, hostas and *Alchemilla mollis* – introduced into the Wilderness was strongly influenced by Russell.

Although the designs for the seaside garden and the Italian garden were never implemented, the one place where Russell made his mark was in the Walled Garden. He concurred with Lady Haddington in 1959 that the double herbaceous border, the pride of Tyninghame when Robert Brotherston was Head Gardener, should go. The high standard its maintenance required was proving impossible to attain. 'Rather than doing away with the splendid yew hedges we decided to form a green alleyway in place of the flowers, thus it was only necessary to cut the grass.'[24] On one of their trips to Italy, stone statues were brought back and erected in niches cut into the hedges. With the marble fountain at its centre, the result indeed saved labour and created a dramatic vista along the whole length of the garden.

The Head Gardener at this time was Jock Stewart; four gardeners worked in the Walled Garden and the greenhouses, and another three tended the areas around the house.[25] Together they tended a gardened area of some forty-five acres – plenty of work for seven men as not all tasks were fully mechanised. Considerable man-hours were spent on maintenance: cutting the lawns, the verges of the mile-long drive, the hedges,

Opposite: The Walled Garden green alleyway

and sweeping and collecting leaves in winter.

The garden that had graced the pages of *Country Life* in 1902 had not survived two world wars unscathed. Besides the deterioration of the herbaceous borders in the Walled Garden, a large section behind the yew hedge had been turned over to growing raspberries. When Peter Verney, author of *The Gardens of Scotland*, visited the garden in the early 1970s, the western half of the garden behind the yew hedge was 'a new planting. Laid out by the eminent landscape gardener, James Russell, and the huge, irregular curved beds hold a treasury of plants.'[26] When he was first asked to design an informal garden in this area, Russell wrote that a garden within a formal wall was always difficult to make convincingly wild and he felt it was preferable to keep a formal mown grass path inside the existing wall. Within that rectangular framework of roughly an acre, Russell designed a broad, gently sinuous grass path stretching its whole length, with other wide curving paths dividing the long broad borders on either side. Included were a selection of what were then unusual or slightly tender trees and shrubs which he thought would survive in the shelter of the site: several different varieties of acer and magnolia, *Corylopsis pauciflora* and *C. wilmottiae*, *Drymis winteri latifolia*, *Idesia polycarpa*, *Styrax japonicus*, *S. obassia*, *Stuartia pseudo-camellia* and *Viburnum furcatum* for example. He also suggested two varieties of eucalyptus, *E. coccifera* and *E. Dalrympleana*, which could be cut down 'so that you have multiple stems shooting up to perhaps 20ft or 30ft which I feel would be the required height here'.[27]

Although Lady Haddington was the one who took the initiative and the responsibility for the gardens, trees were the domain of the 12th Earl. As a keen forester, he took a special interest in establishing a collection of eucalyptus in the Walled Garden. Peter Verney noted: '*Eucalyptus gunnii*, *parviflora*, *pauciflora* . . . *subcrenulata*. Less likely but still doing well at Tyninghame are *E. perriniana* and *E. coccifera*.'[28] While trees were the passion of the Earl, his wife, on the other hand, was a great lover of old-fashioned roses.

These, together with 'acceptable' modern varieties, were introduced everywhere in Tyninghame, not just into the Walled Garden, where some old roses were already established but into what had been a purely herbaceous border on the south lawn and into the Wilderness. The former was widened and given a new serpentine edge: horseshoe-shaped rose arbours were introduced along its length, planted with pink climbing roses 'Aloha', 'New Dawn' and 'Parade', and in the centre the yellow 'Casino' and 'Lady Hillingdon', with honeysuckle in each one and occasional *Vitis coignetiae*. Between the arches were mixed plantings of shrub roses, lilies, delphiniums, *Romneya couteri*, lavenders, penstemons and agapanthus, edged with low, grey-leaved shrubs including cotton lavender, *Senecio* and *Artemesia*.

At the western end of this long border and at the terrace above, the garden came to a rather unsatisfactory boundary area on the edge of the Wilderness. It was a rough area of long grass of about an acre. Lady Haddington finally settled on the idea of creating an enclosed garden dedicated in the main to old roses and where she could 'work happily alone without calling in too much help'.[29] In this she was participating in the revival of interest in old roses in the late 1950s and 1960s. She had undoubtedly received advice on roses from Graham Stuart Thomas, whose book *The Old Shrub Roses* (written while he was working with James Russell at Sunningdale Nursery) had proved so popular it had gone into four editions and two reprints between 1955 and 1966. The foreword was by Vita Sackville-West whose own transformation of the garden at Sissinghurst and her gardening column for *The Observer* had done much to revive and expand interest in old roses, rather than the hybrid teas which were then proliferating.

Lady Haddington wrote: 'I studied many layouts and finally found my inspiration in Rapin's poem, "Of

Gardens" and in John James' translation of *The Theory and Practice of Gardening*, an eighteenth-century French book with garden designs, adapting a drawing to my own more simple taste'.[30] Rapin's poem, inspired by Virgil's *Georgics*, was originally written in Latin in 1665 to reflect the French style of gardening in the seventeenth century. It was immediately popular and translated into English, though it was an unusual incentive for a twentieth-century garden, if indeed it was. It is hard to pinpoint its inspiration for the new rose garden other than in a general way. In the library, the translation would have probably occupied the same shelf as the other translation to which she referred, John James' English version of *La Théorie et La Practique du Jardinage* (1709). This was the book that provided the direct inspiration for the layout.

Thomas Hamilton, the 6th Earl, had subscribed to its translation in 1712 and acquired it for the library at Tyninghame. The original was written by Antoine-Joseph Dézallier d'Argenville in 1709 and quickly became a best-seller in mainland Europe. Of its many designs engraved by the architect Jean Baptiste Alexandre le Blond, the one that most closely resembles the drawing adapted for the rose garden is found in the second plate. It was one of four outer 'sections' of a garden, originally intended as 'a Wood-work, planted in a very handsome Compartment'.[31]

When it came to setting out the design on the ground, rather than follow Rapin's advice and

> . . . engage a Master's Hand,
> Whose artful Pencil shall on Parchmont trace
> The whole Design, and figure out the place[32]

Lady Haddington described how she and her 'capable gardener . . . started the long and tedious job of measuring to get the right size for each bed, then placing the thin ropes into the shapes'.[33] When digging began they found that a pick-axe was needed to get through the stone and rubble which was thought to

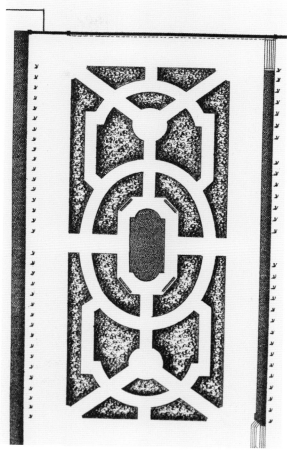

'A very handsome Compartment', from *The Theory and Practice of Gardening*

be the foundation of an old Victorian tennis court.

Roses and herbaceous plants instead of trees filled the beds; rose arches spanned the paths, others gave height to the beds; a statue of Flora, brought from Vicenza and representing Summer, was placed beneath a wooden trellis arbour made on the estate; the central axis terminated in a wide rose arbour above a grotto where a thin jet of water splashed gently into an antique stone basin and into the pool below. A long apple walk formed a boundary to the west, with a curving path and a lawn beneath an ancient horse-chestnut tree. This western section was added on to

The Secret Garden

the original d'Argenville design to fill out the space. A small gate led from the western cross-axis into the Wilderness.

In this space of roughly an acre, the main groups of old roses, together with climbing varieties, were represented: Bourbon, Hybrid Perpetual, Hybrid Musk, Alba, Centifolia, Damask, Gallica and Noisette. There was also a certain amount of cheating, with the inclusion of modern shrub roses to prolong the season of flowering. The colours were pinks, purples, deep reds and white, and the herbaceous planting of geraniums, campanula, lilies, peonies and lavender complemented these muted colours. All jostling for position in the narrow beds of the eighteenth-century design, they clambered up arches and tripods and stretched their stems where space allowed.

Together with roses, Lady Haddington's other favourite was the lilac. 'I have always loved flowers and gardens, perhaps because my earliest recollection is associated with our home which stood on the banks

'Heavily-scented maze', with climbing rose 'Rambling Rector' in the Secret Garden

of the swift flowing River St Lawrence in Canada . . . To this day, when passing a lilac tree and catching its exquisite scent, memories of those happy childhood days return.'[34] Not surprisingly, her favourite, the single white lilac, 'Vestale', was planted throughout the garden. The southern boundary was enclosed by a yew hedge, the other sides by a fence masked by evergreen shrubs. It was christened 'The Secret Garden' and finished in 1968.

The 12th Earl and his Countess, together with their head gardeners Jock Stewart and Tom Morris, did much to revitalise the gardens at Tyninghame. Three years later, when Peter Verney visited, he was entranced: 'every grouping, every corner and border reveals a gardening and designing talent . . . of a very high order'. And when he entered the Secret Garden, he wrote, '[T]he effect is being in Arcady, a glorious, heavily-scented maze in a country far-removed from Scotland.'[35]

CHAPTER 14

Another Beginning

After the death of the 12th Earl in 1986 the future of the estate hung in the balance. His only son, John, Lord Binning, inherited the title together with around £2 million of estate duty taxes. This was the third time in the twentieth century that the estate had been hit with crippling taxation.

Lloyd George's People's Budget (1910) introduced taxation on the value of land for the first time. Death duty for the largest estates, those valued at over £2 million, doubled to forty per cent in 1919. Austen Chamberlain, the Chancellor responsible for the increases, concluded his summary of the proposed alterations with the words: ' . . . these are very onerous rates of duty. They constitute, taken in conjunction with the Income Tax, a further differentiation between wealth derived from continuing personal exertion and wealth derived from accumulated capital.'[1] After the Second World War and the landslide victory of the Labour government, estate duty and inheritance taxes were increased even further. Capital Transfer Tax replaced Estate Duty in 1975; this was later abolished by the Conservative government of Margaret Thatcher and replaced with Inheritance Tax in 1986.

When the 11th Earl and his son died within three months of each other in 1917, this had forced the sale of about 10,000 acres. Had the then Lord Binning died on the battlefield in France, rather than at home of a war-incurred disease, much of the estate duty might have been wiped out. On average, the estates of officers or men killed in action could be relieved of roughly fifty per cent of duty.

Lady Binning, grandmother of the 13th Earl, had stayed on at Tyninghame, keeping the estate going from 1917 until her death in 1954. For the second time, the estate was faced with heavy taxes, this time amounting to eighty per cent of the value of her possessions.[2]

Several houses on neighbouring estates disappeared around this time: Smeaton House, Prestonkirk, the home of the Hepburns, was sold to contractors and demolished in 1948. Hedderwickhill House was blown up a little later in 1961. Dunglass House, having been requisitioned during the Second World War, was later stripped of its roof and left as a ruin until it was blown up by its owner in 1958. With its 100 rooms, his family found it too expensive to renovate and to heat after the war: 'The house had become a dinosaur . . .'[3]

Country wide, dozens of great houses were sold to raise the money to pay taxes and duties; many were abandoned. 'Out of a total of 1,116 country houses in Britain demolished between 1875 and 1974, 63 were

Opposite: John Baillie-Hamilton, 13th Earl of Haddington, by A. T. Festing (Courtesy of the Earl of Haddington)

lost before 1918, an estimated 458 between 1918 and 1945, and 595 after 1945.'[4] In Scotland, over 500 country houses have been lost since 1875.

To the 13th Earl, the tax bill of £2 million sounded like the death knell for Tyninghame, or for Mellerstain. He felt that the upkeep of two stately homes was no longer possible, given the rental income. 'Which arm do you cut off?' was how he put it.[5] He decided to keep Mellerstain, where he had been brought up and where he had also farmed for several years. Would the Tyninghame estate be carved up like the neighbouring Broxmouth estate? What would happen to the village whose population was dwindling?

Some of the Tyninghame farms had already been sold in the early 1980s – Easter and Wester Broomhouse, Lochhouses and Hedderwick – in order to meet the earl's divorce settlement, but the estate did not have limestone wealth, nor was it suitable for extensive housing development like Broxmouth. There were at that time no options for building new houses apart from developing existing farm buildings.

However, the lengthy, sandy shore boundary attracted developers including Jack Nicklaus, the famous golfer and (later) golf-course designer, who 'planned to transform the estate into a world class golf-resort with a links style course built along the shore and the main house converted into a club-house complex'.[6] Such a transformation was anathema to the 13th Earl as he felt it would have destroyed the house and the garden that his family, and in particular his mother, had worked so hard to create. Even if another single buyer had come forward, he was concerned that one person would not be able to keep up the expense, or if she or he did, it would only be a matter of time before the house was sold again to someone who would have no regard for the place. Tyninghame had been in the family since 1628 and even though the earl had spent more time at Mellerstain, where he lived with his wife Jane, he had a deep affection for Tyninghame where the family had always spent their summers.

In the end, the house and surrounding garden at the heart of the designed landscape were sold in 1987 for a song: £250,000. The contents and, sadly, some of the fittings of the house, were sold by Sotheby's in an auction that took place on 28 and 29 September 1987 and that raised over £2 million. The sale included fine furniture, tapestries, chandeliers, china and silver. Among the paintings sold were portraits by Sir Peter Lely, Sir John de Medina, William Aikman, Allan Ramsay, Sir Godfrey Kneller, Sir Henry Raeburn, Thomas Gainsborough and Sir Joshua Reynolds. Separately, the National Library of Scotland purchased the collection of books which had belonged to the 1st Earl of Haddington.

The purchaser of the house was the architect, developer and restorer of historic country houses, Kit Martin. In 1976, Martin had rescued and restored Dingley Hall, a Grade 1 Listed ruined mansion in Northamptonshire. He sympathetically divided it vertically into ten separate houses, keeping the landscape and garden intact. Marcus Binney, the indefatigable campaigner for endangered country houses was impressed with the way Martin worked and suggested they write a book together. *The Country House: To Be or Not to Be?* was the eventual result, published in 1982. The aim of the book was to prevent further demolition of country houses by presenting some workable solutions, giving a new lease of life to a range of disused, neglected properties which no longer suited the needs of their owners. Based on actual examples from his practice, Kit Martin provided outline plans to show how problem houses could be divided and repurposed in a cost-effective way. In some cases, development could take place unit by unit, with the profit from the sale of the first units then invested in the next and so on, thus reducing capital expenditure. A further saving could be made employing labour directly, with trades following on from each other and moving from one unit to the next. There was no pot of gold to be made, but Martin proved that it was possible to save some of

New homes in the east courtyard

the nation's architectural heritage and that it could be achieved on a commercial basis.

He was an architect by training but it had soon become impossible to combine time-consuming, detailed drawing with his work as a property developer. By the time Tyninghame was purchased Martin had already bought and divided two further houses in England and two in Scotland – Cullen House, Banff-shire, and Keith Hall, Aberdeenshire. Local architectural practices with expertise in conservation were appointed to execute his masterplans: for Tyninghame, he chose Simpson and Brown.

One of the solutions for empty country houses proposed in *The Country House: To Be or Not to Be?* and the one in which Kit Martin excelled, was 'The Residential Community'. Obviously, the viability of this solution depended on the layout of the house: a sympathetic conversion needed to retain the principal elevations of the house, preserve interiors of special character and respect the main internal divisions of the house. 'If the division follows the structural lines of the building it is possible (and important) to provide a range of houses and apartments of different sizes and prices . . . The aim is in fact to establish a mixed community.'[7]

This is what happened at Tyninghame House, which was originally divided vertically into ten apartments: The West Wing, The Library Wing, The North

Wing, The Tower, The East Wing, The McLaren Wing, The Turret, The Butlers, and two sections of the Kitchen Wing (now merged as The Old Kitchen).

Each had its own portion of roof and its own front door. Garages were sited discreetly at the sides so as not to obstruct views to or from the house. Outlying buildings were converted into separate dwelling houses: The Clock House, The Head Gardener's House, The Bothy and The Potting Shed. A new house was built adjacent to the Walled Garden, on the site of the old apple stores and bothy. The stable block was upgraded and remained in possession of the Haddington family, making a varied community of fifteen households.

One of the features that set Kit Martin's treatment of historic houses apart from those of other developers was that he understood the value of maintaining the setting of the house. This was the key to long-term success. He understood that a castle or country house without its garden and landscape setting would lose its attraction to potential purchasers, some of whom would be investing considerable sums for the more prestigious apartments. In order to ensure that the gardens immediately surrounding the house were kept in good order for the benefit of all, and to avoid friction between neighbours, Martin's solution was the establishment of a management company called the 'Garden Company', whose purpose is to 'maintain the grounds, and all the shared parts of the building and to control any future development. No occupant can extend or alter his house externally without reference to the Garden Company.'[8] Each purchaser would be an equal shareholder in the company and membership would be conditional on agreement to contributing the required amount to pay for the shared upkeep of the garden.

In the case of Tyninghame, the boundary of this 'kernel' of the estate encompassed approximately thirty-eight acres, including the Wilderness, the north and south lawns, the Secret Garden and the driveways.

The Tyninghame Garden Company has successfully managed and maintained the gardens since 1989 following these principles. A management committee, elected by the residents, together with a factor, oversees the running of the gardens and employs two gardeners: the head gardener and one other. Albert Johnston, who had worked at Tyninghame since 1979, became head gardener until he retired in 2013, since when the post has been occupied by Chas Lowe. He is aided by two part-time assistant gardeners.

As far as the wider landscape setting was concerned, successive Earls of Haddington had been the masters of all the surrounding parkland and agricultural land for generations and had, at least since 1761 when the parish was united with Whitekirk, controlled the views to and from the house. For example, the views from the terrace of the house, looking south over the Tyne towards the Lammermuir Hills, had been established in the eighteenth century and had been carefully maintained since then. Clumps of trees, shelter belts and embankments hide the old A1 (now A199), the new A1 and the main railway line from view.

Fortunately, at Tyninghame, when the house and gardens were sold, the surrounding 'belt' of parkland, including the farms of Kirklandhill and the Knowes, were retained by the earl. Kit Martin believed it was essential to secure by some form of agreement (he recommended a covenant) that the owner(s) of the surrounding land should not construct any new buildings within view of the house nor change the use of the land. Thus the maintenance of the parkland setting, with grazing animals, was enshrined in a clause of the deeds of The Stables to prevent it going under the plough. By 1990, when all the apartments in the house were sold, it seemed that the house and its setting were secured, but the problems for the larger estate remained.

In an interview with the American landscape architect John Simpson, John Baillie-Hamilton, the 13th Earl of Haddington, was very frank: 'You can't

Tyninghame village hall

maintain a huge house and everything that goes with the ownership of large properties like this on rental income or, indeed, on income from in-hand farms. It simply doesn't work anymore, so you must find other means of raising cash.'[9] The sale of the house and its contents was the first step. Further sales in the village were to follow.

Once the house and gardens were sold, there was no longer a reason for the earl to own accommodation in the village for new employees. Back in the eighteenth century when the village began gradually to take shape, with almshouses (from 1715), a sawmill (*c.*1754 rebuilt in 1828) and farm workers' cottages followed by a bake-house (rebuilt in 1842) which became the village hall, a smiddy, an ale house and a school, this expanding

agricultural community depended on employment generated by the estate. Most of the buildings had been rebuilt by Thomas and James Hannan between 1828 and 1850.[10] They were skilled stonemasons who lived in the village and had worked with William Burn, remodelling Tyninghame House and the estate build-ings for the 9th Earl. It is largely their work which gives homogeneity to the village as it appears today.

The village had always been small; by the mid twen-tieth century there were still only thirty-three cottages, all belonging to the earl. By the 1980s the village was shrinking, with few children and cottages standing empty as the estate could only support a dwindling number of the former population. Eight cottages were then sold. A plan for the redevelopment of the village followed in 1991. Two years later permission was finally granted for ten new houses and nine conversions. These included the development of the Mains' farm steading adjacent to Whitberry House, traditionally the home of the estate factor, at the eastern end of the village. The factor, John Hume, retired in 1988, but stayed on there until finally moving to a detached house in Main Street some ten years later. He was succeeded by Alistair Milligan, who had assisted him since 1968 and who lived in the farmhouse at Lawhead. Tyninghame farm steading, estate office and the doocot, were converted into five dwellings which sold quickly in 1999. Whitberry House itself was retained and rented before being sold in 2018.

When John Simpson visited Tyninghame in 2001, the new houses (in Braefoot and the Green) were finished, six conversions were completed and the smiddy had been transformed into a coffee shop selling gifts. The estate still owned twenty-five of the cottages; a few retired employees still occupied tied cottages. He noted that very few of the residents were farm or forestry workers with connections to the estate, instead the majority were commuters, retired folk and second homeowners. Nevertheless, the village seemed to him to have been given a new lease of life.

Evidence of this has been the evolution of the village hall, formerly the bakehouse. The hall is leased to the village by the estate for the use of residents. Over the years it has been the scene of village and estate activities including flower shows, funeral wakes, family parties and shoot lunches. Latterly it was managed by a committee and became popular for weddings, weekly classes and craft fairs. However, the building was in need of some internal refurbishment and in order to access community grants available only to charities and to put matters on a sound legal footing, a successful application was eventually made for Tyninghame Village Hall to become a Scottish Charitable Incorporated Organisation (SCIO) in 2017. It has been a substantial fundraising undertaking for the committee who, besides managing community events, oversee the renting out of the hall to generate income as well as making grant applications. Their success has led to refurbishment including secondary glazing, new LED lighting and replacement heaters. Plans are in progress for roof insulation – which must also accommodate the long-eared bats who roost in part of the roof space! – together with renovation of the toilets and the kitchen. As a result, the hall has become a magnet for an increasing range of different community interest groups: monthly pub nights, Harvest and Burns' Night suppers and occasional concerts, yoga classes and craft workshops.

The life of the wider estate, on the other hand, has hung in the balance. The earl himself had predicted that its future was limited: 'I can foresee the end of the estate. We have governments now that are increasingly unsympathetic towards the land and landowners . . . the future of the estates is very shaky, though I'd hate to see them broken up.'[11] Quite suddenly in 2003, the estate agents Strutt and Parker announced the sale of 'the major part of the Tyninghame Estate', as a whole or in five lots. The sale of 1,642 acres (664 hectares) comprised farmland to the north of the Tyne: Lawhead Farm, Links Wood, Brownrig Wood and Lochhouses links, Binning Wood, and some fishing on the Tyne and in Belhaven Bay. The park and woodland to the north and south of the house were not included.

John Simpson wryly noted that when estates were broken up in Scotland and the land was sold, it rarely went to 'commoners'. Instead, it was usually sold in large chunks to businessmen from home or abroad. He was wrong in this case, on both counts: although a community 'buy-out' for the Binning Wood failed, the lots were sold to a consortium of two closely related neighbouring farming families: the Dales and the Grays. The Dales have farmed nearby in East Lothian for seven generations – in West Barns from the late eighteenth century and from 1834 at Auldhame. Robert Dale had already bought the bulk of the

Lochhouses estate in 1984 and his brother Alec bought Hedderwick at the same time. The Grays, originally from Stirlingshire, farmed on the outskirts of Edinburgh before moving to East Fenton in the 1930s and to Smeaton, Prestonkirk, in 1962.[12] The two families became permanently joined when Anne Dale married George Gray in 1945 and George's sister, Gladys, married Anne's brother, Tommy.

The new owners have faced exactly the same problems as the earl but have found different solutions. Farming continues, although Lawhead Farmhouse was sold and the adjacent steading buildings converted into separate dwellings as at Tyninghame Mains. Responsibility for the land is shared between different generations. Younger family members, cousins with strong ties to the landscape through their shared histories, now play important roles.

One solution has been the formation of a company to provide glamping holidays by the beach at Lochhouses, owned by the Dale family. Whereas there is a presumption against building new houses in the countryside, holiday rentals in the form of treehouses and beach cabins behind the dunes at Lochhouses have been permitted. The company also arrange beach or woodland weddings. The original log cabin still survives and is available for hire. It is regularly used with a marquee as a wedding venue.

The Binning Wood presented different challenges. Forestry as an investment is long term; it might generate capital gains (but it might not) and the timber market might hold up (but it might not), during which time the woodland needs management. Having been so carefully replanted by the 12th Earl, following the original design, options for generating extra income were limited and maintenance is costly. Rhododendrons that were such a curse when the wood was replanted continue to menace and their roots still prove difficult to eradicate, even with modern machinery. Some areas have needed thinning.

Today the avenues or rides are frequented by families, mountain bikers, dogwalkers and anyone else who appreciates woodland. The new owner of the Binning Wood, John Gray, is happy for low-impact public use to continue but the family realised that further investment was needed in order to ensure the survival of the woodland for future generations. He applied for permission to create a green burial site, Binning Memorial Wood, which is run by his son Ben Gray and his wife Sarah. With the help of forestry consultant Robert Gray (no relation), an area of beech on the northern boundary was identified and cleared of undergrowth. Plots are identified by an engraved stone, almost flush with the ground so that the cemetery almost disappears into the natural woodland. The number of plots is controlled, but since 2010 woodland burials have been taking place regularly and their popularity shows no sign of declining.

The 13th Earl died on 5 July 2016 and was buried at Mellerstain. He was succeeded by his son, George. What then for the future of the Tyninghame Estate? Like many other landscapes that were once in the hands of a single, aristocratic family, today ownership is divided and parts are owned by farmers, small businesses, the Tyninghame Garden Company and individual homeowners; other stakeholders include the tenant farmer at Kirklandhill, the farmer who leases the pasture around Tyninghame House, contractors who lease land for crops – arable, vegetable, turf – and East Lothian Council, responsible for the John Muir Country Park. The diversity suggests durability as long as different interests do not create tensions that threaten the coherence of the whole.

It is astonishing that the designs that Helen and her husband Thomas devised for the landscape at the beginning of the eighteenth century, with the tree planting and hedge planting that accompanied it, have mostly survived intact. Having been looked after by the same family for 350 years has meant that the 'long view' could be taken in most management decisions.[13]

Some fields have been amalgamated but many

small six- and seven-acre fields, together with their hedgerows, survive. That this has been possible is partly because Tyninghame remained in the ownership of a single family who cherished it. In 1987 it was recognised as having national significance when it was included in the *Inventory of Gardens and Designed Landscapes* maintained by Historic Environment Scotland (HES). There are now nearly 400 sites on the Inventory in Scotland; the majority are estate landscapes, like Tyninghame. Unlike listed building status, inclusion in the Inventory does not give protection in law but it does require any Local Planning Authority to consult HES on any 'development which may affect a historic garden or designed landscape'.[14]

Tyninghame is one of only a handful of sites in the country, and the only East Lothian site, deemed to have 'Outstanding' interest in all categories by which they are assessed. At the time of its inclusion, the house and gardens had just been sold and there was some anxiety as to whether the standard could be maintained.

At the time of writing, the fragmentation of the estate has not resulted in any detrimental effects on the coherence of this small part of Scotland's historic environment. However, the pressure for this coastline to become a playground is forceful. The 'wild' coastline which the John Muir Country Park seeks to embody is at odds with the ever-increasing visitor numbers arriving from all over the country, usually by car. Visitor numbers to the beach trebled in 2020–1. The old steading at Tyninghame Links, by the car park for the beach at Ravensheugh, is on the 'Buildings at Risk Register for Scotland' while planning permission is being sought for its conversion into a retail space with a café and holiday lets. For this legacy to be valued, cared for and enjoyed by future generations, there is a need for understanding and an appreciation of its

Opposite: Binning Memorial Wood

Overleaf: The Tyne, flowing into Hedderwick Bay
(Courtesy of Andy Semple)

fragility. As always, it is a delicate balancing act.

Hitherto, the stewardship of the Tyninghame estate, now shared between so many, has been sensitive to the different aspects of the landscape heritage. The sense of place that Tyninghame has engendered over the centuries, and which reinforces our cultural identity today, spans several thousand years, multifaceted and ever changing. The ancient standing stone, pointing its finger above the crops at Kirklandhill, recalls the early settlers who came some 5,000 years ago and is a reminder of the hidden archaeology lying beneath the fields. St Baldred and his monastic settlement conferred a sanctity on the land that held sway for over 1,000 years. The twelfth-century kirk was the centre of the parish and the 'toun' for over 500 years, until it was dismantled to become a picturesque ruin and the village of New Tyninghame gradually emerged. The introduction of woodland and hedges for enclosure fundamentally changed the character of the coastal landscape, increasing the biodiversity in ways unimaginable at the beginning of the eighteenth century.

The tenacity shown by Helen Hope who insisted on planting trees, followed by her husband's conversion to her cause, laid the foundations for the next 400 years. Her 'great love of planting' inspired subsequent generations of the Hamilton and Baillie-Hamilton families, together with their gardeners and foresters, to support horticulture and forestry in the gardens and wider estate. From simple beginnings as a tower which doubled as a bishop's palace, Tyninghame House grew and eventually emerged from its plain, seventeenth-century stone chrysalis as a romantic vision of Scottish baronial architecture.

Continuity and change have been the themes of the Tyninghame story. More changes will follow in order to meet as yet unforeseen challenges. Can those who value this heritage, and those who share in it, work together to ensure that it remains as resilient in the future as it has in the past? May future stewards be sensitive to this generous legacy.

Select Bibliography

PRIMARY SOURCES

National Records of Scotland:
    NRS GD124/15/632 Letters of the 6th Earl of Haddington
    NRS GD220/5/614 Letter from Lord Haddington to the Duke of Montrose
    NRS GD220/5/90 Letter from Helen Hope to the Duke of Montrose
    NRS GD420/1–15 The Ancient Fraternity of Free Gardeners of East Lothian
    NRS RH15/39/195 Estimate of fruit at Tyninghame
    NRS CH2/358/1 Tyninghame Kirk Session Minutes 1759–1820
    NRS CH2/359/1 Tyninghame Kirk Session Minutes 1615–1650
National Library of Scotland (NLS) MSS14833 Factors Book, Tyninghame Estate, Earl of Haddington
National Register for Archives for Scotland (NRAS) 3503 Baillie Hamilton. Various
The Archive of James Russell, Borthwick Institute, University of York JR/1/173

SECONDARY SOURCES

Abernethy, L., *Lady Grisell Baillie Mistress of Mellerstain*, Kibworth Beauchamp: Troubador, 2020.
Anderson, M. L., *A History of Scottish Forestry*, London: Nelson, 1967.
—— (ed.), *Forest Trees: Some directions about Raising Forest Trees by Thomas Hamilton*, London: Thomas Nelson and Sons, 1953.
Binney, M., and Martin, K., *The Country House: To Be or Not to Be?* London: Save Britain's Heritage, 1982.
Brotherston, R., *The Book of Cut Flowers*, Edinburgh: T. N. Foulis, 1906.
Brown, M., *Scotland's Lost Gardens*, Edinburgh: RCAHMS, 2012.
Campbell, S., *A History of Kitchen Gardening*, London: Frances Lincoln, 2005.
Crone, A., Hyndmarch, E. and A. Woolf, *Living and Dying at Auldhame – The Excavation of an Anglian Monastic Settlement and Medieval Parish Church*, Edinburgh: Society of Antiquaries of Scotland, 2016.
Dodd, J. 'From Old to New: The Creation of the Present Village of Tyninghame', *Transactions of the East Lothian Antiquarian and Field Naturalists' Society*, vol. xxxii, 2019, pp. 94–111.
Fawcett, R., *The Architecture of the Scottish Medieval Church, 1100–1560*, New Haven and London: Yale University Press, 2011.
Fraser, W., *Memorials of the Earls of Haddington*, 2 vols, Edinburgh: privately printed, 1889.
Glendinning, M., and MacKechnie, A., *Scotch Baronial: Architectural and National Identity in Scotland*, London: Bloomsbury, 2021.
Haddington, Earl of, 'Notes on Binning Wood, East Lothian', *Scottish Forestry*, vol. 22, 1968.
Hately Waddell, P., *An Old Kirk Chronicle. Being a history of Auldhame, Tyninghame and Whitekirk*, Edinburgh: Blackwood & Sons, 1893.
James, A. G., 'Scotland's *-ham* and *-ingham* names: a reconsideration', *The Journal of Scottish Name Studies*, vol. 4, 2010, pp. 103–30.
Kelsall, H. and K., *Scottish Lifestyle 300 Years Ago*, Aberdeen: Scottish Cultural Press, 1993.
Lees-Milne, A., and Verey, R., *The Englishwoman's Garden*, London: Chatto and Windus, 1980.

Lang, J. T., 'Hogback monuments in Scotland', *Proceedings of the Society of Antiquaries of Scotland*, vol. 105, 1974, pp. 206–35.

Legg, K., *The Archive of James Russell, Garden Designer deposited at the Borthwick Institute, University of York*, York: Borthwick Publications, 2003.

Lelong, O., and MacGregor, G., *A Journey through East Lothian's Past – Archaeology along the A1*, Edinburgh: Society of Antiquaries of Scotland, 2007.

Loudon, J. C., *Encyclopaedia of Gardening*, London: Longman, 1825.

Lowe, C., *Angels Fools and Tyrants*, Edinburgh: Canongate, 1999.

Macquarrie, A., *Lives of Scottish Saints in the Aberdeen Breviary*, Scottish Church History Society, vol. 31, 1996.

McWilliam, C. (ed.), *The Buildings of Scotland: Lothian*, London: Penguin, 1978.

Marshall, R., *John de Medina*, Edinburgh: National Gallery of Scotland, 1988.

Ralston, I., 'Going back in time: Re-assessment of the timber halls at Doon Hill, Dunbar', *Transactions of the East Lothian Antiquarian and Field Naturalists' Society*, vol. xxxii, 2019.

Reid, J., *The Scot's Gard'ner*, (ed.) A. Hope, Edinburgh: Mainstream Publishing, 1988.

Ritche, A. E., *The Churches of St Baldred: Auldhame, Tyninghame, Whitekirk, Prestonkirk*, Edinburgh: J. Moodie Miller, 1881.

Robertson, F., *Early Scottish Gardeners and Their Plants 1650–1750*, East Linton: Tuckwell Press, 2000.

Robinson, W., *The English Flower Garden*, A. Hope (ed.), London: Hamlyn, 1984.

Rollason, D. (ed.), *Princes of the Church: Bishops and Their Palaces*, London: Routledge, 2017.

—— (ed.), *Symeon of Durham: Historian of Durham and the North*, Stamford: Studies in Northeastern History, 1998.

Scott-Moncrieff, R., *The Household Book of Lady Grizell Baillie 1692–1733*, Edinburgh: Scottish Historical Society, 1911.

Simpson, J., *Yearning for the Land*, New York: Vintage Books, 2003.

Smout, T., *A History of the Scottish People 1560–1830*, Glasgow: Fontana, 1987.

Stevenson, R., 'The Inchyra Stone and other early Christian Monuments', *Proceedings of the Society of Antiquaries of Scotland*, vol. 92, 1961, pp. 33–55.

Stewart, M., *The Architectural, Landscape and Constitutional Plans of the Earl of Mar, 1700–32*, Dublin: Four Courts Press, 2016.

Story, J., 'Symeon as annalist', from Rollason, D. (ed.), *Symeon of Durham: Historian of Durham and the North*, Stamford: Studies in Northeastern History, 1998.

Tait, A., *The Landscape Garden in Scotland 1735–1835*, Edinburgh: Edinburgh University Press, 1980.

Tindall, F., *Memoirs and Confessions of a County Planning Officer*, Ford: The Pantile Press, 1998.

Trevor-Roper, H., *Tyninghame Library*, 1977 NLS MMSID: 992328933804341

Turnbull, G., *The Diary of George Turnbull, Minister of Alloa and Tyninghame, 1657–1704*, Paul, R. (ed.), Edinburgh: Scottish Historical Society, 1893.

Verney, P., *The Gardens of Scotland*, London: Batsford, 1976.

Notes

CHAPTER 1

1 Canmore ID 57750 Kirklandhill
2 Canmore ID 212799 Bci North-east Quarry
3 Ralston, I., 'Going back in time: Re-assessment of the timber halls at Doon Hill, Dunbar', *Transactions of the East Lothian Antiquarian and Field Naturalist's Society*, vol. xxxii, 2019, pp. 4–27
4 Historic Environment Scotland (HES) Scheduled Monument SM 5875
5 Lowe, C., *Angels Fools and Tyrants*, Edinburgh: Canongate, 1999, p. 32
6 Canmore ID 57766 Hedderwick
7 Canmore ID 77777 Tyninghame Bridge
8 Lelong, O. and MacGregor, G., *A Journey through East Lothian's Past – Archaeology along the A1*, Edinburgh: Society of Antiquaries of Scotland, 2007
9 Ibid. p. xx, Table 5.1
10 Ibid. p. 213
11 Ibid. pp. xx, 89
12 Ibid. p. 13
13 Ibid. p. 12
14 Canmore ID 56270 Drylawhill
15 Canmore ID 573779 Knowes Farm, the Traprain Law Environs Project
16 Baldwin, J., *Lothian and Borders*, Edinburgh: HMSO, 1997; Piggott, S., *Scotland Before History*, Edinburgh University Press, 1982

CHAPTER 2

1 *Annales Lindisfarnenses et Dunelmenses. Monumenta Germaniae Historica*, 1866, vol. xix, p. 505

2 James, A., 'Scotland's *-ham* and *-ingham* names: a reconsideration', *The Journal of Scottish Name Studies*, vol. 4, 2010, pp. 103–4
3 Ibid. p. 111
4 James, A., 'New thoughts on old place-names', *Transactions of the East Lothian Antiquarian and Field Naturalists' Society*, vol. xxxii, 2019, pp. 28–35
5 Crone, A., Hyndmarch, E. and A. Woolf, *Living and Dying at Auldhame*, Edinburgh: Society of Antiquaries of Scotland, 2016, p. 132
6 Bede, *Ecclesiastical History of the English People*, London: Penguin Books, 1990, pp. 129–30
7 Ibid. p. 146
8 Crone, Hyndmarch and Woolf, p. 139
9 Brown, M., *Scotland's Lost Gardens*, Edinburgh: RCAHMS, 2012, p. 18
10 Crone, Hyndmarch and Woolf, p. 137
11 Ibid. p. 59
12 Ibid. p. 169
13 Stevenson, R., 'The Inchyra Stone and other early Christian Monuments', *Proceedings of the Society of Antiquaries of Scotland*, vol. 92, 1961, pp. 33–55; Canmore ID 1009764
14 Story, J., email correspondence; Story, J., 'Symeon as annalist' from Rollason, D. (ed.), *Symeon of Durham: Historian of Durham and the North*, Stamford: Studies in Northeastern History, 1998, pp. 202–13
15 Briggs, E., *Religion, Society and Politics and the* Liber vitae *of Durham*, vol. 1, PhD, University of Leeds, 1987, p. 12
16 Ibid. p. 28
17 Godman, P. (ed.), *Alcuin: The Bishops, Kings and Saints of York*, Oxford: Clarendon Press, 1982, pp. 107–10
18 Macquarrie, A., *Lives of Scottish Saints in the Aberdeen Breviary*, Scottish Church History Society, 1996, p.31

19 Anderson, A. O., *Early Sources of Scottish History, AD 500–1286*, Edinburgh: Oliver & Boyd, 1922, p. 73

20 Lang, J. T., 'Hogback monuments in Scotland', *Proceedings of the Society of Antiquaries of Scotland*, vol. 105, 1974, p. 233

21 Crone, Hyndmarch and Woolf, p. 14

22 Johnson South, T. (ed.), *Historia de Sancto Cuthberto: a history of Saint Cuthbert and a record of his patrimony*, Cambridge: D. S. Brewer, 2002, p. 1

23 Ibid. pp. 47, 202

24 National Manuscripts of Scotland, vol. i, plate ii, p. 4. Collection: Sir William Fraser Facsimiles of Scottish Charters and Letters

CHAPTER 3

1 Ash, M., 'The Diocese of St Andrews under its "Norman" bishops', *Scottish Historical Revue*, vol. 55, 1976, p. 105

2 Skene, W. (ed.), *Chronicles of the Picts, Chronicles of the Scots, and other Early Memorials of Scottish History*, Edinburgh: HM General Register House, 1867, p.193

3 Ash, p. 109

4 Fraser, W., *Memorials of the Earls of Haddington*, vol. 1, Edinburgh, 1889, p. xxv

5 Fawcett, R., *The Architecture of the Scottish Medieval Church, 1100–1560*, New Haven and London: Yale University Press, 2011, p. 28

6 Ibid. p. 46

7 Ibid., p. 52

8 Ibid. p. 55

9 Ibid. figs 23–6

10 McWilliam, C. (ed.), *The Buildings of Scotland: Lothian*, London: Penguin, 1978, p. 455

11 Fawcett, p. 53

12 Bliss, W. H (ed.), *Calendar of Entries in the Papal Registers Relating to Great Britain and Ireland: Papal Letters*, vol. i, 1893, p. 61. https://www.british-history.ac.uk/cal-papal-registers/brit-ie/vol1/pp57-73 (accessed 23 September 2019)

13 Dransart, P., 'Bishops' residences, Saints' cults, and the legacy of Sacred Authority in the Medieval Dioceses of St Andrews and Glasgow', from Rollason, D. (ed.), *Princes of the Church*, London: Routledge, 2017, p. 82

14 Ash, p. xxii

15 Ibid. pp. 125–6

16 Fawcett, R., Luxford, J., Oram, R. and Turple, T., *A corpus of Scottish Medieval Parish Churches*, https://arts.st-andrews. ac.uk/ corpusofscottishchurches/index.php?id=158924

17 Dunlop, A. (ed.), 'Bagimond's Roll: Statement of the Tenths of the Kingdom of Scotland', *Miscellany of the Scottish History Society*, vol. vi, p. 33

18 Fawcett, Luxford, Oram and Turple (accessed 27 September 2019)

19 Ibid.

20 NRAS 3503/4/5 Memorial for the Earl of Haddington to the Revd Presbytery of Dunbar

21 Fraser, vol. 2, pp. 255–6

22 Ibid., vol. 1, p. xxxii

23 NRS CH2/359/1 12 October 1617, and Ritchie, A. E., *The Churches of St Baldred: Auldhame, Tyninghame, Whitekirk, Prestonkirk*, Edinburgh: J. Moodie Miller, 1881, pp. 165–6

24 Ibid. 14 October 1621, and p. 199

25 Ibid. 10 March 1622, and p. 201

26 Trevor-Roper, H., *Tyninghame Library*, 1977 NLS MMSID: 992328933804341 Unfoliated

27 Fraser, vol. 1, p. 37

28 Ibid. p. 132

29 Calderwood, D., *History of the Kirk of Scotland*, vol. vii, p. 360, quoted in Fraser, vol. 1, p. 130

30 Ibid. p.175

31 Chambers, R., *Reekiana*, pp. 308–9, quoted in Fraser, vol. 1, p. 130

32 Fraser, vol. 1, p. 163

33 NRAS 3503/1/55/7

34 Fraser, vol. 2, pp. 300–4

35 McKean, C., *The Scottish Chateau*, Stroud: Sutton, 2004, pp. 196–7

36 McGregor, A., unpublished paper given to the East Lothian Antiquarian and Field Naturalists' Society on 7 September 2019

37 McKean, p. 67

38 Ibid. p. 64

39 Ibid. pp. 66–7

40 Ibid. p. 299

41 Trevor-Roper *Tyninghame Library*

42 Ritchie, p. 149

43 Dodd, J. (ed.), *Tynninghame St Baldred's Kirk East Lothian Marriages 1615–1750*, Edinburgh: Scottish Genealogy Society, vol. 95, 2017

44 Brown, M., *Scotland's Lost Gardens*, Edinburgh: RCAHMS, 2012, p. 143

45 Fraser, vol. 2, p. 311

CHAPTER 4

1 Child, F., *The English and Scottish Popular Ballads*, vol. 4, pp. 61–74

2 Ibid.

3 Marshall, R., *John de Medina*, Edinburgh: National Gallery of Scotland, 1988, p. 4
4 Ibid. p. 8
5 Brown, M., *Scotland's Lost Gardens*, Edinburgh: RCAHMS, 2012, p.150
6 Ibid. p. 50
7 Ibid. p. 245
8 Kelsall, H. and K., *Scottish Lifestyle 300 Years Ago*, Aberdeen: Scottish Cultural Press, 1993, p. 90
9 Rock, J., 'John Hope's House in Edinburgh 1680', https://sites.google.com/site/joerocksresearchpages/home (accessed 1 December 2019)
10 Ibid.
11 Ibid.
12 Skinner, B., 'John Hope and the Wreck of the Gloucester', University of Edinburgh, 1992
13 Kelsall, p.210
14 Historic Scotland, *Inventory for Gardens and Designed Landscapes in Scotland*, vol. ii, 2007, p. 377
15 Marshall, p. 4
16 NRAS 3503/3/76
17 Ibid.
18 Robertson, F., *Early Scottish Gardeners and Their Plants 1650–1750*, East Linton: Tuckwell Press, 2000, p. 116; and GD45/18/746
19 Ibid. p. 123
20 Dodd, J. (ed.), *Tynninghame St Baldred's Kirk East Lothian Marriages 1615–1760*, p. 20
21 Dodd, J. (ed.), *Tynninghame St Baldred's Kirk East Lothian Burial and Mortcloth Records 1676–1762*, p. 18
22 RH15/39/195
23 NRAS 3503/3/76
24 Ibid.
25 Anderson, M. L. (ed.), *Forest Trees: Some directions about Raising Forest Trees by Thomas Hamilton*, London: Thomas Nelson and Sons, 1953, pp. 89–90
26 Ibid. p. 1

CHAPTER 5

1 Turnbull, G., *The Diary of George Turnbull, Minister of Alloa and Tyninghame, 1657–1704*, Edinburgh: Scottish Historical Society, 1893, p. 378
2 Ritchie, A. E., *The Churches of St Baldred: Auldhame, Tyninghame, Whitekirk, Prestonkirk*, Edinburgh: J. Moody Miller, 1881, p. 9
3 Fraser, W., vol. 1, p. 211
4 Anderson, (ed.), p. 89
5 Gibson, R., *The Scottish Countryside: its changing face, 1700–2000*, Edinburgh: John Donald, 2007, p. 36
6 Anderson (ed.), p. 89
7 Fraser, vol. 1, p. 247
8 Ibid. p. 248
9 Ibid. p. 251
10 Ibid. p. 250
11 GD/124/15/632/2 18 July 1707
12 GD/124/15/632/5 16 October 1707
13 GD/124/15/632/6 11 December 1707
14 Stewart, M., *The Architectural, Landscape and Constitutional Plans of the Earl of Mar, 1700–32*, Dublin: Four Courts Press, 2016, pp. xxii, xxiv–v
15 Ibid. p. xxv
16 Anderson (ed.), p. 90
17 Stewart, p. 97
18 Ibid. p. 71
19 Anderson (ed.), p. 90
20 Ibid. p. 91
21 Ibid. p. 92
22 Kelsall, p. 90
23 Ibid.
24 Ibid.
25 Ibid. p. 93
26 Reid, J., *The Scots Gard'ner*, (ed.) A. Hope, Edinburgh: Mainstream, 1988, p. 2
27 Anderson (ed.), p. 93
28 Stewart, p. 205
29 NRS GD220/5/90 Letter from Helen Hope to the Duke of Montrose
30 Fraser, vol. 1, p. lvii
31 NRS GD220/5/90 6 August 1715
32 Ibid. 28 November 1715

CHAPTER 6

1 Macmillan, D., *Scottish Art 1460–1990*, Edinburgh: Mainstream, 1990, pp. 95–8
2 NRS GD220/5/614 Letter from Lord Haddington to the Duke of Montrose
3 Abernethy, L., *Lady Grisell Baillie Mistress of Mellerstain*, Kibworth Beauchamp: Troubador, 2020, p. 117
4 Scott-Moncrieff, R., *The Household Book of Lady Grizell Baillie 1692–1733*, Edinburgh: Scottish Historical Society, 1911, p. 191
5 Abernethy, p.115
6 Mellerstain letters (private archive)
7 Scott-Moncrieff, pp. 251–5
8 NRS GD420/1-15 The Ancient Fraternity of Free Gardeners of East Lothian
9 *Edinburgh Evening Courant*, 26 December 1721
10 Anderson, (ed.), p. 61
11 Ibid. pp. 71–2
12 Ibid. p. 2

13 Holmes, H., 'The circulation of Scottish agricultural books during the eighteenth century', *The Agricultural History Review*, 2006, p. 60

14 Anderson (ed.), p. 7

15 Ibid. p. 9

16 Ibid. p. 30

17 Ibid. p. 40

18 Ibid. p. 54

19 Mellerstain letters (private archive)

20 Ibid.

21 Ibid.

22 Fraser, W., vol. 1, p. 257

23 Rock, J., https://sites.google.com/site/joerocksresearch pages/home (accessed 25 February 2020)

24 Anderson (ed.), p. viii

25 Scott-Moncrieff, pp. lxiii–iv, 12

26 Smout, p. 189

27 Ritchie, p. 99

28 Ibid. pp. 99–100

29 Ibid.

30 Smout, p. 189

31 Dodd, J. (ed.), *Tyninghame St Baldred's Kirk East Lothian Burial and Mortcloth Records 1676–1762*, p. 35

32 NRS CH2/358/1 Tyninghame Kirk Session Minutes

33 Hately Waddell, P., *An Old Kirk Chronicle. Being a history of Auldhame, Tyninghame and Whitekirk*, Edinburgh: Blackwood & Sons, 1893, p. 81

34 NRS CH2/358/1 Tyninghame Kirk Session Minutes 4 February 1649

35 Ibid. May 1712

36 Gibson, p. 53

37 Old Statistical Account (OSA), vol. 17, p. 578

CHAPTER 7

1 Abernethy, p. 164

2 Ibid. pp. 192–3

3 Ibid. p. 205

4 Fraser, p. 272

5 Abernethy, p. 227

6 Ibid. p. 237

7 Dodd, J. (ed.), *Tyninghame St Baldred's Kirk East Lothian Baptisms 1615–1776*, p. 41

8 McWilliam, C. (ed.), *The Buildings of Scotland: Lothian*, London: Penguin, 1978, p. 455

9 Dodd, J., 'From Old to New: The Creation of the Present Village of Tyninghame', *Transactions of the East Lothian Antiquarian and Field Naturalists' Society*, vol. 32, pp. 94–111

10 Fraser, vol. 1, p. lvii

11 Ibid. p. lviii

12 NRS CH2/99/4 Dunbar presbytery

13 NRS E69/9/1/11 East Lothian Hearth Tax 1691–95

14 NRAS 3503/4/5 Thomas Miller Letter from Lord Advocate

15 Ibid. Memorial for the Earl of Hadinton to The Revd Presbytery of Dunbar

16 Ibid. Plan of the Glebe . . . Robert Ainslie

17 Dodd, 'From Old to New . . .', p. 109

18 Ibid. p. 107

19 Turnbull, G., 1893

20 NRS CH2/358/1 Tyninghame Kirk Session Minutes

21 Smout, T., *A History of the Scottish People 1560–1830*, Glasgow: Fontana, 1987, p. 113

22 NRAS 3503/1/355/2 Book of the messuage of Tyninghame 1608

23 Dodd, 'From Old to New . . .', p.100

24 Gibson, R., p. 53

CHAPTER 8

1 Tait, A., *The Landscape Garden in Scotland 1735–1835*, Edinburgh: Edinburgh University Press, 1980, p. 64

2 Ibid. p. 64 note 61

3 NRAS 3503/1/75 Timber and Pruning Book January 1755

4 http://portal.historicenvironment.scot/designation/ GDL00070 (accessed 1 May 2020)

5 Lausen-Higgins, J., 'Sylva Botanica: Evaluation of the lost eighteenth-century Leith Walk Botanic Garden Edinburgh', *Garden History*, vol. 43, no. 2, 2015, pp. 218–36

6 Campbell, S., *A History of Kitchen Gardening*, London: Frances Lincoln, 2005, p. 50

7 Binney, M., 'Tyninghame House', *Country Life*, 2 May 1991, p. 98

8 'Tyninghame, Haddingtonshire', *Country Life*, 16 August 1902, pp. 208–14

9 Reid, p. 24

10 NRAS 3503/1/181 Accounts and Vouchers of John Wauchope W.S. as agent

11 Campbell, p. 134

12 Ibid. p. 61

13 Campbell, pp. 168–9

14 Brotherston, R. P., 'The Greenhouse, Hothouse and Stove', *Gardeners' Chronicle*, 18 February 1922, p. 78

15 Fraser, vol. 1, p. 277

16 https://collections.vam.ac.uk/item/O62464/stove-adam-robert/ (accessed 10 May 2020)

17 Mitchell, D., *Conservation of Architectural Ironwork*, Abingdon: Routledge, 2017, pp. 4–5

18 NRAS 3503/1/181 Accounts and Vouchers of John Wauchope W.S. as agent

19 Loudon, J. C., *Encyclopaedia of Gardening*, London: Longman, 1825, p. 748
20 Ibid. p. 353
21 Campbell, p. 177
22 NRAS 3503/1/75 Timber and Pruning Book
23 NLS MSS14833 Factors Book, Tyninghame Estate, Earl of Haddington
24 Anderson, p. 40
25 Boutcher, W., *A Treatise on Forest-Trees*, 2nd Edition, Edinburgh, 1778, p. 185

CHAPTER 9

1 Buxbaum, T., *Scottish Garden Buildings*, Edinburgh: Mainstream, 1989, pp. 151–5
2 Wordsworth, D., *Recollections of a Tour Made in Scotland A.D. 1803*, Edinburgh, 1874, pp. 37–8
3 Tait, A., p. 146 note 34
4 NRAS/3503/1/74 Notebook, including measurements of path
5 Fraser, pp. 282–3
6 John Baxter entry, *Dictionary of Scottish Architects*, http://www.scottisharchitects.org.uk/index.php (accessed 26 May 2020)
7 Smith, J., *Old Scottish Clockmakers from 1453 to 1850*, Edinburgh: Oliver & Boyd, 1921
8 *Freemasons' Quarterly Review*, London, 1842, p. 34
9 Ross, T., 'Ancient Sundials of Scotland', *Proceedings of the Society of Antiquaries of Scotland*, 1890, vol. 24, pp. 161–273
10 HES Newbattle Abbey Policies, south sundial LB14563, description
11 Somerville, R., 'The ancient Sundials of Scotland', *Proceedings of the Society of Antiquaries of Scotland*, 1987, vol.117, pp. 251–2
12 Ibid. p. 233
13 Packer, J., *Influences of Ancient Egypt on Architecture and Ornament in Scotland*, PhD Thesis, University of Edinburgh, 2012, p. 99
14 *The Gentleman's Magazine*, London, vol. 143, p. 363
15 Fraser, vol. 1, p. 288
16 NRAS 3503/1/195 and NRAS 3503/1/196
17 NRAS 3503/1/62/1
18 Miller, J., *The Lamp of Lothian*, Haddington: James Allan, 1844, p. 314
19 Fraser, vol. 1, pp. 285–6
20 Ibid. p. 232
21 Ibid.p. 299
22 *The Scotsman*, 22 August 1818 and reprinted 8 September 1824
23 Ibid. 16 April 1823
24 *London Evening Standard*, 26 September 1831
25 *Caledonian Mercury*, 22 July 1843

CHAPTER 10

1 NRAS 3503/1/94 Vouchers of Accounts of James Hope WS
2 NRAS 3503/1/90 Vouchers of Accounts of James Hope WS
3 Ibid.
4 Colvin, H., *Biographical Dictionary of British Architects 1600–1840*, New Haven: Yale University Press, 1995, p. 875
5 'William Burn 1789–1870', *Dictionary of Scottish Architects*, http://www.scottisharchitects.org.uk/architect_full.php?id=200136 (accessed 5 June 2020)
6 Glendinning, M., and MacKechnie, A., *Scotch Baronial: Architectural and National Identity in Scotland*, London: Bloomsbury, 2021, p.146
7 https://scotlandsplaces.gov.uk/digital-volumes/ordnance-survey-name-books/roxburghshire-os-name-books-1858-1860/roxburghshire-volume-28/99 (accessed 11 June 2020)
8 Glendinning and MacKechnie, p. 145
9 McWilliam, (ed.), p. 456
10 McKean, p. 211
11 Glendinning and MacKechnie, p. 148
12 Ibid. p. 146
13 McWilliam, p. 336
14 Fraser, vol. 1, p. 355
15 *Dictionary of Scottish Architects*, http://www.scottisharchitects.org.uk/architect_full.php?id=200136
16 McWilliam, p. 457
17 Ibid.
18 NRAS 3503/1/90 Vouchers of Accounts of James Hope WS 1833
19 Ibid.
20 NRAS 3503/1/90 Vouchers of Accounts of James Hope WS 1833
21 Cowtan Pattern Books no. 692, p. 274; (E. 1863–1946)
22 https://collections.vam.ac.uk/item/O178968/wallpaper-unknown/ (accessed 28 May 2021)
23 Buxbaum, T., p. 108
24 McNeill, F. Marian, *The Scots Kitchen*, Edinburgh: Birlinn, 2015, p. 270
25 Buxbaum, p. 113
26 Repton, H., *Fragments on the Theory and Practice of Landscape Gardening*, London: T. Bensley, 1805, p. 531
27 Ibid. pp. 141–2
28 James, J., *The Theory and Practice of Gardening*, London, 1712, p. 33

29 Loudon, J. (ed.), *The Gardeners' Magazine*, vol. 17, p. 370
30 NRAS 3503/1/94
31 Packer, p. 197

CHAPTER 11

1 Floud, R., *An Economic History of the English Garden*, London: Penguin Books, 2019, p. 154
2 NRAS Old Parish Registers Births 730/2010 Chirnside
3 *Memoirs of the Caledonian Horticultural Society*, vol. 1. p. 20
4 Ibid. vol. 2, pp. 31, 32
5 *The Scots Magazine*, 1 October 1813
6 *The Caledonian Mercury*, 18 September 1823
7 Campbell, p. 195
8 Wilson, D., *John Hay 1758–1836*, MA Thesis, Institute of Historical Research, p. 51. https://sasspace.sas.ac.uk/6879/1/MA%20Dissertation_Patricia%20Doreen%20Wilson_154578700_Merit.pdf (accessed 5 August 2020)
9 Loudon, p. 512
10 *The Caledonian Mercury*, 23 September 1837
11 Ibid. 16 October 1843
12 Moshenska, G., 'Esoteric Egyptology, Seed Science and the Myth of Mummy Wheat', *Open Library of Humanities*, 3(1), p. 1. http://doi.org/10.16995/olh.83
13 *Haddingtonshire Courier*, 30 April 1886
14 Haddington, The Countess of, 'A Garden on the east coast of Scotland: Tyninghame', *Journal of the Royal Horticultural Society*, vol. 96, p. 338
15 *The Scotsman*, 9 September 1869
16 Hogg, R., *The Fruit Manual*, 1884, p. 398
17 Leslie, A., *The International Rhododendron Register & Checklist*, RHS, 2004, p. 289
18 *Transactions of the Botanical Society of Edinburgh*, vol. 16., pp. 311–12
19 *The Gardeners' Chronicle*, suppl. ill., May 19 1888, p. 626
20 Ibid. 16 September 1905, p. 212
21 Elliot, B., 'Rhododendrons in British Gardens: A Short History', in Postan, C. (ed.), *The Rhododendron Story*, RHS, 1996, pp.162–3
22 Fortune, A., 'Green Burials in Binning Wood', *East Lothian Life*, Autumn 2009, p. 24
23 *Southern Reporter*, 7 November 1878
24 Fraser, vol. 1, p. 360
25 *Statistical Account of Scotland*, 1834–45, vol. 2, p. 30
26 Ibid. p. 34
27 Sabine, J., 'An Account of some Remarkable Holly Hedges and Trees in Scotland', *Transactions of the Horticultural Society of London*, vol. vii, 1830, pp. 194–7
28 Croal, D., *Sketches of East Lothian*, Haddington, 1904, p. 75

CHAPTER 12

1 Brotherston, R. P., *The Gardener*, 1877, pp. 265–7
2 Brotherston, R. P., 'Hardy Flowers for July and August', *The Gardener*, August 1874, pp. 364–8
3 Robinson, W., *The English Flower Garden*, London: Hamlyn, 1984, p. xxxviii
4 Ibid. p. xxii
5 Ibid. p. 266
6 Cox, E. H. M., *A History of Gardening in Scotland*, London: Chatto & Windus, 1935, p. 129
7 *Country Life*, August 16 1902, p. 213
8 Ibid.
9 Arnott, S., and Brotherston, R., *Gardening in the North*, London: Cassell & Co.,1909, p. 198
10 *The Gardeners' Chronicle*, 16 September 1905, p. 211
11 *Transactions of the Highland and Agricultural Society of Scotland*, 4th Series, vol. xvii, pp. 256–7
12 *The Gardeners' Chronicle*, 16 September 1905, pp. 211–12
13 Brotherston, R. P., 'The Flower-Garden', *The Gardener*, June 1881, p. 254
14 Brotherston, R. P., 'The Herbaceous or Mixed Border', *The Garden*, January 1914, p. 19
15 Brotherston, R. P., *The Book of Cut Flowers*, Edinburgh: T. N. Foulis, 1906, p. 276
16 Ibid. p. 22
17 Ibid. p. 25
18 *The Gardeners' Chronicle*, 1 September 1923, p. 126
19 *The Journal of Botany*, 1924, p. 149
20 *Country Life*, 16 August 1902, p. 214
21 Macmillan, D., and Moffat, A., *Robert Noble*, East Lothian Print Services, 2017
22 *The Gardeners' Chronicle*, 25 January 1924, p. 13

CHAPTER 13

1 https://www.birmingham.ac.uk/research/warstudies/research/projects/lionsdonkeys/b.aspx (accessed 27 October 2020)
2 Bunyan, S., 'The Lothians and Border Horse Yeomanry – An illustrious history recognised', *East Lothian Life*, Autumn 2019, p. 45
3 Karsgard, A., 'Loathsome and Bloody – the Story of the Lothian and Border Yeomanry in France 1940', *East Lothian Life*, Winter 2017
4 Ibid. p. 54
5 https://canmore.org.uk/insites/187 (accessed 22 October 2020)
6 Ibid.
7 Earl of Haddington, pp. 45–52
8 Ibid. p. 46

9 Ibid. p. 46

10 Ibid. p. 47

11 Conversation with Alastair Milligan, assistant factor 1968–85 and factor 1985–2004, 19 March 2019

12 Queen Victoria, *More Leaves from the Journal of A Life in the Highlands from 1862–1883*, London: Smith, Elder & Co, 1884, p. 376

13 Legg, K., *The Archive of James Russell, Garden Designer deposited at the Borthwick Institute, University of York*, York: Borthwick Publications, 2003, pp. 7, 71 and 19

14 JR/1/173 Letter 15 October

15 Ibid.

16 Ibid. Letter 3 November

17 Tindall, F., *Memoirs and Confessions of a County Planning Officer*, Ford: Pantile Press, 1998, p. 46

18 Ibid.

19 The Countess of Haddington, 'A Garden on the east coast of Scotland: Tyninghame', *Journal of the Royal Horticultural Society*, vol. 96, August 1971, pp. 338–44

20 Lees-Milne, A., and Verey, R., *The Englishwoman's Garden*, London: Chatto & Windus, pp. 56–60

21 Countess of Haddington, p. 339

22 Lees-Milne and Verey, p. 58

23 Countess of Haddington, p. 343

24 Ibid.

25 Conversation with Alastair Milligan, 19 March 2019

26 Verney, P., *The Gardens of Scotland*, London: Batsford, 1976, pp. 126–7

27 JR/1/173 Letter 8 November 1965

28 Verney, p. 127

29 Countess of Haddington, p. 342

30 Lees-Milne and Verey, p. 59

31 James, J., *The Theory and Practice of Gardening*, London, 1712, p. 24

32 Rapin, R., *Rapin of Gardens*, trans. by J. Gardiner, London, 1728, p. 8

33 Lees-Milne and Verey, p. 60

34 Ibid. p. 58

35 Verney, p. 122

CHAPTER 14

1 https://api.parliament.uk/historic-hansard/commons/1919/apr/30/death-duties (accessed 5 January 2021)

2 Simpson, J., *Yearning for the Land*, New York: Vintage Books, 2003, p. 195

3 Ibid.

4 Binney, M., and Martin, K., *The Country House: To Be or Not to Be?*, London: Save Britain's Heritage, 1982, p. 10

5 Simpson, J., p. 201

6 Ibid.

7 Binney and Martin, p. 40

8 Ibid. p. 42

9 Simpson, p. 200

10 Ibid. p. 299; Dodd, J., 'From Old to New . . .', p. 110

11 Simpson, p. 211

12 Martine, R., *This too shall pass*, Edinburgh: Birlinn, 2009, pp. 80, 181

13 Land Use Consultants, *An Inventory of Gardens and Designed Landscapes in Scotland: A report to the Countryside Commission for Scotland and Historic Buildings and Monuments Directorate, Scottish Development Department*, vol. 5, Lothian and Borders, 1987, p. 239

14 Historic Environment Policy Statement, 2016, pp. 24–6, para 2.77

Acknowledgements

My thanks to the staff at the John Gray Centre, Haddington, and in particular to David Anderson, Stephanie Leith and Fran Woodrow for all their help and patience. Also to Lesley Abernethy, Geoff Bailey, Lady Briggs, Marilyn Brown, Rick Clarke, Hilary and Peter Cochrane, Judi Coe, Billy Crawford, Robert and Tommy Dale, Joy Dodd, Christopher Dingwall, Ben Gray, Charnisay Gwyn, Graham Hardy, Fiona Mariota Leslie, Angus Macgregor, Aonghus McKechnie, Joanne and John McNeill, Alastair Milligan, Joe Rock, Andy Semple, Joanna Story, Sabina Struthers, and to friends at Scotland's Garden and Landscape Heritage (SGLH).

I am deeply grateful to all at Birlinn, in particular to Hugh Andrew for his enthusiastic support and guidance, and to Andrew Simmons for his skilful editing.

Index